Diversity *of* Perspectives

Eileen Taylor, EdD

Cover images and design by Ken Strickland.

Kendall Hunt
publishing company

www.kendallhunt.com
Send all inquiries to:
4050 Westmark Drive
Dubuque, IA 52004-1840

ISBN: 978-1-7924-5647-3

Published in the United States of America

Contents

Preface

Dear Learner:

You were my inspiration to write this book, so it is genuinely dedicated to you! I kept you in mind while writing so I could provide information that may help you prepare for Workforce 2030. It feels like it's just around the corner! By then, the majority of the workforce will be people of color according to the U.S. Census Bureau (Vespa et al, 2020, p. 13). I share what I have personally learned while teaching in higher education and working in practical careers. This book is framed with helpful information for you to make a positive, meaningful contribution to Workforce 2030 and beyond.

I believe in life-long learning! First, I encourage you to embrace the wisdom to build a strong foundation of a growth mindset (Dweck, 2016) throughout the journey of workforce change. At this point in your life, you have acquired academic learning and perhaps workforce experiences. You know a lot, but there is so much more to learn to help you achieve your personal goals.

Second, the changing workforce that will include others who may not look, think, or act like you provides the opportunity to learn about diversity of and with other people (Taylor, 2021). Third, this book is especially written with the premise that you may have more than one job in your lifetime as the workforce continues to change toward 2030 and beyond. You will discover eight competencies defined by the National Association of Colleges and Employers (2021) that will help strengthen your knowledge, skills, and abilities for any career path you choose.

Fourth, embracing a strong foundation of a growth mindset of learning will also help you journey through the Bloom's Taxonomy lower-order thinking skills to higher-order thinking skills (Anderson & Krathwohl, 2001). This is an academic model of personal development through learning.
Finally, regardless of what course you are taking while reading this book, you will build upon your previous academic learning and experiences in life to discover your personal diversity is added value to Workforce 2030 and beyond. Diversity of Perspectives will help you develop mindfulness and inclusion while working in any profit or nonprofit organization producing goods or services to customers. So come on, let's take this journey toward Workforce 2030 and beyond. It feels like it's just around the corner!

Take good care...and be well.

Dr. Eileen Taylor

TAYLOR CONCEPT MODEL

Your Course
Your Learning
Your Experiences
Bloom's Taxonomy
Diversity of Perspectives
NACE Competencies
Growth Mindset
versus
Fixed Mindset

Anderson, L. W., & Krathwohl, D. R. (2001). *A taxonomy for learning, teaching, and assessing: A revision of bloom's taxonomy of educational objectives* (Complete). Longman.
Dweck, C. S. (2016). *Mindset : the new psychology of success* (Updated). Random House.
National Association of Colleges and Employers (NACE). (2021). *Career readiness: Competencies for a career-ready workforce.* http://naceweb.org/career-readiness-competencies
Taylor, E. (2021). *Diversity of Perspectives.* Kendall Hunt Publishing Company.
Vespa, J., Medina, L., & Armstrong, D. M. (2020). *Demographic turning points for the United States: Population projections for 2020 to 2060.* U.S. Department of Commerce, U.S. Census Bureau. https://www.census.gov/content/dam/Census/library/publications/2020/demo/p25-1144.pdf

CHAPTER 1

Workforce 2030

OVERVIEW

Human Diversity and Mindfulness
Individual Development Plan
Working in a Rapidly Changing Workforce
Chapter Takeaways
Application Exercises

Human Diversity and Mindfulness

The year 2030 feels like it's right around the corner! By then, the majority of the workforce will be people of color according to research. The 21st century of globalization where technology continues to transform the method and scope of communication has resulted in increased discussions about human diversity while working alongside others. It is significant whether you are a current member or soon to be member of a profit or nonprofit organization. Regardless of your current level in any organization (traditional student, adult learner, intern, entry-level, employee, manager, or leader), you will soon experience a changing workforce that will become majority minority as early as the year 2030. Perhaps you are working on a student project that requires the ability to demonstrate an effective call to action to others, a businessperson needing to close deals that increase company revenue, a manager that has to make decisions about which department will use limited resources most effectively, or a leader who understands organizational change is imminent in any business. The ability to work with other people to achieve intended outcomes is required for all of these scenarios. In fact, the Bureau of Labor Statistics Career Builder Survey (n.d.) reports that Americans between the ages of 18 to 52 will have 12.3 jobs. Change is imminent! As we experience this unique change in our world history, the Diversity of Perspectives unique model of mindfulness and inclusion will help you navigate change as you journey toward Workforce 2030 and beyond.

According to Buris and Turman (2010), "When something significant changes in our world, it is human nature to try to explain what is happening" (p. 4). "The year 2030 marks a demographic turning point for the United States" according to the U.S. Census Bureau (Vespa et al., 2020, p. 13). This means you will begin to experience more people of color from different backgrounds working to provide products and services for customers. Regardless of being a worker or customer, you will experience the changing workforce. The essence of successful organizations may be human diversity and mindfulness, which is introduced in this chapter.

Race relations, cultural diversity, affirmative action, and equal employment opportunity were terms that described some aspect of human diversity in the 20th century. More recently, in the 21st century, terms like diversity, multicultural, cross-cultural, intercultural, inclusion, and equity have all been used. Regardless of the shift in terminology used to describe human diversity, it has existed for centuries. Greater access to technology as a norm has increased exposure to diversity.

Some people have limited exposure to interacting with different people and more recently have begun working with others who do not look, think, or act exactly like them while trying to meet the goals of producing goods and services for customers. This vulnerability is at risk to both employers and workers and is covered under "federal laws that make it illegal to discriminate against a job applicant or an employee because of the persons' race, color, religion, sex (including pregnancy, transgender status, and sexual orientation), national origin, age (40 or older), disability or genetic information" (U.S. EEOC, 2020). There is a lot of research about diversity as it relates specifically to these federal protected classes and working in profit and nonprofit businesses. However, this book does not discuss the federal protected classes in detail. Rather, it provides information and persuasion about change, organizational communication, leadership, followership, and other relationship theories to bring about awareness and embracing of human diversity in the workforce. How do you develop workforce unity? Diversity of Perspectives is a way to achieve those organizational results.

This book offers the Diversity of Perspectives model as a practical approach to self-discovery of existing personal experiences with diversity and a development opportunity to gain new knowledge. The framework and design of the model is implicitly rooted in empathy necessary to be mindful in self-discovery and learning about others who do not look, think, or act exactly like you. Challita (2014) offers the following definition of empathy that relates to the Diversity of Perspectives model.

> Empathy is a motivational force to action—an action fully oriented towards the good and totally free from any bias or selectivity—triggered by the awareness to perceive beyond our own perspective the emotional state of the other, to share this state and to act on it appropriately. (p. 518)

The foundation of the Diversity of Perspectives model focuses on human beings equipped with a mind that controls the body which are actions. The one human equalizer is that no matter who you are, where you come from, or resources you may or may not have, you only get 168 hours a week (24 hours a day times 7 days a week). Reflection opportunities to explore how you engage your mind during 168 hours a week as you communicate with others and outcomes of those interactions will be provided while reading this book.

You are also provided opportunities to grow in self-awareness of what you bring to others while working together. The concept of a *growth mindset versus fixed mindset* (Challita, 2014; Dweck & Reppucci, 1973) will be discussed later in this book when learning more about diversity to increase your intrinsic desire for knowledge. Overall, this book is structured to provide information and a Diversity of Perspectives *toolkit* of self-assessments in Chapter Nine to help guide you to an outcome of increasing confidence in your self-awareness, new knowledge of human diversity, freedom of choice in your behaviors, and connect accountability to interacting with people who do not look, think, or act exactly like you using mindfulness.

I offer the following definition for human diversity. Any person who does not look, think, or act exactly like you is considered a diverse human being. This profound statement became every person's reality upon birth and will last until the end of their life. Simply put, no two people are the same. This includes members of your immediate family. If you think about it, did anyone in your family look, think, or act exactly alike? Of course not! It is possible that when you were young, you may have believed that every family member shared the same values, assumptions, beliefs, and expectations. As you grew older, you may have noticed family differences in these same areas. Taking the giant leap outside of your family home into preschool/kindergarten may have been your earliest awareness of human diversity. People in preschool/kindergarten did not look, think, or act exactly like your family. Respectfully, homeschoolers may not have experienced others who may not look, think, or act exactly alike until much later unless they participated in outside home activities.

You may have experienced additional diversity awareness in grade school, high school, college, and/or the workforce internship or career jobs. Even more people continued to not look, think, or act exactly like you. Regardless of how vast or small the differences, you have been experiencing diversity all your life. Perhaps this book is your introduction to the concept of human diversity or is a refresher on the topic. The pondering question is: Have you experienced diversity throughout your life with mindfulness?

Two definitions of mindfulness are offered as it relates to experiencing diversity. Both definitions are useful to help focus your thoughts while reading this book and as you journey toward the year 2030 when employees in the workforce will shift from being minority majority to become majority minority. People of color who have typically been the minority of the workforce will comprise the majority of the workforce by 2030 (Burtis & Turman, 2010). If you prepare now with mindfulness for this major shift from minority majority, you may discover positive, meaningful value throughout the journey to a more diverse workforce. The first definition is "Mindfulness is a flexible state of mind in which we are actively engaged in the present, noticing new things and sensitive to context, with an open, nonjudgmental orientation to experience" (Langer, 1989, p. 220). Self-reflection is beneficial and may prevent judging others. Begin with consciously reflecting upon the current composition of your family, classrooms, workforce, and experiences. Prior to reading this book, did you notice a change to more people of color in your family, classrooms where you are learning, the workforce where you may have an internship or career job, or as a customer receiving products and services? Alright, it is possible that diversity change has not occurred or been obvious. This presents an opportunity to start paying attention to the imminent changes where you live, learn, work, or receive products and services.

This awakening experience may or may not be initially welcomed. However, using the first mindfulness definition may inspire you to have an individual "open, nonjudgmental orientation to experience" (Langer, 1989, p. 220) just like you did as a preschooler/kindergartener that began to explore the world outside of your family home. Your knowledge about diversity during that time in life was limited and experiences led you to interacting with new people who do not look, think, or act exactly like you. Typically, a young mind is innocent and nonjudgmental due to lack of experiences which may lead to an easier navigation through change. It is much more difficult to navigate change as we grow older and have more life experiences. The status quo is the comfort zone for many people. However, reflecting back upon your younger mind and how you began to navigate new experiences may be a starting point for your journey toward the changing workforce. An open mind provides opportunity to learn more about diversity while working alongside others. Workforce 2030 is imminent, and we will all experience the change in some way. You may already be a leader, become a leader, or believe you have individual choice about what leaders you choose to follow. Do you believe current leaders in your life are mindful about human diversity?

The second definition is "mindfulness refers to an open state of mind where the leader's attention, informed by a sensitive awareness, merely observes what is taking place: worry about the future and negative ruminations or projections are brought back to the present moment where the situation is seen for what it is" (Roche et al., 2014, p. 477). This section of the book focuses on leadership mindfulness of human diversity and decisions to follow a leader on the journey toward Workforce 2030 and beyond. It is important to discuss the relationship between leadership and followership that may be fragile during times of change. The journey toward Workforce 2030 will inevitably present challenges to leader and follower relationships. "People will not make sacrifices, even if they are unhappy with the status quo, unless they think the potential benefits of change are attractive and unless they really believe that a transformation is possible" (Kotter, 1996, p. 9). The health of leaders' and followers' relationships may vary in positivity or negativity that ultimately impacts their customers. A leader who has vision of Workforce 2030 embracing the potential strengths and challenges throughout the journey of its change and helps followers navigate each step of the way with a shared purpose may demonstrate the essence of human diversity with mindfulness that results in a healthy work environment ultimately benefiting its customers. This is why leadership matters when navigating human diversity change in the workforce.

The ability to influence others to be inspired within to act upon a vision of intended outcomes is effective leadership at every level of any organization. This is why followership also matters when people constantly make decisions about how they spend their 168 hours a week. When working is required for the basic needs of life, people make choices of where they work, how long they are interested in staying at a job, and seek healthy work environments. The following section discusses how both leaders and workers can contribute to healthy work environments using mindfulness during the journey toward Workforce 2030. It begins with developing an Individual Development Plan specifically to learn more about diversity as it relates to working alongside others.

Individual Development Plan

One way to change/sustain personal behavior is through an opportunity to discover and track your individual development. You are encouraged to delve deep to discover vast and diverse opportunities that may or may not have been experienced related to diversity. Reflections upon past experiences and a desire for future development will help in creating a meaningful Individual Development Plan.

The following questions are offered for you to reflect upon your journey toward Workforce 2030 and areas that may need development. How do you work alongside other people without convincing them to think and act like you? Do you have a *growth mindset* that is open to learning more *knowledge* about diversity as it relates to working with other people or do you have a *fixed mindset* (U.S. EEOC, 2020; Challita, 2014) while working with others that may contribute to limiting organizational success (Dweck & Reppucci, 1973)? It is important to have a willingness to listen to understand other perspectives. Are you mindful that you have individual freedom of choice and decision-making as it relates to another person's view? How do you make the connection of your behavior to personal accountability?

No one knows you better than you know yourself. So this is your Individual Development Plan and not another person's vision of your development. When you think about the foundation of the Diversity of Perspectives model, think about your mind that controls your body and you are accountable for your own actions. The next section of the model is Self-Awareness of what you bring to others. Only you can reflect upon your current values, assumptions, beliefs, and expectations. Your Individual Development Plan is personal, because only you know your current knowledge and experience with diversity and will be the one to achieve your Plan. Regardless of where you are in life (traditional student, adult learner, intern, entry-level, employee, manager, or leader), there is no shame in limited knowledge or experiences with diversity. Rather, it is an opportunity to grow and learn more about human diversity. Wherever your knowledge is at this time, try to be inspired with a sense of confidence that when you know better, you probably do better. Increased learning about human diversity should illuminate its value to informal and formal relationships with others.

Life-long learning is an opportunity to achieve personal growth and professional development. Exploring your mindset may reveal strengths and abilities to overcome challenges encountered in a journey toward personal and professional goals. Whether you are a first-year college student or have been in your career for several years, you can experience personal growth and professional development while reading this book and participating in application exercises about human diversity at the end of each chapter. Stephen R. Covey (2007) suggests that effective leaders "begin with the end in mind" (p. 48). This concept is also relevant to anyone developing an Individual Development Plan. When you begin with envisioning personal growth and professional development, you are able to reflect upon what you know and seek ways to discover new learning about diversity.

You will begin to develop your Individual Development Plan at the end of this chapter in the Application Exercise. Before you begin your Plan focused on your Workforce 2030 journey, consider your personal brand identity. Do you even have a brand? As the workforce shifts to a majority of people of color, what will you be known for as you meet new people and navigate toward 2030? Kim and Kim (2020) offer the following description about personal brand identity.

> Similarly, throughout your life, you will craft a very clear, personal brand for yourself. A brand identity that you want people to identify you with and to remember you by. As you grow and thrive, you will deepen the relationship you have with your brand and it will not only become a reflection of who you are, but also the characteristic by which others will associate with you and everything you do. (p. 258)

Your Individual Development Plan can be used as a tool to help define your brand identity. When you share your story, it will be based upon personal experiences that inform your decision-making, who you are, what you do, and what matters to you (Burtis & Turman, 2010, p. 171).

Working in a Rapidly Changing Workforce

Making the time to intrinsically reflect upon who you are helps to illuminate self-awareness of what you bring to other people. Today you may be consciously or subconsciously interacting with people who do not look, think, or act exactly like you. This is an opportunity to confidently settle into who you are and how you will act alongside other people in the near future when "The year 2030 marks a demographic turning point for the United States" according to the U.S. Census Bureau (Vespa et al., 2020, p. 13). This will be significant to workforce organizations. "Beginning that year all baby boomers will be older than 65 and, within the decade, older adults (65 years and older) are projected to outnumber children (under 18 years) for the first time in U.S. History" (p. 13). In addition, "by 2030, immigration is projected to become the primary driver of population growth: more people are projected to be added to the population through net international migration than from natural increase" (p. 13). The U.S. Census Bureau states, "The rapid aging of the population between 2020 and 2040 will have a substantial democratic impact on the country" (p. 13).

Products and services needed by consumers will certainly change over time as "the population grows slowly, ages considerably, and becomes more racially and ethnically pluralistic" (Vespa et al.,

2020, p. 13). During this same time period, The Economy Policy Institute reports "people of color will become a majority of the American working class in 2032" and includes the "Bureau of Labor Statistics (BLS) in its projections" (Wilson, 2016, pp. 1, 21). Working in a diverse organization that provides products and services to an increasing diverse demographic is becoming a reality that employees should be thinking about now and the opportunity for personal growth of change during these unique times. According to Chrobot-Mason & Aramovich (2013), "employees will realize their full potential at work and greater creativity and innovation will result from the variety of perspectives, experiences, backgrounds, and work styles that a diverse workforce may bring, positively impacting the bottom line" (p. 660).

Organizations that value diversity of perspectives may communicate it as a norm and relate it to employee performance expectations (Minkes et al., 1999, p. 328). In discussing diversity, Ely & Thomas (2001) suggest: "It is based on the assumption that cultural differences give rise to different life experiences, knowledge, and insights, which can inform alternative views about work and how to best accomplish it" (p. 265). The following are more questions for you to consider for your Individual Development Plan. Are you prepared to work within a majority minority workforce? Do you currently have an inclusive mindset in this 21st century of globalization where technology continues to transform the method and scope of communication? Are you willing to strengthen your personal *foundation* of individual values, assumptions, beliefs, and expectations that add value to any organization? Do you believe in individual freedom of choice for your behavior that results in actualizations that you are ultimately held accountable? Are you willing to reflect upon past experiences and position yourself for new ones that will help you be prepared for Workforce 2030? The answers to these questions determine your willingness to learn about and understand others who may be different from you which is a crucial skill in an ever-growing global market. The Diversity of Perspectives *toolkit* in Chapter Nine is intended to help you be better prepared for the impending Workforce 2030 and beyond.

Regardless of where you are at this stage in your life (traditional student, adult learner, intern, entry-level, employee, manager, or leader), it is helpful to know there are employment competencies defined by the National Association of Colleges and Employers (NACE, 2021) that may be helpful to identify areas of development you may need for your Individual Development Plan. These are called competencies which are knowledge and skills necessary to be able to perform in a job. NACE conducts periodic surveys with employers of profit and nonprofit organizations and compiles data of the most relevant competencies. Although these competencies are needed of college graduates, you may discover you possess many and need development in others. Some people go straight into the workforce out of high school. Some college students have internships with employers and want to ensure classroom learning helps develop competencies. Some people reading this book may have been in the workforce for a long time but may find the NACE competencies helpful for professional development. This chapter ends with an introduction of the eight competencies defined by NACE.

TABLE 1.1 National Association of Colleges and Employers (NACE): Career Readiness: Competencies for a Career-Ready Workforce

Competencies	Description
Career & Self-Development	Proactively develop oneself and one's career through continual personal and professional learning, awareness of one's strengths and weaknesses, navigation of career opportunities, and networking to build relationships within and without one's organization.
Communication	Clearly and effectively exchange information, ideas, facts, and perspectives with persons inside and outside of an organization.
Critical Thinking	Identify and respond to needs based upon an understanding of situational context and logical analysis of relevant information.
Equity & Inclusion	Demonstrate the awareness, attitude, knowledge, and skills required to equitably engage and include people from different local and global cultures. Engage in anti-racist practices that actively challenge the systems, structures, and policies of racism.
Leadership	Recognize and capitalize on personal and team strengths to achieve organizational goals.
Professionalism	Knowing work environments differ greatly, understand and demonstrate effective work habits, and act in the interest of the larger community and workplace.
Teamwork	Build and maintain collaborative relationships to work effectively toward common goals, while appreciating diverse viewpoints and shared responsibilities.
Technology	Understand and leverage technologies ethically to enhance efficiencies, complete tasks, and accomplish goals.

CHAPTER TAKEAWAYS

- People of color who have typically been the minority of the workforce will comprise the majority of the workforce by 2030.
- Race relations, cultural diversity, affirmative action, and equal employment opportunity were terms that described some aspect of human diversity in the 20th century. Diversity, multicultural, cross-cultural, intercultural, inclusion, equity, and intercultural have been used more frequently in the 21st century.
- Human diversity risk to both employers and workers is covered under "federal laws that make it illegal to discriminate against a job applicant or an employee because of the person's race, color, religion, sex (including pregnancy, transgender status, and sexual orientation), national origin, age (40 or older), disability or genetic information" (U.S. EEOC, 2020).
- The framework and design of the Diversity of Perspectives model is implicitly rooted in empathy necessary to be mindful.
- The foundation of the Diversity of Perspectives model focuses on human beings equipped with a mind that controls the body which are actions.
- The one human equalizer is that no matter who you are, where you come from, or resources you may or may not have, you only get 168 hours a week (24 hours a day times 7 days a week).
- Any person who does not look, think, or act exactly like you is considered a diverse human being.
- The first definition is "Mindfulness is a flexible state of mind in which we are actively engaged in the present, noticing new things and sensitive to context, with an open, nonjudgmental orientation to experience" (Langer, 1989, p. 220).
- The second definition is "mindfulness refers to an open state of mind where the leader's attention, informed by a sensitive awareness, merely observes what is taking place: worry about the future and negative ruminations or projections are brought back to the present moment where the situation is seen for what it is" (Roche et al., 2014, p. 477).
- Regardless of where you are in life (traditional student, adult learner, intern, entry-level, employee, manager, or leader), there should be no shame in limited knowledge or experiences with diversity. Rather, it is an opportunity to grow and learn more about human diversity.
- Personal brand identity is a reflection of who you are and everything you do.
- An Individual Development Plan is a personal document of goals and development needs.

- Employment competencies defined by the National Association of Colleges and Employers (NACE, 2021) that may be helpful for identifying areas of development you may need for your Individual Development Plan.
- The journey toward Workforce 2030 will inevitably present challenges to leader and follower relationships. "People will not make sacrifices, even if they are unhappy with the status quo, unless they think the potential benefits of change are attractive and unless they really believe that a transformation is possible" (Kotter, 1996, p. 9). The health of leaders' and followers' relationships may vary in positivity or negativity that ultimately impacts their customers. A leader who has vision of Workforce 2030 embracing the potential strengths and challenges throughout the journey of its change and helps followers navigate each step of the way with a shared purpose may demonstrate the essence of human diversity with mindfulness that results in a healthy work environment ultimately benefiting its customers.

APPLICATION EXERCISES

Each chapter will have one or more practical exercises focused on your journey to Workforce 2030. The purpose of the application exercises for Chapter One is for you to begin to build your brand identity by confidently acknowledging and embracing your current stage in life (traditional student, adult learner, intern, entry-level, employee, manager, or leader). You will begin to develop your Individual Development Plan from your perspective. Remember, this is your Plan and not someone else's development ideas for you. Periodically through reading this book, you will have continued opportunities to further develop your Plan with a goal of completing it by the end of reading this book.

1. Locate the Individual Development Plan template in Chapter Nine.

2. Enter your first and last names.

3. Enter your current position (traditional student, adult learner, intern, entry-level, employee, manager, or leader).

4. Enter your current education level. The following are a few examples:
   - High School graduate
   - Certificate in General Education

- ► Associate of Arts in Music
- ► Bachelor of Science in Early Childhood Education
- ► Master of Science in Nursing
- ► Doctor of Philosophy (PhD) in Organizational Leadership

5. Enter your department or organization. If you are a student, enter the department for the degree you are working toward or even a student organization where you are active. If you are in the workforce, enter the department where you work.

6. Enter your university or business. If you are in college, enter the college/university name. If you are in the workforce, enter the name of the business where you are employed.

Once you have completed the exercises, it is now time to begin to develop your brand identity starting with Section I—Career Goals in your Individual Development Plan.

1. Review the competencies in Table 1.1 for skills and abilities needed to prepare for Workforce 2030. Identify which competencies you demonstrate strengths. Next, demonstrate which competencies you are challenged with limited or no experience. Your list of competencies strengths and challenges will be used in Section II—Plan as an Application Exercises in another chapter. However, making the list early will help you think about competencies that need further development as you continue reading about Diversity of Perspectives and Workforce 2030.

2. Think about how you would like to spend your 168 hours a week for the next 2 years preparing for Workforce 2030. What is a personal or professional goal(s) you can set to develop a *growth mindset* versus a *fixed mindset* for interacting with others who do not look, think, or act like you? Select one to two realistic goals to achieve over the next 2 years. Remember, this is your Individual Development Plan. No one knows you better than you know yourself, so be authentic in establishing your goal(s) over the next 2 years.

Stop working on your Individual Development Plan at this point. You will have an opportunity to continue working on your Individual Development Plan in Application Exercises as you continue reading this book.

CHAPTER 2

Diversity Reimagined

OVERVIEW

Journey to Workforce 2030
Storytelling Diversity
Defining Generations
Shaping Generational Experiences
Evolution of Diversity Terminology
Chapter Takeaways
Application Exercises

Journey to Workforce 2030

This chapter offers an opportunity to engage a *growth mindset* by reimagining diversity as a benefit to Workforce 2030. In a similar situation, colleges and universities have already been preparing for the effects of a dramatic decrease in first-year enrollment of traditional high school graduates which is caused by a decline in birth rates in recent years. Reimaging their business models has included expanding the type of student enrollment by offering adult learner education certificates and online degrees. There have been numerous other solutions to obtaining new enrollments.

Employers will experience the decline in birth rates in a different way through the workforce changing into a majority of people of color. "The National Association of Colleges and Employers (NACE), through a task force comprised of representatives from both the higher education and corporate sides, has developed a definition and identified competencies associated with career readiness for the new college graduate" (2019). Equity and Inclusion is one of the competencies, and even high school graduates who do not go to college can benefit from knowing its NACE definition as a guide to personal and professional development about diversity. "Demonstrate the awareness, attitude, knowledge, and skills required to equitably engage and include people from different local and global cultures. Engage in anti-racist practices that actively challenge the systems, structures, and policies of racism" (NACE, 2021). This definition illuminates the framework and design of the Diversity of Perspectives model that is implicitly rooted in empathy necessary to be mindful. The middle section of the model that is knowledge of what we learn is part of our human diversity experience. Some people have vast and others limited experiences with diversity. Generational storytelling may help reimagine diversity.

Storytelling Diversity

To reimagine diversity as a benefit will require taking initiative to prepare for it with a *growth mindset*. A *fixed mindset* would be resistance to change and limit personal and professional development. Typically the workforce is comprised of employees of different ages which mean diverse life experiences. That is why you may have noticed a communication theme in this book so far that regardless of your current level in any organization (traditional student, adult learner, intern, entry-level, employee, manager, or leader) you will soon experience a changing workforce that will become majority minority as early as the year 2030. Human life experiences span across generations and are a priceless benefit to any workforce organization. This benefit is only as good as the understanding of the past, present, and vision for the future. This chapter reimagines the emerging diversity in the United States using brief generational storytelling of its human history. Storytelling is defined to make sense of its purpose.

"Working with storytelling requires us to be sensitive to context and relationships, as well as to historical and cultural influences" (Hersted & Frimann, 2016, p. 160). When sharing the United States story on our journey toward Workforce 2030, Baker and Boyle (2009) remind us, "That is the power of a shared story. It transports you, and the story, eventually, transcends the experience itself, taking on a higher power and greater degree of meaning because, while the experience can only happen once, the story can be retold again and again" (p. 79). What personal stories will we tell our children, grandchildren, and generations to come about the journey toward Workforce 2030 and beyond?

Prior to reading this book, you may have been keenly aware about the emerging workforce of majority people of color. Perhaps it's a discovery that you now face and are perplexed about how this situation occurred. Salicru (2018) offers, "The genesis of sensemaking, then, is chaos and confusion, as people attempt to answer the question, 'what's the story?', by mapping the context and the ongoing unpredictable experiences thrown at them. Ultimately, sensemaking involves turning circumstances into a situation that is understood explicitly in words, which serves as a springboard for action" (p. 132). Humans use words to share their phenomena about life. "Stories express how and why life unfolds. They assist us to shape our own identities and make sense of others' actions. 'In organizations, storytelling is the preferred sense-making currency of human relationships among internal and external stakeholders'" (p. 133). How will you contribute to your organization's storytelling?

Muindi et al. (2020) argue there is power in storytelling, because "Stories are an essential cornerstone of the universal human experience" (p. 249). Human beings communicate using words often used for storytelling. "The richness and meaning of stories reveals the tremendous diversity of the human experience" (p. 249). Leaders use storytelling to share experiences of challenges, triumphs, and vision for the future. Wilson (2019) states that "Storytelling is in our nature; it is in our genes" (p. 390). People who have been in the same workplace share stories they have experienced within the company. "Storytelling is defined as a recollection of events with collective associations that involve interactions of individuals to produce meaning that is applicable to future experiences" (p. 390). Each person may be diverse, but the commonality of their shared stories is what makes them similar. "Storytelling is one way to open space for the dialogue (Sole and Wilson, 2002) given that stories motivate, inspire and provide an external event through which one can relate to their own reality" (Synder, et al., 2017, p. 494).

Defining Generations

Examining generations through storytelling illuminates the probability that multiple age cohorts make up the workforce at any given time in history. "Generations provide the opportunity to look at Americans both by their place in the life cycle—whether a young adult, a middle-aged parent or a retiree—and by their membership in a cohort of individuals who were born at a similar time" (Dimock, 2019). Senior-level, mid-level, and entry-level workers are capable of sharing stories. Table 2.1 defines generations based on year of birth and offers two perspectives. Strauss and Howe (1991, 1997) provide an earlier perspective of generational cohorts. Dimock of the Pew Research Center (2018, 2019) offers a more recent perspective of generational cohorts that further defined the Millennial cohort with a cutoff date of 1966. Pew Research Center (Dimock, 2018, 2019) generational cohorts will be used with discussions in this chapter.

TABLE 2.1 Defining Generations Based on Year of Birth

Generation	Strauss & Howe (1991, 1997)	Dimock (2019) Pew Research Center
Silent		1928–1945
Baby Boomer	1943–1960	1946–1964
Generation X	1961–1981	1965–1980
Millennials	1982–2004	1981–1996
Generation Z	2005–Present	1997–Present

Shaping Generational Experiences

For the purpose of reimaging diversity, the United States and its changing human landscape will be the focus of the next discussion. A brief reflection of the past and how the country arrived at this point and shaped generational experiences is important. We begin in the 1700s long before the Silent Generation. "Alexander Hamilton, the nation's secretary of treasury, believed that industrialization was vital for the United States economy to prosper" (McCormick, 2014, p. 20). Hamilton's diversity of perspectives was so unique that "not even the most farsighted inventors and businessmen of the late 1700s could have foreseen the dramatic changes that the Industrial Revolution would eventually bring. By 1900, it would transform the United States from an agricultural nation into one of the wealthiest industrial nations in the world" (p. 9). McCormick sums up the impact of the Industrial Revolution on future generations as follows:

> The Industrial Revolution made life easier and more exciting in many ways. But the telephones, televisions, radios, autos, airplanes, and other inventions that came into use during the later years of the Industrial Revolution did something else too. They took away the isolation of the single-family farm, and made communication with neighbors, friends, and even strangers around the world possible. They opened the horizons of nearly every American to the sights, sounds, and thoughts of people they might never have known without them. (p. 84)

The industrial era influenced the silent (traditionalist) generation who then influenced rapidly changing future generations. The information era is sometimes referred to as the knowledge era. "The Knowledge Era is characterized by a new competitive landscape driven by globalization, technology, deregulation, and democratization" (Halal & Taylor, 1999).

Generational experiences may be considered the framework for perspectives in storytelling. However, just because you are born within a certain time period, does not mean you think or act exactly like everyone born at that time. You may discover that just because you are born in a particular generation, your life experiences may result in a perspective from a different generation. To gain a better understanding of generations, the Association of Colleges and Educators (ACUE) use the following Pew Research Center (2015) information to explain generations.

TABLE 2.2 Pew Research Center: Defining Generations

Generation	Description
Silent Generation (Traditionalists)	Born between 1928 and 1945, members of the Silent Generation experienced the impact of post WWI, the Depression, and the political forces building to WWII. This generation became known for their determination, willpower, and adherence to personal beliefs. They place value on hard work and economic resourcefulness.
Baby Boomers	Born between 1946 and 1964, the Baby Boomers grew up as television, the transistor radio, and music expanded, changing their connection to the world in fundamental ways. The civil rights movement, ongoing wars, space race, and assassination of an American president dramatically impacted their lifestyles, social and political thinking, and expectations. They've experienced and adopted a range of new technologies.
Generation X	Born between 1965 and 1980, Generation X was not born into a technological world, but grew through it. It's been written they were the last to experience an "old-time" childhood and became early consumers of technology. Sandwiched between two larger generations, they came of age in a time of an uncertain economy, two-income families, increasing divorce, Watergate, energy crises, and being the first after-school "latch-key" kids.
Millennials (Generation Y)	Millennials were born between 1981 and 1996. By the time they were born, technological revolutions had settled in as a norm. Millennials saw the rise of the internet, text-messaging, and email; and experienced the evolution of cell phones and new wireless technologies to name just a few.
Generation Z	Generation Z includes those born after 1996. They have been exposed to digital technologies (internet, social networks, mobile systems) their entire lives. As a result of this exposure, this generation of learners is extremely comfortable with networking, crowd-sourcing, collecting and cross-referencing many sources of information, and integrating virtual and offline experiences in their lives. They witnessed the rise of augmented reality, virtual immersive environments, and enhancements in 3D technology; as well as voice recognition and video chatting. The implications of growing up in an "always on" technological environment are only now coming into focus.

NOTE. https://www.pewresearch.org/politics/2015/09/03/the-whys-and-hows-of-generations-research/.

Evolution of Diversity Terminology

We transition to human diversity and language to have a broad understanding of related terminology. You may recall from Chapter One that race relations, cultural diversity, affirmative action, and equal employment opportunity were terms that described some aspect of human diversity in the 20th century. More recently, in the 21st century terms like diversity, multicultural, cross-cultural, intercultural, inclusion, and equity, have all been used. Regardless of the shift in terminology used to describe human diversity, it has existed for centuries. Greater access to technology as a norm has increased exposure to diversity and terminology has also evolved. The following are descriptions of diversity terminology.

Bebber (2020) states "**Race relations**, as defined by the IRR [Institute of Race Relations], combined academic, journalistic, and policymaking approaches to emerging questions of international relations and racial conflict in Britain and the world from the early 1950s onward" (pp. 319–320).

Ely and Thomas (2001) argue

> "...**cultural diversity** is a potentially valuable resource that the organization can use not only at its margins, to gain entrée into previously inaccessible niche markets, but at its core, to rethink and reconfigure its primary tasks as well. It is based on the assumption that cultural differences gives rise to different life experiences, knowledge, and insights, which can inform alternative views about work and how to best accomplish it." (p. 265)

Affirmative Action was an early method used to diversify organizations. Kravitz (et al., 1997) defined Affirmative Action as "a body of policies and procedures designed to eliminate employment discrimination against women and ethic minorities, and to redress the effects of past discrimination" (p. vii). This method did not achieve its stated objective in all organizations due to complex challenges related to a diverse workforce.

Maya et al. (2020) explain the complexities of diversity in the workforce **Equal Employment Opportunity** law that "prohibit discrimination against a job applicant or an employee because of the person's race, color, religion, sex (including pregnancy, gender identity, and sexual orientation), national origin, age (forty or older), disability, or genetic information" (p. 239). There is no perfect work environment, and this complexity offers the following protection in a diverse workforce. "It is also illegal for employers to discriminate against employees for complaining about discrimination, filing a complaint of discrimination, or participating in an employment discrimination investigation or lawsuit" (p. 239).

Quinn et al. (2018) express a reimagined explanation of **diversity** that demonstrates a *growth mindset.*

> Social identities overlap, and we are not just a race or ethnicity, but also a sexual orientation, a socioeconomic status, a gender (or lack of identification with gender), a religion, a fan, and so on. When multiple dimensions of these co-occurring (concurrent) social identities coexist among

individuals, groups, or communities, the trust dynamics escalate in complexity and opportunity for mistrust. (p. 47)

Spring Institute (2016)—a nonprofit organization of intercultural learning—states, "The differences in the meanings have to do with the perspectives we take when interacting with people from other cultures." It offers the following terminology definitions in Table 2.3.

TABLE 2.3 Spring Institute: Cultural Terminology Defined

Cultural Terminology	Description
Multicultural	**Multicultural** refers to a society that contains several cultural or ethnic groups. People live alongside one another, but each cultural group does not necessarily have engaging interactions with each other. For example, in a multicultural neighborhood people may frequent ethnic grocery stores and restaurants without really interacting with their neighbors from other countries.
Cross-cultural	**Cross-cultural** deals with the comparison of different cultures. In cross-cultural communication, differences are understood and acknowledged, and can bring about individual change, but not collective transformations. In cross-cultural societies, one culture is often considered "the norm" and all other cultures are compared or contrasted to the dominant culture.
Intercultural	**Intercultural** describes communities in which there is a deep understanding and respect for all cultures. Intercultural communication focuses on the mutual exchange of ideas and cultural norms and the development of deep relationships. In an intercultural society, no one is left unchanged because everyone learns from one another and grows together.

Peterson (2016) describes **inclusion** as "Having diversity of thought, approach and thinking, and being inclusive in making sure everyone feels they can make a meaningful contribution to the ultimate outcome, are some of the most important things that you as a leader can do" (p. 42).

Research for a definition of **equity** resulted in diverse descriptions related to health care, student education, finance, mathematical programming, transportation, and so forth. Merriam-Webster Dictionary (n.d.) offers the following definitions of equity: "Justice according to natural law or right" and "something that is equitable."

Reimagining diversity through the industrial era and defining generations is a beginning to realizing diversity has existed for centuries. People are living longer, working longer, and bring diverse perspectives to a diverse workforce. Eras and generational thinking may be gateways to a *growth mindset* about diversity in the workplace. This thinking is not conclusive; it is a way to imagine how you have co-existed with people of diverse generations that have different perspectives as early as the beginning of your life. You were able to eventually leave your family home and function in society. It will just look different in 2030 when the majority will be the minority. Continue reading and participating in the Application Exercise as you journey toward Workforce 2030.

CHAPTER TAKEAWAYS

- The NACE definition of equity and inclusion illuminates the framework and design of the Diversity of Perspectives model that is implicitly rooted in empathy necessary to be mindful.
- Human life experiences span across generations and are a priceless benefit to any workforce organization. This benefit is only as good as the understanding of the past, present, and vision for the future.
- People are living longer, working longer, and bring diverse perspectives to a diverse workforce.
- "Working with storytelling requires us to be sensitive to context and relationships, as well as to historical and cultural influences" (Hersted & Frimann, 2016, p. 160).
- "Generations provide the opportunity to look at Americans both by their place in the life cycle—whether a young adult, a middle-aged parent or a retiree—and by their membership in a cohort of individuals who were born at a similar time" (Dimock, 2019).
- Greater access to technology as a norm has increased exposure to diversity and terminology has also evolved.
- Generational experiences may be considered the framework for perspectives in storytelling. However, just because you are born within a certain time period, does not mean you think or act exactly like everyone born at that time.

APPLICATION EXERCISES

In this chapter, you learned that people are working longer and Americans will average 11.4 jobs between 18 and 48 years old. This means multiple generations already comprise the workforce and life experiences bring diverse perspectives. Delivering products and services to profit and nonprofit businesses effectively will be determined by the ability to effectively work alongside others who do not look, think, or act like you. The following exercise provides an opportunity to reimagine diversity through a generational perspective as you journey toward Workforce 2030 when people are working longer and the majority will be people of color.

- Write a one-page paper about a personal experience working alongside someone who did not look, think, or act like you. Reflect upon (a) the situation that required you to work together, (b) strengths and/or challenges when working together, and (c) whether you achieved the outcome that required you to work together.

CHAPTER 3

Cost of Diversity Challenges

OVERVIEW

Emotional and Financial Costs
E-Race and Other EEOC Initiatives
Employment Practices
Types of Race/Color Discrimination
Chapter Takeaways
Application Exercises

Emotional and Financial Costs

Chapters One and Two introduced and brought awareness to Workforce 2030 when people of color will be the majority. It provided a reflection opportunity that we have co-existed with human diversity as a norm and used age or generational diversity as an example. This chapter discusses the emotional (qualitative) and financial (quantitative) costs when inclusion and Diversity of Perspectives is deficient.

> We commonly hear people dividing the world into right and wrong, good and bad, self and other, etc., as though these terms help us eliminate any ambiguity and as though the terms themselves self-declare mutually exclusive descriptions of the manner in which we experience our world." (Carr & Ann, 2011, p. 241)

Chapters Five through Eight discuss the Diversity of Perspectives model that should be considered a method to avoid the emotional and financial costs when we do not effectively work with others who may or may not look, think, or act like you.

This chapter presents the work of Educating Racism and Colorism From Employment (E-RACE) which is an initiative from the United States Equal Employment Opportunity Commission (EEOC) that describes it as follows:

> In enforcing Title VII's prohibition of race and color discrimination, the EEOC has filed, resolved, and adjudicated a number of cases since 1964. Under the E-RACE Initiative, the Commission continues to be focused on the eradication of race and color discrimination from the 21st century workplace and is seeking to retool its enforcement efforts to address contemporary forms of overt, subtle and implicit bias. Below is an inexhaustive list of significant EEOC private or federal sector cases from 2003 to present. These cases illustrate some of the common, novel, systemic and emerging issues in the realm of race and color discrimination. (n.d.)

The following information from E-RACE represents $291.5 million in significant financial costs due to race and color discrimination in the workplace from the years 2002 to 2020. There are table and case descriptions for categories. Highlights of the financial costs in each category are: $195.6 million Systemic, $1.6 million Youth at Work, $89.3 million Employment Practices, and $11 million in types of Race/Color Discrimination. Each table below will provide more details of the financial costs in private and federal businesses.

TABLE 3.1 Educating Racism and Colorism from Employment (E-RACE), 2002–2020

E-RACE and Other EEOC Initiatives

Category	Financial Costs
Systemic	$195,605,500
Youth @ Work	1,668,000
Total	**$197,273,500**

NOTE. U.S. Equal Employment Opportunity Commission. https://www.eeoc.gov/initiatives/e-race/significant-eeoc-racecolor-casescovering-private-and-federal-sectors

E-Race and Other EEOC Initiatives

Systemic

- In March 2020, Porous Materials, a manufacturer in Ithaca, NY, must pay $93,000 in monetary relief and report any future harassment allegations directly to the EEOC to settle claims that it engaged in pervasive harassment based on race, sex, and national origin, according to a recent EEOC lawsuit. The extreme bullying and harassment allegedly included a manager using racial slurs toward his employees, calling foreign workers "terrorists," telling immigrants to leave America, and making unwanted sexual advances toward female employees. The EEOC further claims the owner of Porous Materials did nothing to put a stop to the harassment. ***EEOC v. Porous Materials, Inc.*, Civil Action No. 3:18-cv-01099 (N.D.N.Y. Mar. 3, 2020).**

- In March 2020, Prewett Enterprises, Inc., doing business as B&P Enterprises, and Desoto Marine, LLC, rail services and disaster response companies, paid $250,000 and furnished other relief to settle a race harassment case brought by the EEOC. According to the EEOC's lawsuit, Prewett and Desoto supervisors and managers subjected African American employees to daily harassment and humiliation because of their race by calling them racially offensive and derogatory names and assigned Black employees the more dangerous job duties. Under the 2-year consent decree, the businesses will revise their anti-racial harassment policies; create an 800-hotline number for employees to report complaints about discrimination, harassment, and retaliation; and conduct exit interviews of employees who leave the company. The decree also mandates training of employees and the reporting of any future complaints of race harassment to the EEOC. ***EEOC v. Prewett Enterprises, Inc. d/b/a B&P Enterprises, and Desoto Marine, LLC*, Civil Action No. 3:18-cv-213 (N.D. Miss. Mar. 18, 2020).**

- In January 2020, Jacksonville Plumbers and Pipefitters Joint Apprenticeship and Training Trust (JPPJATT), which sponsors an apprenticeship program that trains participants to work in the plumbing and pipefitting industries in Northern Florida, revised its selection process, paid $207,500, and provided other significant equitable relief to settle EEOC's class race discrimination lawsuit which sought relief for applicants who allegedly were denied apprenticeship positions because they were Black. In addition to the monetary relief, the 4-year consent decree provides for extensive injunctive relief to help secure a diverse workforce; requires JPPJATT to hire a consultant to review and revise its selection process and implement and train employees in the new process; enjoins JPPJATT from discriminating against Black applicants on the basis of race in the future; and requires the company to hold information sessions at locations in the Black community. ***EEOC v. Jacksonville Plumbers and Pipefitters Joint Apprenticeship and Training Trust*, Case No. 3:18-cv-862-J-32JRK (M.D. Fla. Jan. 2020).**

- In January 2020, Falcon Foundry Company agreed to resolve a racial harassment class case which was filed against it by the Youngstown Branch of the National Association for the Advancement of Colored People (NAACP) and the EEOC. The NAACP filed an EEOC charge on behalf of some employees and the EEOC's investigation found that a top company official subjected employees to derogatory racial comments and that there was a noose hanging in the facility. The EEOC also found that Black and Hispanic employees were disciplined for violating company policies while Caucasian employees who violated the same policies were not disciplined. On these bases, the EEOC found that a class of individuals were harassed and discriminated against because of their race, Black; their national origin, Hispanic; or their association with a Black or Hispanic employee in violation of Title VII of the Civil Rights Act of 1964. The company conducted an internal investigation, trained its employees, and terminated the company official to address the claims filed against it. Additionally, the EEOC, the NAACP and Falcon Foundry signed a conciliation agreement that requires Falcon Foundry to pay substantial monetary relief to identified victims; hold managers and supervisors accountable for discrimination in the workplace and provide ongoing training to all employees; revise its policies and procedures for dealing with discrimination; and report to the EEOC for the agreement's multi-year term.

- In November 2019, Janitorial Service Provider Diversified Maintenance Systems, LLC paid $750,000 and furnished significant equitable relief to settle a federal race discrimination, harassment, and retaliation lawsuit. The complaint alleged that since at least January 2012, Diversified engaged in an ongoing pattern or practice of race discrimination against African American job applicants in Maryland, Washington, DC, and Philadelphia metropolitan areas by refusing to hire Black applicants for custodian, lead custodian, or porter positions and racially harassing a Black janitorial supervisor in the presence of customers and employees. The lawsuit also alleged that when he complained, the company demoted the Black supervisor, changed his work assignments, hours, and conditions and then fired him. The 30-month consent decree enjoins Diversified from discriminating against or harassing anyone based on race or engaging in retaliation and requires the company to designate an internal monitor to ensure compliance with the consent decree. Additionally, Diversified must implement a targeted hiring plan that tracks the number and race of applicants, and reason(s) why they are not hired. It also must create a policy to prohibit harassment and retaliation and provide training on preventing discrimination, harassment, and retaliation. ***EEOC v. Diversified Maintenance Systems, LLC.*, Case No. 8:17-cv-01835 (D. Md. settlement announced Nov. 25, 2019).**

- In November 2019, a federal judge approved the settlement of the 2013 EEOC lawsuit challenging the way a discount retailer conducted criminal background checks of job applicants because the process allegedly discriminated against Black workers with criminal histories. In addition to paying $6 million, the company agreed to hire a criminologist to develop a new background check process that accounts for job applicants' actual risk of recidivism. ***EEOC v. Dolgencorp LLC d/b/a Dollar General*, Civil Action No. 13 C 4307 (N.D. Ill. Nov. 18, 2019).**

- In November 2019, a federal judge approved a $1.2 million settlement resolving the EEOC's racial harassment suit against Nabors Corporate Services Inc. and another Houston-based oil field services company. Nine Black employees and a White coworker received payments. The EEOC lawsuit alleged that Black employees assigned to fracking and coiled tubing oilfield service operations in Pleasanton, Texas, were subjected to a hostile work environment based on race since at least 2012 and that Nabors and C&J Well Services Inc. retaliated against employees who complained about the harassment. Although they deny the allegations, the companies also agreed to provide the affected workers with neutral employment references; maintain social media and information policies that prohibit the use of email, software, or hardware or any company-owned devices to be used for racially offensive communications or similar misconduct; and maintain procedures that encourage workers to come forward with race bias complaints. ***EEOC v. Nabors Indus., Ltd.* No. 5:16-cv-00758 (W.D. Tex. consent decree approved Nov. 12, 2019).**

- In October 2019, Breakthru Beverage Illinois, LLC (BBI), a distributor of alcoholic beverages, agreed to pay $950,000 to resolve an investigation of race and national origin discrimination conducted by the EEOC. Based on its investigation, the EEOC had found reasonable cause to believe that BBI discriminated against Illinois sales employees by offering them account and territory assignments that, when accepted, resulted in national origin or race discrimination, which violates Title VII of the Civil Right Act of 1964. Pursuant to this settlement, BBI will The settlement provides monetary relief to the class identified by the EEOC and ensures the company will take proactive measures to prevent such discrimination from occurring in the future. Pursuant to the terms of the settlement, BBI also will conduct anti-discrimination training for its Illinois sales force; put in place systems to further encourage diverse applicants for open positions; revise its anti-discrimination policy to expressly reference that it prohibits segregating or making assignments based on race and/or national origin, and distribute the revised policy to its Illinois sales force; hire a monitor to track the demographics of employees applying for and receiving offers for specified Illinois sales positions; provide periodic reporting on the demographics of its Illinois sales force for the next 2 years; and post an internal notification to its Illinois employees of this resolution.

- In February 2019, the Jacksonville Association of Firefighters, Local 122, IAFF agreed to pay $4.9 million to settle a race discrimination lawsuit. The EEOC's 2012 lawsuit against the union alleged that the union advocated for an unlawful promotional process that had a disparate impact on African American promotional candidates even after it learned that the EEOC had received charges challenging the city's promotion practices. ***EEOC v. Jacksonville Association of Firefighters, Local 122, IAFF*, No. 3:12-cv-491-J-32MCR (M.D. Fla. Feb. 5, 2019).**

- In December 2017, Laquila Group Inc., a Brooklyn-based construction company, paid $625,000 into a class settlement fund and took measures to eliminate race bias and retaliation against Black construction laborers. In its lawsuit, the EEOC alleged that Laquila engaged in systemic discrimination against Black employees as a class by subjecting them to racial harassment, including referring to them using the N-word, "gorilla," and similar epithets. The Commission also alleged that the company fired an employee who complained about the harassment. The consent decree also requires Laquila to set up a hotline for employees to report illegal discrimination, provide anti-discrimination training to its managers, adopt revised anti-discrimination policies and employee complaint procedures and report all worker harassment and retaliation complaints to the EEOC for the 42-month duration of the agreement. ***EEOC v. The Laquila Grp., Inc.*, No. 1:16-cv-05194 (E.D.N.Y. consent decree approved Dec. 1, 2017).**

- In November 2017, after an extensive 5-year, complicated systemic investigation and settlement efforts, the EEOC reached an agreement with Lone Star Community College covering recruitment, hiring, and mentoring of African American and Hispanic applicants and employees. The terms of the agreement were designed to enhance the College's commitment to the recruitment of African Americans and Hispanics and to engage in meaningful monitoring of the College's efforts to reach its recruitment and hiring goals. The agreement included some novel relief, such as: implementation of a new applicant tracking system; establishing an advisory committee focused on the recruitment, development, and retention of minority groups; hiring of recruitment firms; developing new interview protocol training; establishing a mentoring program for recently hired minority employees; and updating job descriptions for all college manager positions to require as a job component the diversity of its workforce.

- In August 2017, Ford Motor Company agreed to pay nearly $10.125 million to settle a sex and race harassment investigation by the EEOC at two Ford plants in the Chicago area. In its investigation, the EEOC found reasonable cause to believe that personnel at two Ford facilities in the Chicago area, the Chicago Assembly Plant and the Chicago Stamping Plant, had subjected female and African American employees to sexual and racial harassment. The EEOC also found that the company retaliated against employees who complained about the harassment or discrimination. In addition to the monetary relief, the conciliation agreement ensures that during the next 5 years, Ford will conduct regular training at the two Chicago-area facilities; continue to disseminate its anti-harassment and anti-discrimination policies and procedures to employees and new hires; report to the EEOC regarding complaints of harassment and/or related discrimination; and monitor its workforce regarding issues of alleged sexual or racial harassment and related discrimination.

- In July 2017, Bass Pro Outdoor World LLC agreed, without admitting wrongdoing, to pay $10.5 million to a class of African American and Hispanic workers the EEOC alleged it discriminated against by failing to hire because of their race and/or national origin in violation of Title VII. According to the consent decree, Bass Pro will engage in good faith efforts to increase diversity by reaching out to minority colleges and technical schools, participating in job fairs in communities with large minority populations, and post job openings in publications popular among Black and Hispanic communities. Additionally, every 6 months for the next 42 months, Bass Pro is to report to the EEOC its hiring rates on a store-by-store basis. ***EEOC v. Bass Pro Outdoor World LLC*, Case No. 4:11-cv-03425 (S.D. Tex. consent decree filed July 24, 2017).**

- In June 2017, the EEOC investigated a restaurant operating over 100 facilities in the Eastern US involving issues of hiring discrimination against African Americans. The restaurant agreed to pay $9.6 million to class members as part of a conciliation agreement. Additionally, the restaurant will overhaul its hiring procedures and has agreed to institute practices aimed at meeting hiring targets consistent with the labor market in each of the locations in which it has facilities. The new hiring procedures include implementation of an extensive applicant tracking system that will better enable the EEOC and the company to assess whether the company is meeting the targeted hiring levels. The restaurant will also provide an annual report to the EEOC detailing the company's efforts in complying with the agreement and its objectives over the term of the 5-year agreement, including detailed hiring assessments for each facility covered by the agreement.

- In May 2017, Rosebud Restaurants agreed to pay $1.9 million to resolve a race discrimination lawsuit brought by the EEOC against 13 restaurants in the Chicago area. The chain was charged with refusing to hire African American applicants and having managers who used racial slurs to refer to African Americans. The monetary award will be paid to African American applicants who were denied jobs. Pursuant to a consent decree, the chain also agreed to hiring goals with the aim of having 11% of its future workforce be African American. Rosebud is also required to recruit African American applicants as well as train employees and managers about race discrimination. ***EEOC v. Rosebud Rest.*, No. 1:13-cv-06656 (N.D. Ill. May 30, 2017).**

- In April 2017, Sealy of Minnesota paid $175,000 to resolve a charge of racial harassment filed with the EEOC. An investigation by the EEOC's Minneapolis Area Office revealed that the mattress and box spring manufacturing company in St. Paul, MN, subjected its Black and Hispanic employees to severe racial harassment in the form of KKK hoods, nooses, and racial slurs and jokes. The agency also found that the company discriminated against Black and Hispanic employees in the selection of lead positions at the St. Paul facility. ***EEOC v. Sealy of Minn.* (D. Minn. Apr. 20, 2017).**

- In December 2016, Crothall Services Group, Inc., a nationwide provider of janitorial and facilities management services, settled an EEOC lawsuit by adopting significant changes to its record-keeping practices related to the use of criminal background checks. According to the EEOC's complaint, Crothall used criminal background checks to make hiring decisions without making and keeping required records that disclose the impact criminal history assessments have on persons identifiable by race, sex, or ethnic group, a violation of Title VII of the Civil Rights Act of 1965. ***EEOC v. Crothall Servs. Group, Inc.*, Civil Action No. 2:15-cv-03812-AB (E.D. Pa. Dec. 16, 2016).**

- In August 2016, a magistrate judge reaffirmed that "African" has long been recognized as an acceptable class entitled to protection under Title VII. The EEOC alleged that the Defendants, a health-care management system and nursing home discriminated against African employees, specifically employees from Ethiopia and Sudan, when it terminated four personal care providers all on the same day, allegedly for failing to pass a newly instituted written exam. The EEOC brought disparate impact and treatment claims based on race and national origin, and a retaliation claim for a White supervisor who stood up for the African workers and was fired several months before the test was instituted. Defendants moved for dismissal arguing (1) Africa is not a nation and so cannot serve as the basis of a national origin claim; (2) the EEOC failed to allege any shared cultural or linguistic characteristics between the aggrieved individuals so they could not constitute a protected class; and (3) the EEOC's retaliation claim must be dismissed because the EEOC failed to allege protected activity or the Defendants had knowledge of the White supervisor's motivations. The Magistrate Judge recommended that the motion be denied in total. ***EEOC v. Columbine Health Sys. & New Mercer Commons*, Civ. Action No. 15-cv-01597-MSK-CBS (D. Colo. Aug. 19, 2016).**

- In June 2016, the EEOC obtained a $350,000 settlement in its race discrimination lawsuit against defendant FAPS, Inc., a company located at Port Newark, NJ, involved in the processing for final sale of shipped automobiles. In this case, the Commission alleged that the company engaged in a pattern-or-practice of race discrimination by relying on word-of-mouth hiring which resulted in a predominantly White workforce despite the substantial African American available workforce in the Newark area. The agency further alleged that FAPS refused to hire qualified African American candidates, including by telling them that no positions were available when in fact FAPS was hiring. Finally, the EEOC alleged that FAPS' employment application contained improper pre-employment medical inquiries in violation of the ADA. Besides the monetary compensation, the 5-year consent decree requires FAPS to meet substantial hiring goals for African Americans; give hiring priority to rejected class members who are interested in working at the company; use recruiting methods designed to increase the African American applicant pool; and hire an EEO coordinator to ensure compliance with Title VII. ***EEOC v. FAPS, Inc.*, C.A. No. 2:10-cv-03095 (D.N.J. June 15, 2016).**

- In April 2015, Local 25 of the Sheet Metal Workers' International Association and its associated apprenticeship school agreed to create a back pay fund for a group of minority sheet metal workers in partial settlement of race discrimination claims against the local union. Pursuant to the settlement, it is estimated that the union will pay approximately $12.7 million over the next 5 years and provide substantial remedial relief to partially resolve claims made against the union in 1991–2002. The trade union, which is responsible for sheet metal journeypersons in northern New Jersey, allegedly discriminated against Black and Hispanic journeypersons over a multiyear period in hiring and job assignments. An analysis of hours and wages showed African American and Hispanic workers received fewer hours of work than their White coworkers during most of this same time frame. This particular agreement covers from April 1991 through December 2002. ***EEOC v. Local 28 of the Sheet Metal Workers' Int'l Ass'n*, Case No. 71 Civ. 2887 (LAK) (S.D.N.Y. April 2, 2015).**

- In December 2015, Hillshire Brands (formerly known as Sara Lee Corporation) agreed to pay $4 million to 74 workers at the now-shuttered Paris, Texas, plant, including the dozens of people who sought EEOC charges against Hillshire and other aggrieved workers identified by the EEOC and the plaintiffs. This resolution settles claims that the company subjected a class of Black employees to a hostile work environment that included racist graffiti and comments that included the N-word and "boy." The company also agreed to implement training at all of its plants in a bid to end consolidated suits from the EEOC and former worker Stanley Beaty. The consent decree also requires Hillshire to implement anti-racism training and create a mechanism for employees at its existing plants to confidentially report instances of harassment, discrimination, and retaliation. The settlement also requires Hillshire to designate one employee to serve as a point-of-contact for those who feel they've been treated improperly and to punish workers with suspensions and even termination who are found "by reasonable evidence" to have engaged in racial bias or behavior related to it. ***EEOC v. Hillshire Brands Co. f/k/a Sara Lee Corp.*, No. 2:15-cv-01347 (E.D. Tex. consent decree filed 12/18/15) and *Beaty et al v. The Hillshire Brands Co. et al.*, No. 2:14-cv-00058 (E.D. Tex. consent decree filed 12/18/15).**

- In October 2015, a federal judge held that the operators of an Indianapolis Hampton Inn in contempt for failing to comply with five different conditions settling the EEOC's class race discrimination and retaliation lawsuit against the companies. The judge faulted Noble Management LLC and New Indianapolis Hotels for failing to: (1) properly post notices; (2) properly train management employees; (3) keep employment records; (4) institute a new hiring procedure for housekeeping employees; and (5) reinstate three former housekeeping employees. The judge also faulted Noble and New Indianapolis Hotels for commingling of medical records in employee personnel files. As background, the EEOC filed suit against operators New Indianapolis Hotels LLC and Noble Management LLC in September 2010, alleging that their Hampton Inn fired African American housekeepers because of their race and in retaliation for complaints about race discrimination. The agency also charged that the hotel paid lower wages to Black housekeepers, excluded Black housekeeping applicants on a systemic basis, and failed to maintain records required by law in violation of Title VII. In September 2012, the judge entered a 5-year consent decree resolving the EEOC's litigation against the hotel operators. The decree provided $355,000 in monetary relief to approximately 75 African American former housekeeping employees and applicants and required training, notice posting, reinstatement of three former housekeeping employees, a new hiring procedure for housekeeping employees and ordered that the defendants maintain employment-related records. The court also enjoined the operators from race discrimination and retaliation in the future. In March 2014, following the filing of the EEOC's contempt motion, Judge Lawrence ruled that the defendants violated the terms of the 2012 decree and ordered Defendants to pay more than $50,000 in back wages to the three former housekeepers whose reinstatement was delayed. Defendants were also ordered to: (1) provide monthly reporting to the EEOC on compliance with the new hiring procedure, recordkeeping and posting; (2) pay fines for late reporting; (3) allow random inspections by the EEOC subject to a fine, for failure to grant access; (4) pay fines for failure to post, destroying records or failing to distribute employment applications; (5) provide the EEOC with any requested employment records within 15 days of a request; (6) cease comingling medical records; and (7) train management employees. The posting and training provisions of the Decree were also extended by 2 years. In November 2015, the judge awarded $50,515 in fees and $6,733.76 in costs to the EEOC because the "Defendants willfully violated the explicit terms of the Consent Decree and repeatedly failed to comply with it [.]" ***EEOC v. New Indianapolis Hotels LLC and Noble Management LLC*, C.A. No. 1:10-CV-01234-WTL-DKL (N.D. Ind. Nov. 9, 2015) (fee ruling).**

- In September 2015, BMW Manufacturing Co. settled for $1.6 million and other relief in an EEOC lawsuit alleging that the company's criminal background check policy disproportionately affects Black logistics workers at a South Carolina plant. Specifically, the EEOC alleged that after learning the results of the criminal background checks around July 2008, BMW denied plant access to 88 logistics employees, resulting in their termination from the previous logistics provider and denial of hire by the new logistics services provider for work at BMW. Of those 88 employees, 70 were Black. Some of the logistics employees had been employed at BMW for several years, working for the various logistics services providers utilized by BMW since the opening of the plant in 1994. Under the terms of a consent decree signed by Judge Henry M. Herlong of the U.S. District Court for the District of South Carolina, the $1.6 million will be shared by 56 known claimants and other Black applicants the EEOC said were shut out of BMW's Spartanburg, SC, plant when the company switched to a new logistics contractor. In addition to the monetary relief, the company will provide each claimant who wishes to return to the facility an opportunity to apply for a logistics position. BMW will also notify other applicants who have previously expressed interest in a logistics position at the facility of their right to apply for work, the decree states. BMW has implemented a new criminal background check policy and will continue to operate under that policy throughout the 3-year term of the decree. The company is expressly enjoined from "utilizing the criminal background check guidelines" challenged by the EEOC in its lawsuit, the decree states. The agreement also imposes on BMW notice-posting, training, record-keeping, reporting and other requirements. ***EEOC v. BMW Mfg. Co.*, No. 7:13-cv-01583 (D.S.C. consent decree filed Sep. 8, 2015).**

- In August 2015, Target Corp. settled for $2.8 million an EEOC charge that the retailer's former tests for hiring for professional jobs discriminated against applicants based on race, sex, and disability. Three assessments used by Target disproportionately screened out female and racial minority applicants, and a separate psychological assessment was a pre-employment medical examination that violated the Americans with Disabilities Act, the EEOC had charged. Target also violated Title VII of the 1964 Civil Rights Act by failing to maintain the records sufficient to gauge the impact of its hiring procedures. Under the 3-year conciliation agreement, reached before any lawsuit was filed, Target has discontinued the use of the tests and made changes to its applicant tracking system, the EEOC said. About 4,500 unsuccessful applicants affected by the alleged discriminatory tests now are eligible to file claims for monetary relief.

- In March 2015, a Texas-based oil and gas drilling company agreed to settle for $12.26 million the EEOC's lawsuit alleging discrimination, harassment, and retaliation against racial minorities nationwide. According to a complaint filed by the EEOC the same day as the proposed decree, Patterson-UTI had engaged in patterns or practices of hostile work environment harassment, disparate treatment discrimination, and retaliation against Hispanic, Latino, Black, American Indian, Asian, Pacific Islander, and other minority workers at its facilities in Colorado and other states. Under the proposed 4-year consent decree, the drilling company also will create a new vice president position to be filled by a "qualified EEO professional" who will facilitate, monitor, and report on the company's compliance with certain training, management evaluation, minority outreach, and other remedial measures. ***EEOC v. Patterson-UTI Drilling Co.*, No. 1:15-cv-00600 (D. Colo. consent decree filed Mar. 24, 2015).**

- In January 2015, Skanska USA Building, Inc., a building contractor headquartered in Parsippany, NJ, paid $95,000 to settle a racial harassment and retaliation lawsuit brought by the EEOC. According to the EEOC's suit, Skanska violated federal law by allowing workers to subject a class of Black employees who were working as buck hoist operators to racial harassment, and by firing them for complaining to Skanska about the misconduct. Skanska served as the general contractor on the Methodist Le Bonheur Children's Hospital in Memphis, where the incidents in this lawsuit took place. The class of Black employees worked for C-1, Inc. Construction Company, a minority-owned subcontractor for Skanska. Skanska awarded a subcontract to C-1 to provide buck hoist operations for the construction site and thereafter supervised all C-1 employees while at the work site. The EEOC charged that Skanska failed to properly investigate complaints from the buck hoist operators that White employees subjected them to racially offensive comments and physical assault. ***EEOC v. Shanska USA Building, Inc.*, No. 2:10-cv-02717 (W.D. Tenn. Jan. 29, 2015).**

- In December 2014, two Memphis-based affiliates of Select Staffing, employment companies doing business in Tennessee, agreed to pay $580,000 to settle allegations they engaged in race and national origin discrimination. The EEOC's lawsuit charged that the staffing firms had discriminated against four Black temporary employees and a class of Black and non-Hispanic job applicants by failing to place or refer them for employment. The four temporary employees said while seeking employment through the company's Memphis area facilities, they witnessed Hispanic applicants getting preferential treatment in hiring and placement. ***EEOC v. New Koosharem Corp.*, No. 2:13-cv-2761 (W.D. Tenn. consent decree filed Dec. 5, 2014).**
- In December 2014, three related well-servicing companies agreed to pay $1.2 million to settle allegations by the Equal Employment Opportunity Commission of verbal abuse of minority employees. The EEOC complaint alleged that J&R employees regularly used racial slurs to refer to Black, Hispanic, and Native American employees. Employees of these racial groups on company rigs regularly heard racist terms and demeaning remarks about green cards and deportation, the EEOC complaint said. Several individuals complained to management, but their complaints were minimized or ignored, the complaint alleged. For example, an area supervisor responded to employee complaints by telling the complainants they could quit or by saying that he was sick of everyone coming to him and that everyone simply needed to do their jobs. In addition, the complaint stated that several men were demoted or fired after taking their complaints of discrimination to the Wyoming Department of Workforce Services' Labor Standards Division. ***EEOC v. Dart Energy Corp.*, No. 13-cv-00198 (D. Wyo. consent decree filed Dec. 1, 2014).**
- In November 2014, a Rockville, MD-based environmental remediation services contractor paid $415,000 and provided various other relief to settle a class lawsuit alleging that the company engaged in a pattern or practice of race and sex discrimination in its recruitment and hiring of field laborers. Under a 3-year consent decree signed Nov. 10 by Judge Paul W. Grimm of the U.S. District Court for the District of Maryland, ACM Services Inc. will pay a combined $110,000 to the two Hispanic female workers who first brought the allegations to the EEOC's attention and will establish a class fund of $305,000 for other potential claimants to be identified by the agency. According to the EEOC, the company has relied exclusively on "word-of-mouth recruitment practices" for field laborer positions, with the intent and effect of restricting the recruitment of Black and female applicants. ACM also subjected the

two charging parties to harassment based on sex, national origin, and race, and it retaliated against them for opposing the mistreatment—and against one of them based on her association with Black people—by firing them, the commission alleged. The agreement applies to all ACM facilities and locations nationwide and has extra-territorial application to the extent permitted by Title VII of the 1964 Civil Rights Act. In addition to the monetary relief, the decree requires the company to set numerical hiring goals for its field laborer positions, recruit Black and female applicants via print and internet advertisements, and report to the EEOC regarding its attainment of the numerical hiring goals and other settlement terms. ***EEOC v. ACM Servs., Inc.*, No. 8:14-cv-02997 (D. Md. consent decree filed Nov. 10, 2014).**

- In November 2014, Battaglia Distributing Corporation paid $735,000 to a group of current and former African American employees. In this case, the EEOC alleged that Battaglia tolerated an egregious race-based hostile work environment, requiring African American dock workers to endure harassment that included racial slurs (including the "N" word). Among other relief provided under the decree, Battaglia also will provide its managers with training on Title VII and report regularly to the EEOC on any complaints it has received, as well as provide other data to demonstrate that it has not retaliated against any of the participants in the litigation. ***EEOC v. Battaglia Distrib. Corp.*, No. 13-cv-5789 (N.D. Ill. consent decree entered Nov. 10, 2014).**

- In October 2014, Prestige Transportation Service L.L.C., a Miami company that provides transportation services to airline personnel to and from Miami International Airport, paid $200,000 to settle a race discrimination and retaliation lawsuit, in connection with actions allegedly committed under different ownership. The EEOC charged in its suit that Prestige's predecessor company, Airbus Alliance Inc., repeatedly instructed its human resource manager to not hire African American applicants because they were "trouble" and "would sue the company." ***EEOC v. Prestige Transp. Service L.L.C.*, No. 1:13-cv-20684(JEM) (S.D. Fla. consent decree filed Sept. 26, 2014).**

- In September 2014, McCormick & Schmick's settled a 2008 EEOC lawsuit, alleging a pattern or practice of race discrimination against African American job applicants by refusing to hire them for front-of-the-house positions and by denying equal work assignments because of their race. The consent decree established a claims fund of $1.3 million and provides substantial injunctive relief, including goals for hiring of Black job applicants for front-of-the-house positions, targeted recruitment efforts, and extensive self-assessment of hiring and work assignment practices to ensure non-discrimination and compliance with the terms of the consent decree. McCormick & Schmick's also must designate an outside monitor to oversee compliance with the consent decree and submit reports to the EEOC. ***EEOC v. McCormick & Schmick's Seafood Restaurants, Inc. and McCormick and Schmick Restaurant Corporation*, No. WMN-09-cv-984 (D. Md. Sep. 12, 2014).**

- In September 2013, U-Haul agreed to pay $750,000 to eight African American current and former employees and to provide other relief to settle a race and retaliation discrimination lawsuit filed by the EEOC. According to the EEOC's suit, Black employees were subjected to racial slurs and other racially offensive comments by their White supervisor, at U-Haul's Memphis facility. The EEOC's complaint charged that the supervisor regularly referred to Black employees with the "N" word and other derogatory slurs. The suit further alleged that the company engaged in retaliation by firing one employee when he complained of racial harassment to the company president. Under the 2-year consent decree, U-Haul Company of Tennessee must maintain an anti-discrimination policy prohibiting race discrimination, racial harassment, and retaliation, and provide mandatory training to all employees regarding the policy. Additionally, the marketing company president will receive training on race discrimination and on obligations to report race discrimination, racial harassment, and retaliation. Finally, the company will provide written reports to the EEOC regarding any race discrimination or racial harassment complaints by employees. ***EEOC v. U-Haul Co. Int'l & U-Haul Co. of Tenn.*, No. 2:11-cv-02844 (W.D. Tenn. Sep. 25, 2013).**

- In September 2013, a Kentucky coal mining company paid $245,000 to 19 total applicants and amended its hiring practices to settle a racial discrimination suit brought by the EEOC. River View Coal LLC, a unit of Alliance Resource Partners LP, also will have to regularly report to the EEOC on its hiring practices for 2 years to escape the suit, which alleged that the company refused to hire a class of African American applicants for coal mining jobs at its Waverly, KY, location since 2008. The consent decree also requires River View to refrain from any future racial discrimination in its hiring procedures. ***EEOC v. River View Coal, LLC*, No. 4:11-cv-00117(JHM)(HBB) (W.D. Ky. Sep. 26, 2013).**

- In December 2012, a South Dallas, TX, mill agreed to pay $500,000 to a class of 14 Black employees to settle an EEOC race discrimination suit alleging that the mill exposed Black employees to violent, racist graffiti and racial slurs by coworkers, such as "KKK," swastikas, Confederate flags, "white power," and other racist terms, including "die, n----r, die," as well as the display of nooses at an employee workstation. Black employees alleged that the supervisors allowed the behavior to continue unchecked. The consent decree permanently enjoins the company from discriminating against employees on the basis of race and requires the company to enact a graffiti abatement policy and undergo annual reviews of its compliance for 2 years. ***EEOC v. Rock-Tenn Services Co.*, No.3:10-cv-01960 (N.D. Tex. filed Sep. 29, 2012).**

- In November 2012, a federal court ordered Caldwell Freight Lines, a now defunct company, to pay $120,000 to settle a race discrimination complaint stemming from its alleged refusal to hire Black applicants to work on its loading dock even though it is no longer in business. According to the EEOC's lawsuit, 51 African American applicants sought work with Caldwell Freight and none was hired even though many had previous dock experience and were qualified for the positions. An EEOC investigation revealed that the company hired no Black dock workers during the period studied and that one high-level manager allegedly said he "didn't want any [B]lacks on the dock." Under the terms of the consent decree, if the company resumes operations, it will have to implement an anti-discrimination policy and report to the EEOC all discrimination complaints and information regarding its hiring practices during the term of the decree. ***EEOC v. Caldwell Freight Lines,*** **Case No. 5:11CV00134 (W.D.N.C. Aug. 3, 2012).**

- In October 2012, a federal district court in Texas ordered AA Foundries Inc. to take specific measures to prevent racial harassment of Black employees at its San Antonio plant following a $200,000 jury verdict finding the company liable for race discrimination under Title VII. According to the EEOC, evidence at trial indicated that a White supervisor used "the N word" in reference to Black employees, called male Black employees "motherfucking boys," posted racially tinged materials in an employee break room, and accused Black employees of "always stealing and wanting welfare." After several employees filed racial harassment charges with the EEOC, a noose was displayed in the workplace. When some employees complained, the supervisor allegedly replied the noose was "no big deal" and that workers who complained were "too sensitive." Additionally, at trial, he also admitted it did not bother him to hear racially derogatory language in the workplace. In a judgment entered Oct. 9, the district court upheld the jury verdict that AA Foundries must pay punitive damages of $100,000 to former employee Christopher Strickland, $60,000 to former employee Leroy Beal, and $40,000 to former employee Kenneth Bacon. Because trial evidence also showed that AA Foundries lacked effective internal procedures to handle discrimination complaints, it must conduct at least 1 hour of equal employment opportunity training for all employees within 60 days of the court's Oct. 9 order. The company must distribute copies of its revised written anti-harassment policy to all current and future employees and post the policy in the break room of its San Antonio manufacturing facility. Every employee shall be notified of the procedure for initiating racial harassment or other bias complaints, including notice of their right to file EEOC charges if the company does not resolve their complaint. ***EEOC v. AA Foundries Inc.,*** **No. 11-792 (W.D. Tex. judgment and injunction entered Oct. 9, 2012).**

- In September 2012, two California-based trucking firms agreed to settle for $630,000 an EEOC lawsuit alleging one company violated Title VII by permitting the harassment of African American, Latino, and East Indian workers and by otherwise discriminating based on race, national origin, and religion. In its original complaint, EEOC alleged that since at least 2003, management officials and employees at Scully Distribution referred to Black drivers as "niggers," East Indian drivers as "Taliban" and "camel jockeys," and a Latino manager as a "spic." The EEOC also charged Scully gave non-White drivers less favorable job assignments than their White counterparts. The EEOC claimed Scully also fired one of the three employees who filed EEOC charges complaining about the alleged harassment in retaliation for his protected activity. Scully denied all of the EEOC's allegations, but it and its successor Ryder System Inc. agreed to resolve the suit. ***EEOC v. Scully Distribution Servs. Inc.,*** **No. 11-cv-08090 (C.D. Cal. proposed consent decree filed Sep. 25, 2012).**

- In August 2012, a Tampa, FL-based environmental services company agreed to settle a race discrimination and harassment case brought by the EEOC and 11 intervening plaintiffs for $2,750,000 and other relief. In the lawsuit, the EEOC alleged that the harassment of African American employees included multiple displays of nooses, the repeated use of the "N-word," and physical threats. The EEOC also claimed that four White employees were harassed by their White coworkers because they associated with African American employees. Two African American employees also alleged they were fired because of their race and two White employees asserted they were fired for engaging in protected activity and in retaliation for associating with African American employees. At summary judgment, the district court denied in part the company's motion, stating that the company ignored both the extreme symbolism of a noose and that a reasonable jury could conclude that the worksite had at least some racial tension given the other nooses, threats, and racial epithets that each African American employee experienced, and that the noose was intended to intimidate all African Americans. The court also found that a reasonable jury could decide that Defendant failed to exercise reasonable care to prevent or remedy the harassment since it did not distribute its written policy forbidding racial harassment to its employees, post it at the job-site, or train the employees about what constitutes harassment and how to report it. The court, however, determined that Defendant was entitled to summary judgment on the hostile work environment claims brought on behalf of the White employees because injury must be personal and thus a White employee cannot sue for harassment of African American employees that the White employee happened to see. Lastly, intervening Plaintiff provided direct evidence that the supervisor who fired him did so because of his race (through the supervisor's comment that he could get rid of "that . . . nigger." 2011 U.S. Dist. LEXIS 110149 (N.D. Ill. Sept. 27, 2011). Although the company denied liability for the harassment, the 3-year consent decree enjoins the company from engaging in further retaliation, race discrimination, or racial harassment, including associational bias. The company also must revise its anti-discrimination policy; provide employee training on the revised policy; and develop a procedure for investigating complaints of race discrimination and harassment and evaluating supervisors' compliance with the revised anti-discrimination policy. ***EEOC v. WRS Infrastructure and Env't Inc. d/b/a WRS Compass*****, No. 1:09-cv-4272 (N.D. Ill. consent decree filed Aug. 23, 2012).**

- In June 2012, Yellow Transportation Inc. and YRC Inc. agreed to settle for $11 million an EEOC suit alleging that the trucking companies permitted the racial harassment of Black employees at a now-closed Chicago Ridge, IL, facility. The proposed consent decree would settle both the EEOC's suit and a private suit filed in 2008 by 14 Black employees under the Civil Rights Act of 1866 (42 U.S.C. § 1981), which were consolidated for purposes of settlement. In its complaint, the EEOC claimed that Black employees at the Chicago Ridge facility, which closed in 2009, were subjected to multiple incidents of hangman's nooses and racist graffiti, comments, and cartoons. The EEOC claimed that Yellow and YRC also subjected Black employees to harsher discipline and closer scrutiny than their White counterparts and gave Black employees more difficult and time-consuming work assignments. Although numerous Black employees complained about these conditions, Yellow and YRC failed to act to correct the problems, the EEOC alleged. The court granted preliminary approval of a proposed consent decree, but it must grant final approval following a fairness hearing before the decree takes effect. ***EEOC v. Yellow Transp. Inc.*, No. 09 CV 7693 (N.D. Ill. preliminary approval granted June 28, 2012).**

- In January 2012, Pepsi Beverages Company, formerly known as Pepsi Bottling Group, agreed in a post-investigation conciliation to pay $3.13 million and provide training and job offers to victims of the former criminal background check policy to resolve an EEOC charge alleging race discrimination in hiring.

> The EEOC's investigation revealed that more than 300 African Americans were adversely affected when Pepsi applied a criminal background check policy that disproportionately excluded Black applicants from permanent employment. Under Pepsi's former policy, job applicants who had been arrested pending prosecution were not hired for a permanent job even if they had never been convicted of any offense.
>
> Additionally,
>
> Pepsi's former policy also denied employment to applicants from employment who had been arrested or convicted of certain minor offenses. The use of arrest and conviction records to deny employment can be illegal under Title VII of the Civil Rights Act of 1964, when it is not relevant for the job, because it can limit the employment opportunities of applicants or workers based on their race or ethnicity.

- In December 2011, a New York City retail-wholesale fish market agreed to pay $900,000 and institute anti-discrimination measures to settle an EEOC lawsuit charging it with creating a hostile work environment for Black and African male employees. The lawsuit alleged that management at the company's Brooklyn facility routinely subjected more than 30 Black and African male loaders and drivers to sexual and racial harassment and retaliated against employees who complained. The harassment was both physical and verbal and included offensive comments based on race and national origin such as "nigger" and "African bastard" as well as explicit sexual expressions. The Commission also alleged that the company engaged in retaliation against workers who joined in the complaint. In addition to the monetary relief, M. Slavin agreed to submit to 5 years of monitoring by the EEOC; retain an independent EEO coordinator to investigate complaints; conduct one-on-one training for the worst harassers; and provide annual training for all staff. ***EEOC v. M. Slavin & Sons Ltd.*, No. 09-5330 (E.D.N.Y. filed consent decree 12/15/11).**

- In December 2010, Roadway Express, a less-than-truckload motor carrier with terminals throughout North America, settled the claims of two lawsuits alleging racial harassment of Black employees and race discrimination in terms and conditions of employment at two Illinois facilities. The claims included: (1) awarding Black employees less favorable assignments (both terminals); (2) assigning them more difficult and demanding work (both terminals); (3) enforcing break times more stringently (Chicago Heights); (4) subjecting their work to heightened scrutiny (Chicago Heights); and (5) disciplining them for minor misconduct (both terminals). Roadway also assigned Chicago Heights employees to segregated work groups. The 5-year decree, which applies to Roadway and YRC, Roadway's identity after it merged with Yellow Transportation, includes $10 million in monetary relief, $8.5 million to be paid upon preliminary approval of the decree and the remainder in three subsequent installments due on or before November 1 of 2011, 2012, and 2013. In addition to prohibiting race discrimination and retaliation against Black employees at YRC's Chicago Heights facility, the decree also requires YRC to provide all Chicago Heights employees annual training on racial harassment and race discrimination and engage a Work Assignment Consultant and a Disciplinary Practice Consultant to assist it in reviewing and revising the company's work assignment and disciplinary policies and practices at the Chicago facility. ***EEOC v. Roadway Express, Inc., and YRC, Inc.*, Nos. 06-CV-4805 and 08-CV-5555 and *Bandy v. Roadway Express, Inc., and YRC, Inc.*, No. 10-CV-5304 (N.D. Ill. Dec. 20, 2010).**

- In October 2010, Austin Foam Plastics, Inc. (AFP), a producer and distributor of corrugated box and cushion packaging, agreed to pay $600,000 to resolve a number of racial and sexual harassment charges. In pertinent part, the EEOC alleged that Black employees at AFP were subjected to intimidation, ridicule, insults, racially offensive comments and jokes, and cartoons and images that denigrated African Americans. White employees and managers regularly emailed racially derogatory jokes, cartoons, and other materials to coworkers, and posted racially offensive photographs on the bulletin board outside the human resources office. They also engaged in threatening and intimidating conduct toward Black employees, such as tampering with the brake lines and air hoses of one CP's truck. The 2-year consent decree also enjoins race and sex (male) discrimination under Title VII, as well as retaliation. Defendant will submit to EEOC an EEO policy that prohibits race and sex discrimination and retaliation. Defendant will file annual audit reports with the EEOC summarizing each complaint of race or sex (male) discrimination, or retaliation, it receives at its Pfluggerville, TX, location and its disposition. ***EEOC v. Austin Foam Plastics, Inc.*, No. 1:09-CV-00180 (W.D. Tex. Oct. 15, 2010).**

- In September 2010, a mineral company agreed to pay $440,000 and other relief to settle a class race discrimination and retaliation lawsuit. Allegedly, the company disciplined an African American quality control supervisor for having facial hair and using a cell phone during work, while Caucasian employees were not reprimanded for similar conduct. In addition to management subjecting the Black supervisor to heightened and unfair scrutiny, the company moved his office to the basement, while White employees holding the same position were moved to higher floors. Other African American employees were subjected to racial harassment, such as a White supervisor placing a hangman's noose on a piece of machinery. ***EEOC v. Mineral Met, Inc.*, No. 1:09-cv-02199 (N.D. Ohio Sept. 23, 2010).**

- In August 2010, the EEOC and the largest commercial roofing contractor in New York state settled for $1 million an EEOC suit alleging the company discriminated against a class of Black workers through verbal harassment, denials of promotion, and unfair work assignments. According to the lawsuit, the EEOC alleged from at least 1993 to the present, a White foreman repeatedly used racial slurs toward Black workers, that the company assigned Black employees to the most difficult, dirty, and least desirable jobs, that the roofing contractor systematically excluded Black employees from promotion opportunities, and that the company retaliated against those who complained. Additionally, nooses were displayed and portable toilets featured racially offensive graffiti with swastikas and "KKK" references at the job sites, the EEOC alleged. Although it admitted no wrongdoing and said that it settled the case for financial reasons, the company agreed to hire an equal employment opportunity coordinator to provide employee EEO training, monitor future race discrimination complaints, and file periodic reports with the EEOC regarding hiring, layoffs, and promotions. ***EEOC v. Elmer W. Davis Inc.*, No. 07-CV-06434 (W.D.N.Y. consent decree filed Aug. 10, 2010).**

- In December 2009, a national grocery chain paid $8.9 million to resolve three lawsuits collectively alleging race, color, national origin, and retaliation discrimination, affecting 168 former and current employees. According to the lawsuits, minority employees were repeatedly subjected to derogatory comments and graffiti. Blacks were termed "n-----s" and Hispanics termed "s---s"; offensive graffiti in the men's restroom, which included racial and ethnic slurs, depictions of lynchings, swastikas, and White supremacist and anti-immigrant statements, was so offensive that several employees would relieve themselves outside the building or go home at lunchtime rather than use the restroom. Black and Hispanic employees also were allegedly given harder work assignments and were more frequently and severely disciplined than their Caucasian coworkers. Lastly, the EEOC asserted that dozens of employees complained about the discriminatory treatment and harassment and were subsequently given the harder job assignments, were passed over for promotion and even fired as retaliation. ***EEOC v. Albertsons LLC,* Civil Action No. 06-cv-01273, No. 08-cv-00640, and No. 08-cv-02424 (D. Colo 2009).**

- In May 2009, an Illinois construction company agreed to pay $630,000 to settle a class action race discrimination suit, alleging that it laid off Black employees after they had worked for the company for short periods of time, but retained White employees for long-term employment. The 3-year consent decree also prohibits the company from engaging in future discrimination and retaliation; requires that it implement a policy against race discrimination and retaliation, as well as a procedure for handling complaints of race discrimination and retaliation; mandates that the company provide training to employees regarding race discrimination and retaliation; and requires the company to provide periodic reports to the EEOC regarding layoffs and complaints of discrimination and retaliation. ***EEOC v. Area Erectors, Inc.*, No. 1:07-CV-02339 (N.D. Ill. May 29, 2009).**

- In August 2008, a tobacco retail chain agreed to pay $425,000 and provide significant remedial relief to settle a race discrimination lawsuit on behalf of qualified Black workers who were denied promotion to management positions. The 3-year consent decree also requires the company, which has stores in Arkansas, Missouri, and Mississippi, to train all managers and supervisors on preventing race discrimination and retaliation; create job descriptions for manager and assistant manager positions that outline the qualifications for each position; develop a written promotion policy that will include the procedures by which employees will be notified of promotional opportunities; report assistant manager and manager vacancies, the name and race of all applicants for the position, and the name of the successful candidate; report the names of all African Americans who are either hired or promoted to manager or assistant manager positions; and report any complaints of race discrimination and describe its investigation in response to the complaint. ***EEOC v. Tobacco Superstores, Inc.*, No. 3:05 CV 00218 (E.D. Ark. settled Aug. 2008).**
- In July 2008, a Chicago-based leading chemical manufacturer of high-quality surfactants, polymers, chemical specialties, and cosmetic preservatives paid $175,000 to settle a class race discrimination and retaliation lawsuit filed by the EEOC. According to the lawsuit, a class of African American employees had been subjected to race discrimination, racial harassment, and retaliation for complaining about the misconduct. The company agreed to conduct EEO training and refrain from future acts of discrimination and retaliation. ***EEOC v. McIntyre Group, Ltd.*, No. 07 C 5458 (N.D. Ill. settled July 2008).**
- In May 2008, the EEOC obtained a settlement of $1.65 million in a racial harassment case filed against a general contractor and its subsidiaries on behalf of a class of African American employees who were subjected to egregious racial harassment at a construction site in Bethlehem, Pennsylvania. The harassment included a life-size noose made of heavy rope hung from a beam in a class member's work area for at least 10 days before it was removed; the regular use of the "N-word"; racially offensive comments made to Black individuals, including "I think everybody should own one"; "Black people are no good and you can't trust them"; and "Black people can't read or write." Additionally, racist graffiti was written in portable toilets, with terms such as "coon"; "if u not White u not right"; "White power"; "KKK"; and "I love the Ku Klux Klan." Additional remedies were injunctive relief enjoining each defendant from engaging in racial harassment or retaliation; anti-discrimination training; the posting of a notice about the settlement; and reporting complaints of racial harassment to the EEOC for monitoring. ***EEOC v. Conectiv, et al.* Civil Action No. 2:05-cv-00389 (E.D. Pa. settled May 5, 2008).**

- In August 2007, a renowned French chef agreed to pay $80,000 to settle claims that his upscale Manhattan restaurant discriminated against Hispanic workers and Asian employees from Bangladesh in job assignments. The aggrieved employees alleged that they were restricted to "back of the house" positions such as busboys and runners and refused promotions to "front of the house" positions such as captains, which instead went to Caucasian workers with less experience and seniority. They also alleged that they were subjected to racial insults and harassment when they complained. **EEOC v. Restaurant Daniel, No. 07-6845 (S.D.N.Y. August 2, 2007).**

- In June 2007, the EEOC obtained $500,000 from a South Lyon, MI, steel tubing company, which, after purchasing the assets of its predecessor company, allegedly refused to hire a class of African American former employees of the predecessor. Though the company hired 52 of its predecessor's former employees, none of them were Black. The EEOC charged that many of the White employees hired had significantly less experience than the Black former employees represented by the EEOC, and in some cases had actually been trained by the same African American employees who were denied hire. The suit also included other Black applicants who were denied hire in favor of less qualified White applicants. ***EEOC v. Michigan Seamless Tube*, No. 05-73719 (E.D. Mich. June 8, 2007).**

- In February 2007, the EEOC obtained a $5 million settlement resolving two consolidated class action employment discrimination lawsuits against a global engine systems and parts company, asserting that the company engaged in illegal discrimination against African Americans, Hispanics, and Asians at its Rockford and Rockton, IL, facilities with respect to pay, promotions, and training. ***EEOC v. Woodward Governor Company*, No. 06-cv-50178 (N.D. Ill. Feb. 2007).**

- In August 2006, the Commission settled this Title VII lawsuit alleging that since at least 1991, defendant, a manufacturer of precision metal-formed products and assemblies, failed to hire women and Blacks into laborer and machine operator positions at its plant because of their sex and race for $940,000. The complaint also alleged that defendant failed to retain employment applications. The 39-month consent decree requires defendant to consider all female and Black applicants on the same basis as all other applicants, to engage in good faith efforts to increase recruitment of female and Black applicants, and to submit semiannual reports to the EEOC that include applicant flow and hiring data by race and sex. ***EEOC v. S&Z Tool Co., Inc.*, No. 1:03CV2023 (N.D. Ohio Aug. 16, 2006).**

- In August 2006, a major national public works contractor paid $125,000 to settle race, gender, national origin, and religious discrimination and retaliation lawsuits brought by the EEOC on behalf of a class of Black, Asian, and female electricians who were subjected to daily harassment due to their race, national origin, and/or gender by their immediate foremen, racial and otherwise offensive graffiti in plain sight at the workplace, and retaliation for complaining. ***EEOC v. Amelco*, No. C 05-2492 MEJ (N.D. Cal. Aug. 22, 2006).**

- In June 2005, the EEOC obtained an $8 million settlement from Ford Motor Co. and a major national union in a class race discrimination lawsuit, alleging that a test had a disproportionately negative impact on African American hourly employees seeking admission to an apprenticeship program. **See** *http://www.eeoc.gov/press/6-1-05.html*

- In November 2004, the Commission settled for $50 million a lawsuit filed against Abercrombie & Fitch on behalf of a class of African Americans, Asian Americans, Latinos, and women allegedly subjected to discrimination in recruitment, hiring, assignment, promotion, and discharge based on race, color, national origin, and sex. Abercrombie & Fitch also agreed to improve hiring, recruitment, training, and promotions policies; revise marketing material; and select a Vice President of Diversity and diversity recruiters. ***EEOC v. Abercrombie & Fitch Stores, Inc.*, No. CV-04-4731 (N.D. Cal. Nov. 10, 2004).**

- In November 2002, the Commission settled a lawsuit with the Las Vegas hotel for more than $1 million on behalf of African American and Hispanic applicants who allegedly were not hired for server positions because of their race. The hotel also agreed to conduct antidiscrimination training and implement procedures to investigate discrimination complaints. ***EEOC v. The Mirage Hotel & Casino,* No. CV S-02-1554 RLH - LRL (D.Nev. Nov. 27, 2002).**

Youth @ Work

- In September 2006, the Korean owners of a fast-food chain in Torrance, California, agreed to pay $5,000 to resolve a Title VII lawsuit alleging that a 16-year-old biracial girl, who looked like a fair-skinned African American, was refused an application for employment because of her perceived race (Black). According to the EEOC lawsuit, after a day at the beach with her Caucasian friends, the teen was asked if she would request an application on her friend's behalf since the friend was a little disheveled in appearance. The owner refused to give the teen an application and told her the store was not hiring anymore despite the presence of a "Help Wanted" sign in the window. After consultation among the friends, another White friend entered the store and was immediately given an application on request. ***EEOC v. Quiznos,* No. 2:06-cv-00215-DSFJC (C.D. Cal. settled Sept. 22, 2006).**

- In December 2005, the EEOC resolved this Title VII lawsuit alleging that a fast-food conglomerate subjected a Black female employee and other non-White restaurant staff members (some of them minors) to a hostile work environment based on race. The racial harassment included a male shift leader's frequent use of "nigger" and his exhortations that Whites were a superior race. Although the assistant manager received a letter signed by eight employees complaining about the shift leader's conduct, the shift leader was exonerated and the Black female employee who complained was fired. The consent decree provided $255,000 in monetary relief: $105,000 to Charging Party and $150,000 for a settlement fund for eligible claimants as determined by the EEOC. ***EEOC v. Carl Karcher Enterprises, Inc.*, d/b/a Carl's Jr. Restaurant, No. CV-05-01978 FCD PAW (E.D. Cal. Dec. 13, 2005).**

- In October 2005, an elevator manufacturing company agreed to pay $75,000 to an 18-year-old African American welder and $100,000 to 12 other Black employees in an EEOC suit alleging racial harassment of the teen and a pattern of discrimination against African American employees at the Middleton, Tennessee, facility. Harassment of the teen included calling him a "Black [S.O.B.]," telling racially offensive jokes, hiding his safety gloves, placing stink bombs under his workstation, and telling him that the vending machines do not take "crack money." ***EEOC v. Thyssenkrupp Elevator Manufacturing, Inc.*, Civil Action No. 03-1160-T (W.D. Tenn. Oct. 2005).**

- In September 2005, the EEOC obtained a $34,000 default judgment on behalf of a then 19-year-old Black former employee of a manufacturing plant in Illinois who alleged that he had been subjected to derogatory remarks and racial epithets, such as "What are you supposed to be, some kind of special nigger?" or name-calling such as "pencil dick," by his supervisor. The supervisor was the father of the company's president and he insisted that the "n-word" is Latin for "Black person." When the teen complained to the company president about the offensive remarks, the supervisor's son replied that he could not reprimand his father. ***EEOC v. Midwest Rack Manufacturing, Inc.*, No. 05-194-WDS (S.D. Ill. Sep. 21, 2005).**

- In March 2004, a Ruby Tuesday franchise agreed to pay $32,000 to resolve an EEOC lawsuit, alleging race discrimination in hiring against two African American college students who were refused employment as food servers in favor of several Caucasian applicants with less or similar experience and qualifications. According to the lawsuit, when the students met with the store manager, he briefly reviewed their applications and told them they were "not what he was looking for." ***EEOC v. RT KCMO, LLC d/b/a Ruby Tuesday's*, No.03-CV-00983-FJG (W.D. Mo. settled March 30, 2004).**

- In February 2004, the Commission settled a racial and sexual harassment lawsuit for $67,000 plus injunctive relief on behalf of two Black young female employees who alleged that they were subjected to unwelcome touching, degrading sexual and racial comments, and were shown a drawing of a Ku Klux Klan member by their supervisor. After one of the women complained, her hours were cut, and she was eventually terminated. The other employee was forced to resign. ***EEOC v. Planet Wings of Rockland, Inc.*, No. 03 CV 5430 (S.D.N.Y. Feb. 4, 2004).**

TABLE 3.2 Educating Racism and Colorism from Employment (E-RACE), 2002–2020

Employment Practices

Category	Financial Costs
Hiring	$6,326,500
Customer/Patient Preferences	$15794,750
Hispanic/Foreign Preferences	$8,338,700
Job Segregation	$21,688,700
Terms and Conditions	$2,562,500
Compensation Disparity	$25,063,050
Hostile Work Environment	$18,474,019
Retaliation	$4,095,000
Discharge	$1,202,000
Total	**$89,345,219**

NOTE. U.S. Equal Employment Opportunity Commission. https://www.eeoc.gov/initiatives/e-race/significant-eeoc-racecolor-casescovering-private-and-federal-sectors

Employment Practices

Hiring

- In February 2020, a northern Indiana vending and coffee service provider paid $22,000 and provided other significant relief to resolve an EEOC race discrimination lawsuit alleging that the company discriminated against a Black applicant in filling vending service representative positions. ***EEOC v. Coffel Vending Co.,*** **Case No. 3:19-cv-00596-PPS-MGG (N.D. Ind. Feb. 25, 2020).**

- In August 2019, Pier 1 Imports paid a $20,000 settlement to a Black job applicant in San Bernardino County who was denied an assistant manager position based on his race following a background check pursuant to a 2-year conciliation agreement. As part of the agreement terms, the company admitted no liability, and Pier 1 Imports agreed to revise its policies, which include eliminating its background screening processes and removing the question about convictions from its job application. The EEOC will monitor the company's compliance with the agreement.

- In August 2016, an Illinois-based payroll and human resource services firm agreed to a $1.4 million settlement of charges that the company discriminated against Black and Hispanic job applicants and employees. ADP LLC, under a conciliation agreement signed before any lawsuit was filed, also will enhance its recruitment, hiring, and promotion of racial minorities, the EEOC announced July 29. ADP in resolving the charges didn't admit it engaged in any violations of Title VII of the 1964 Civil Rights Act.

- In March 2016, a manufacturing company based in New Ulm, MN, paid $19,500 to settle a race discrimination lawsuit filed by the EEOC, alleging that Windings, Inc. violated Title VII of the Civil Rights Act of 1964 when it refused to hire a biracial (African American and White) applicant for a vacant assembler position, and instead hired a White applicant. According to the EEOC's lawsuit, Kimball applied for a vacant assembler job and interviewed with the company in January 2014. The applicant was qualified for the job as he passed the job-related assessment tests and had previous work experience as an assembler. In addition to the monetary relief, the 2-year consent decree requires Windings to use hiring procedures to provide equal employment opportunity to all applicants including posting vacancy announcements and job listings on its website, and not solely rely on word-of-mouth recruitment or employee referrals. Windings also will use objective standards for hiring, guidelines for structured interviews, and will document interviews. Windings adopted a written affirmative action plan, and will seek out applications from qualified minority applicants, including African Americans. Also, Windings agrees to participate in job fairs and recruiting events that target Black Americans and to provide the EEOC with reports of its applicants, hiring and specific reasons why applicants were not selected during the decree's term. ***EEOC v. Windings, Inc.*, Civil Action No. 15-cv-02901 (D. Minn. consent decree filed Mar. 18, 2016).**

- In September 2015, Cabela's Inc., an outdoor recreation merchandiser based in Sidney, Nebraska, with 60 retail stores in 33 states, agreed to take nationwide measures to increase the diversity of its workforce to settle the EEOC's allegations that the company discriminated in recruitment and hiring of minorities. The settlement agreement resolves an EEOC commissioner's charge filed against the company. Under the agreement, Cabela's is required to appoint a diversity and inclusion director who will report directly to the company's chief administrative officer and set hiring goals designed to achieve parity in the hiring rates of White and minority job applicants. The agreement also requires Cabela's to make equal employment opportunity compliance a component in the performance evaluation of managers and supervisors, to update its EEO policies, and provide annual training on EEO issues for all employees.

- In April 2015, a federal judge denied a motion to dismiss a claim of racial discrimination in hiring against Rosebud Restaurants, the U.S. Equal Employment Opportunity Commission (EEOC) announced today. In its complaint, the EEOC charged that the Chicago-area Italian restaurant chain violated federal civil rights laws by refusing to hire African Americans because of their race. The company's motion to dismiss argued that the EEOC's complaint should be dismissed because it did not identify the victims of the alleged hiring discrimination. The court rejected that argument, concluding that the EEOC's "allegations of intentional discrimination are sufficient to state a claim for Title VII relief . . . even in the absence of the identification of an individual job applicant who was rejected because of his race." ***EEOC v. Rosebud Restaurants, Inc.*, Civil Action No. 13-cv-6656 (N.D. Ill. decision filed Apr. 7, 2015).**

- In September 2014, the EEOC appealed the dismissal of its race discrimination complaints alleging that an employer's withdrawal of a job offer from a qualified Black applicant because she refused to cut off her dreadlocks constituted race discrimination under Title VII. On the appeal, the Commission contends that the district court improperly dismissed its original and amended complaints because they stated plausible claims of intentional discrimination. Specifically, the Commission argued that the employer's application of its grooming policy to prohibit dreadlocks discriminates on the immutable trait of racial hair texture, violates the fundamental right to freedom of racial expression, and promotes unlawful racial stereotyping. ***EEOC v. Catastrophe Mgmt. Solutions*, No. 14-13482 (11th Cir. Brief filed Sept. 22, 2014)**.

- In June 2013, the EEOC and J.B. Hunt Transport Inc. settled a race discrimination charge alleging the nationwide transportation company engaged in unlawful race discrimination by rejecting a Black truck driver applicant because of a prior criminal conviction unrelated to his prospective job duties. The settlement follows conciliation of an EEOC charge under Title VII of the 1964 Civil Rights Act over claims that an African American job candidate was denied a truck driver position at a J.B. Hunt facility in San Bernardino, CA, in 2009 based on a criminal conviction record, which the EEOC contends was unrelated to the duties of the job. The federal agency also reviewed the company's broader policy with respect to the hiring of job applicants with conviction records. Blanket prohibitions are not in accordance with the agency's policy guidance on the subject, which was reissued on April 25, 2010. The EEOC's guidance recommends evaluating: the nature and gravity of the offense or conduct; the time that has passed since the conviction and/or completion of the sentence; and the nature of the job sought prior to disqualifying a candidate with such a record. J.B. Hunt also reached a private settlement with the alleged discrimination victim, who filed an EEOC charge after being denied a job at J.B. Hunt's San Bernardino, CA, facility in 2009. As part of a 5-year conciliation agreement, J.B. Hunt agreed to review and, if necessary, revise its hiring and selection policies to comply with the EEOC's April 2012 enforcement guidance regarding employers' use of arrest and conviction records. The EEOC will monitor compliance with the conciliation agreement. The EEOC entered into a pre-suit conciliation agreement.

- In November 2012, Alliant Techsystems Inc. paid $100,000 to settle an EEOC suit alleging that the company violated Title VII when it refused to hire an African American woman for a technical support job at its offices in Edina because of her race. According to the lawsuit, the alleged victim applied and was interviewed several times for the job in May 2007. After the first interview, the recruiter allegedly advised her to take out her braids to appear more professional. She did so and purportedly was later told by the recruiter that Alliant wanted to hire her and that she would be contacted by the company's Human Resources Department. However, by the time she met with the company's information technology director, she had put her braids back in. The next day, she was informed that she would not be hired. In June 2007, the company hired a White male for the IT job. The 3-year consent decree, which applies to the company's headquarters in Minnesota and Virginia, enjoins Alliant from further discriminating in hiring based on race and from retaliating against persons who oppose practices made unlawful under Title VII. Additionally, the company will review its workplace policies to assure that they comply with Title VII and will train its entire staff on the laws against discrimination. ***EEOC v. Alliant Techsystems Inc.*, Case No. 0:11-cv-02785-DSD-JJG (D. Minn. consent decree filed Nov. 20, 2012).**

- In April 2012, Bankers Asset Management Inc. agreed to pay $600,000 to settle an EEOC lawsuit alleging that the real estate company excluded Black applicants from jobs at the company's Little Rock location based on their race. The firm also allegedly retaliated against other employees and former employees for opposing or testifying about the race discrimination by demoting and forcing one worker out of her job and by suing others in state court. In addition to paying $600,000, the 3-year consent decree settling the lawsuit also requires Bankers Asset Management to hold a mandatory, annual 3-hour training on race discrimination and retaliation in which its president or another officer participates, among other provisions. ***EEOC v. Bankers Asset Mgmt. Inc.*, Civil Action No. 4:10-CV-002070-SWW (E.D. Ark. Apr. 18, 2012).**

- In February 2012, the owners of Piggly Wiggly supermarkets in Hartsville and Lafayette, TN, agreed to pay $40,000 to settle a race and gender discrimination lawsuit filed by the EEOC. In its lawsuit, the EEOC asserted that the Piggly Wiggly locations owned by MWR Enterprises Inc. II violated federal law by maintaining policies and practices that intentionally failed to hire African Americans because of their race for positions at the company's Piggly Wiggly store in Hartsville and Lafayette. The EEOC further charged that the company maintained a segregated workforce and an established practice of not hiring males for cashier positions at the same locations. The 4-year consent decree also requires Defendant MWR Enterprises Inc., II, to establish a written policy which provides that all job assignments will be made without consideration to gender; establish guidelines and procedures for processing employment applications; provide Title VII training on race and gender discrimination to its managers; meet record-keeping and reporting requirements; and post a notice about the lawsuit and settlement at its store locations. ***EEOC v. MWR Enterprises Inc., II*, C.A. No. 3:10-cv-00901 (M.D. Tenn. Feb. 23, 2012).**

- In January 2012, a Johnson City, NY-based cleaning company agreed to pay $450,000 to 15 former employees to settle a hiring discrimination and retaliation case. According to an EEOC lawsuit filed in September 2011 in a federal court in Pennsylvania, the executives of the cleaning company prohibited a White supervisor from hiring Black employees for a client in Concordville, PA. The supervisor continued to hire qualified Black workers, and later was fired for defying her manager's instructions. The EEOC also alleged that the company forced Black workers at the Concordville worksite to sit in the back of the cafeteria during breaks, and ultimately barred them from the cafeteria altogether. The company later fired the entire crew, replacing them with all non-Black workers. The EEOC filed a lawsuit seeking relief for the terminated supervisor and Black employees. In addition to the monetary relief, the company agreed to providing EEO training for its managers and supervisors and to submit a follow-up report on remedial measures being taken at the Concordville worksite. ***EEOC v. Matrix L.L.C.*, Civil Action No. 2:11-cv-06183 (E.D. Pa. Jan. 6, 2012).**

- In January 2012, a marine construction and transportation company located in Dyersburg, TN, will pay an African American job applicant $75,000 to settle a racial discrimination lawsuit filed by the EEOC. According to the EEOC's lawsuit, the company refused to hire a Black job applicant for a deckhand position because of his race in violation of Title VII. In addition to the monetary relief, a 3-year consent decree requires the company to use its best efforts to fill up to 25% of available positions with African Americans. Choctaw has also been ordered to maintain records of discrimination complaints, provide annual reports to the EEOC, and post a notice to employees about the lawsuit that includes the EEOC's contact information. ***EEOC v. Choctaw Transp. Co., Inc.*, 1:10-cv-01248-JDB-egb (W.D. Tenn. Jan. 19, 2012).**

- In September 2011, the EEOC filed suit against Bass Pro Outdoor World, LLC, alleging that the nationwide retailer of sporting goods, apparel, and other miscellaneous products has been discriminating in its hiring since at least November 2005. The EEOC's suit alleged that qualified African Americans and Hispanics were routinely denied retail positions such as cashier, sales associate, team leader, supervisor, manager, and other positions at many Bass Pro stores nationwide and that managers at Bass Pro stores in the Houston area, in Louisiana, and elsewhere made overtly racially derogatory remarks acknowledging the discriminatory practices, including that hiring Black candidates did not fit the corporate profile. The lawsuit also claims that Bass Pro punished employees who opposed the company's unlawful practices, in some instances firing them or forcing them to resign. ***EEOC v. Bass Pro Outdoor World, LLC*, Civil Action No. 4:11-cv-03425 (S.D. Tex. Sep. 21, 2011).**

- In March 2011, a federal district court in Maryland rejected a novel attempt by a national restaurant chain to block the EEOC from airing radio spots seeking Black individuals who applied for a job or worked at the chain's Baltimore location, in connection with its race bias suit against the restaurant. ***EEOC v. McCormick & Schmick's Seafood Rests. Inc.*, No. 1:08-cv-00984 (D. Md. motion denied Mar. 17, 2011).**

- In December 2010, the EEOC filed a race discrimination and retaliation suit against a real estate brokerage and management company alleging that the company refused to hire numerous Black applicants and then retaliated against other employees or former employees for opposing the race discrimination. The lawsuit seeks back pay, compensatory and punitive damages, instatement or reinstatement, as well as an injunction against future discrimination and retaliation. ***EEOC v. Cry-Leike, Inc.*, Civil Action No. 4:10-CV-002070 (E.D. Ark. Dec. 30, 2010).**

- In November 2010, a Chicago janitorial services provider agreed to pay $3 million to approximately 550 rejected Black job applicants under a 4-year consent decree, settling the EEOC's allegations of race and national origin discrimination in recruitment and hiring. The EEOC had alleged that the provider had recruited through media directed at Eastern European immigrants and Hispanics and hired people from those groups over African Americans, and that the provider's use of subjective decision-making had a disparate impact on African Americans. As part of the decree, the provider also agreed to extensive changes in its employment policies, to engage in "active recruitment" of African American employees, to hire previously rejected Black applicants, to implement training on discrimination and retaliation, and to hire an outside monitor to review compliance with the decree. ***EEOC v. Scrub Inc.*, No. 09 C 4228 (N.D. Ill. consent decree entered Nov. 9, 2010).**

- In June 2010, the EEOC obtained a ruling by the Ninth Circuit that permits the Commission to pursue injunctive relief to stop a coal company mining in the Navajo Nation from discriminating in employment against non-Navajo Indians. In this Title VII case, the EEOC claimed mineral lease provisions that require companies mining on the Navajo reservation in Arizona to give employment preferences to Navajos are unlawful. By honoring those provisions and refusing to hire non-Navajo Indians, Peabody discriminates based on national origin, in violation of Title VII of the 1964 Civil Rights Act, the EEOC asserted. The EEOC also can proceed with efforts to secure an injunction against future enforcement of the Navajo hiring preference, the court added. Should a court find a Title VII violation and issue such an injunction, Peabody and the Navajo Nation could file a third-party complaint against the Interior Secretary under Rule 14(a) to prevent the Secretary from seeking to enforce the lease provisions or cancel the leases, it said. ***EEOC v. Peabody W. Coal Co.*, No. 06-17261 (9th Cir. June 23, 2010).**

- In January 2010, an international investment management firm based in Malvern, PA, settled for $300,000 the EEOC's Title VII lawsuit, alleging that the firm failed to hire an African American female applicant for a financial planning manager position at defendant's Charlotte, NC, office because of her race. She was the only African American among four candidates, and according to the EEOC, had met or exceeded all requirements for the job, had received highly favorable comments as she progressed through defendant's interview process, which included multiple in-person and telephone interviews with high level managers, as well as an in-person assessment by a third party on matters such as personality and aptitude. Additionally, at the conclusion of her final interview, defendant's managing director allegedly told the Black applicant she was "obviously qualified for the position." The firm, however, offered the job to two less qualified White applicants—the first declined and the second accepted. The 2-year consent decree also enjoins the firm from making hiring decisions based on race and prohibits retaliation. ***EEOC v. Vanguard Group, Inc.*, No. 09-04424 (E.D. Pa. Jan. 4, 2010).**

- In March 2009, a manufacturer and distributor of food service equipment has offered permanent employment to an African American applicant and furnished other relief to resolve a race discrimination lawsuit alleging that the company refused to hire the Black applicant into a permanent position at its Fayetteville, TN, facility because he disclosed a felony conviction on his application—even though the company hired a White applicant a year earlier who made a similar disclosure. ***EEOC v. Franke, Inc., dba Franke Foodservice Systems,*** **No. 3:08-cv-0515 (M.D. Tenn. Mar. 26, 2009).**

- In October 2008, a department store chain in Iowa entered a consent decree agreeing to pay $50,000 and to provide other affirmative relief. The EEOC had alleged that the store chain refused to hire qualified Black job applicants for sales, truck driver, and other positions in its retail or warehouse facilities for reasons that were not applied to successful White applicants. In addition to the monetary relief, the consent decree requires the store chain to post a remedial notice, provide semi-annual training to managers and supervisors on employee and applicant rights under Title VII and employer obligations under Title VII, and report applicant data and any future complaints related to racial discrimination to the EEOC. ***EEOC v. Von Maur,*** **No. 06-CV-182 (S.D. Iowa Apr. 19, 2006 settled Oct. 29, 2008).**

- In July 2008, the EEOC resolved a race discrimination and retaliation suit for $140,000 against a Mississippi U-Haul company. The company was accused of discriminating on the basis of race when it hired the son of a selecting official rather than a veteran African American manager, to serve as the company's marketing company president. The Black manager had worked for U-Haul for 10 years as a reservation manager, assistant manager, general manager, area field manager, and field relief manager, and held a bachelor's degree in business management as well as having received various awards for performance. The company, however, altered the job's requirements and hired the executive's son who lacked a college degree and had scanty experience compared with the Black manager. The manager complained and the company disciplined and fired him. The company has agreed to adopt an online employee handbook and other documents spelling out company policies and practices; to post all vacancies for marketing company president; to provide training on discrimination and retaliation to all board members; and to provide periodic reports to the EEOC. ***EEOC v. U-Haul Co. of Mississippi,*** **Civil Action No. 3:06cv516 (S.D. Miss. filed July 2008).**

- In June 2008, a beauty supply chain agreed to pay $30,000 to settle a race discrimination lawsuit in which the EEOC charged that it rescinded a job offer after learning the successful applicant was Black. In a deposition, the former acting store manager of the West Orange store gave sworn testimony that she had a telephone conversation with the district manager after the applicant had applied, and the district manager "told [me] she didn't want another Black person working in the store." When the selectee arrived at the store on her starting date, she was informed that she could not be hired due to her race because there would have been too many African Americans at the store. ***EEOC v. Sally Beauty Supply LLC,*** **Civil Action No. 1:07cv644 (E.D. Tex. settled June 23, 2008).**

- In September 2007, the EEOC upheld an Administrative Judge's (AJ) default judgment in favor of complainant, a Staff Nurse Supervisor, who had alleged race discrimination when she was not selected for a Nurse Manager position. The AJ sanctioned the agency for failing to timely investigate the complaint. Relief included retroactive promotion, back pay and a tailored order to allow complainant to submit her request for fees incurred solely for the successful prosecution of the appeal. ***Royal v. Department of Veterans Affairs,*** **EEOC Appeal No. 0720070045 (Sep. 10, 2007).**

- In January 2007, the Commission found discrimination based on race (African American) when a federal employee was not selected for the position of Criminal Investigator despite plainly superior qualifications as compared to the selectee. The manager who recommended the selectee, ignored complainant's qualifications and was reported to have previously told another African American applicant that his "Black ass would never become a special agent." The Commission affirmed the AJ's finding of discrimination and ordered the retroactive promotion of complainant, back pay, compensatory damages ($75,000), attorney's fees, and other relief. ***Green v. Department of Homeland Security,*** **EEOC Appeal No. 0720060058 (January 19, 2007).**

- In November 2006, the Commission found that a federal employee had been discriminated against based on his race (Asian/Pacific Islander) when he was not selected for the position of Social Insurance Specialist. The Commission affirmed the AJ's finding that the agency's articulated reason for failing to select complainant—the selectee was "highly recommended" to the selecting official—was not worthy of belief since complainant was "definitely recommended" and that discrimination more likely motivated the agency's decision. The Commission ordered the retroactive promotion of complainant, back pay, compensatory damages ($5,000), attorney's fees, and other relief. ***Paras v. SSA,*** **EEOC Appeal No. 0720060049 (November 6, 2006).**

- In August 2006, a federal appellate court in Illinois reversed a negative trial court ruling and decided that the EEOC had produced sufficient evidence to proceed to trial in its race discrimination case against Target Corporation, a major retailer. According to the lawsuit, an interviewing official for the company refused to schedule interviews for four Black applicants seeking entry-level management positions because of their race. The Commission's evidence included inculpatory tester evidence and expert testimony indicating that the names and voices of the Black applicants, as well as some of the organizational affiliations (e.g. Alpha Kappa Alpha Sorority, Inc.) disclosed on their resumes, could have served as proxies for race. ***EEOC v. Target Corporation,*** **460 F.3d 946 (7th Cir. 2006).**

Customer/Patient Preference

- In September 2019, Lexington Treatment Associates, a Delaware-based limited liability company that owns and operates methadone clinics in North Carolina, paid $110,000 and provided other relief to settle a racial harassment lawsuit brought by the EEOC. The EEOC had charged that the company violated Title VII when it subjected three Black employees at its Lexington, NC, facility to a racially hostile work environment. According to the EEOC's lawsuit, from February 2017 to at least July 2018, Treatment Centers subjected a Substance Abuse Counselor Allen Parson and two other African American employees were repeatedly and openly subjected to racial slurs by several clients of the facility and race-based counselor assignments to accommodate White clients' racial preferences not to be assigned to Black counselors. ***EEOC v. Treatment Centers, LLC d/b/a Lexington Treatment Assocs.*****, Civil Action No.1:19-cv-00933 (M.D.N.C. Sep. 12, 2019).**
- In September 2013, Hurley Medical Center entered into a 5-year agreement with the EEOC to settle its lawsuit alleging that a White father reportedly demanded no African American nurses treat his newborn baby. Four nurses filed discrimination lawsuits after a Hurley staff member allegedly posted a note with the father's instructions. Pursuant to the agreement, the EEOC will conduct non-discrimination training for all Hurley staff each year and will examine any progress made to see if more needs to be done. Hurley also agreed to pay about $200,000 in March to settle a lawsuit filed by three nurses. "In the Matter of U.S. Equal Employment Opportunity Commission and Tonya Battle, Charging Party, and Hurley Medical Center, Respondent," Detroit Field Office, September 26, 2013. See also Resolution Agreement between the U.S. Department of Health and Human Services Office for Civil Rights and Hurley Medical Center, 13-156114 (July 31, 2014 available at http://www.hhs.gov/ocr/civilrights/activities/agreements/hurley.html).
- In December 2010, a company which provides in-home care certified nursing assistants (CNAs) and non-CNAs to seniors in Anne Arundel County and Howard County, Maryland agreed to settle claims alleging that it discriminated based on race in assigning caregivers. According to the EEOC's lawsuit, the company coded the preferences of clients who requested White caregivers and made assignments based on the preferences. For example, "circle dots" referred to the clients that preferred Caucasian caregivers. The facility claimed that it ceased the coding practice in 2008, but admitted that it continued to take client racial preferences into account in making caregiver assignments. The 5-year consent decree provides $150,000 in compensatory damages to be distributed to claimants (defined as all caregivers employed by defendant from October 2007 through entry of the decree) in amounts determined by EEOC based on length of service and employment status. The decree enjoins the company from racial coding and prohibits race-based caregiver assignments. The injunction survives the decree. Where a client indicates a preference not to have a caregiver of a certain race, and there is a risk that the client will become

violent, the facility will notify the caregiver, who can choose to refuse the assignment. The company also will provide 2 hours of training annually to recruiters and HR personnel on Title VII, with a special emphasis on the discriminatory assignment of caregivers based on the racial preferences of clients. **EEOC v. HiCare, Inc., dba Home Instead Senior Care, No. 1:10-CV-02692 (D. Md. Dec. 10, 2010).**

- In July 2010, Plaintiff Brenda Chaney and the EEOC as amicus curiae obtained a reversal of a summary judgment in favor of an employer in a Title VII case that "pit[ted] a [Black] health-care worker's right to a non-discriminatory workplace against a patient's demand for [W]hite-only health-care providers." In this race-based action, an Indiana nursing home housed a White resident who did not want any assistance from Black health-care staff. The facility complied with the patient's request by informing Plaintiff "in writing everyday that 'no Black' assistants should enter this resident's room or provide her with care." Plaintiff filed suit alleging that the facility's acquiescence to the racial biases of its residents is illegal and created a hostile work environment. She also asserted that her termination was racially motivated. On appeal, the Seventh Circuit unanimously rejected the facility's argument that Indiana's patient-rights law permitted such practice and remanded the case for trial because the "the racial preference policy violates Title VII by creating a hostile work environment and because issues of fact remain over whether race motivated the discharge." ***Chaney v. Plainfield Healthcare Center,* 612 F .3d 908 (7th Cir. 2010).**

- In December 2007, a Minnesota-based frozen food home delivery service agreed to pay $87,250 and provide Title VII training to settle an EEOC race discrimination case alleging that the company discriminated against qualified African American job applicants at its Missouri facility. The EEOC alleged that the company refused to hire Black applicants because it was concerned that its customers would be uncomfortable with a Black man coming to their home and would be intimidated by him. Consequently, despite promising the Black applicant he would be hired for a warehouse position, the company hired a less qualified White applicant. ***EEOC v. Schwan's Home Services, Inc.,* No. 4:07-CV-00221-AGF (E.D. Mo. settled Dec. 17, 2007).**

- In April 2007, a Pennsylvania hot dog franchise entered a consent decree with the EEOC agreeing to pay $7,500, to post a remedial notice in the restaurant, to semi-annually report on any future complaints alleging racial discrimination to the EEOC for a period of 4 years, and to provide Title VII training to all supervisors and managers. In its lawsuit, the EEOC alleged that the franchise ordered the store manager to fire the African American employees because the student patrons did not like to be waited on by them. After firing several of the Black employees, the store manager resigned in protest and the general manager fired the remaining African American employees himself. The consent decree also enjoins The Original Hot Dog Shop from creating, tolerating, or fostering a hostile work environment based on race. ***EEOC v. The Original Hot Dog Shop,* No. 06-CV-1243-JFC-RCM (W.D. Pa. Apr. 19, 2007).**

- In October 2005, the EEOC obtained $650,000 for named claimants and an additional $70,000 for "unknown class members" in a Title VII lawsuit alleging that the owner of assisted living and other senior facilities in 14 states engaged in discriminatory hiring practices based on race and/or color. Specifically, the lawsuit alleged that defendant's former general manager refused to hire Blacks and other non-Caucasian applicants into nursing support, food service, and housekeeping positions at an assisted living facility and coded the applications of minority applicants because she believed residents preferred White employees and did not want minorities to come into their rooms. Additionally, defendant failed to retain employment applications as required by the EEOC's regulations implementing section 709(c) of Title VII. Pursuant to a 42-month consent, defendant is prohibited from discriminating or retaliating and is required to advise recruiting sources that it hires without regard to race or color. ***EEOC v. Merrill Gardens, LLC,* No. 1:05-CV-004 (N.D. Ind. Oct. 6, 2005)**

- In September 2005, the nation's largest maker and retailer of wooden play systems agreed to pay six people a total of $275,000 to resolve an EEOC lawsuit, which alleged that the company's owner pursued a policy of limiting the hiring and promotion opportunities of African Americans and Hispanics and fired a White district manager in retaliation for recommending two Blacks for district manager openings after telling him that "our customers can't relate to minorities and therefore we must be choosy who we hire." ***EEOC v. Creative Playthings, Inc.,* No. 04-cv-3243 (E.D. Pa. press release issued Sep. 15, 2005).**

- In March 2004, the EEOC settled a failure to promote case for $45,000, in which the company's president and CEO defended its action by arguing that the company was in "redneck country" and customers would not accept a Black man as an account manager. ***EEOC v. Frontier Materials Corp.,* No. H-03-856 (S.D. Tex. Mar. 2, 2004).**

Hispanic/Foreign Preference

- In February 2020, a Texas-based fiberglass conduit and strut manufacturer implemented extensive hiring reforms and paid $225,000 to settle allegations by the EEOC that it refused to hire non-Hispanic individuals as laborers. A Black, non-Hispanic man told the EEOC that the company refused to provide him with a job application after it learned he couldn't speak Spanish. The EEOC sued on behalf of an entire class of non-Hispanic job applicants who were allegedly negatively affected by Champion Fiberglass' hiring approach dating back to at least 2013. According to the consent decree, "these policies and practices have resulted in a laborer workforce that is almost 100% Hispanic." In accordance with the agreement, the company will pay a civil penalty and discontinue its "word-of-mouth" referrals to settle the accusations that its behavior stifled diversity in the laborer role. ***EEOC v. Champion Fiberglass, Inc.,* No. 4:17-cv-02226 (S. D. Tx. Feb. 28, 2020).**

- In September 2019, a San Jose, California, food producer and distributor paid $2 million to settle an EEOC race discrimination lawsuit, charging that the company refused to hire non-Hispanic applicants of all races, including Black, White, and Asian applicants, for unskilled production warehouse positions because its affiliates preferred Hispanic job applicants. The lawsuit also alleged that the companies discouraged non-Hispanic applicants for applying for open positions by imposing a language requirement not required for the job in violation of Title VII of the Civil Rights Act of 1964. In addition to the monetary settlement, the company agreed to hire an external monitor and implement hiring goals and measures to ensure hiring transparency and diversification. ***EEOC v. Marquez Brothers International Inc.*, Case No. 1:17-cv-00044-AWI-EPG (E.D. Cal. Sep. 18, 2019).**

- In July 2018, a Miami Beach hotel operator paid $2.5 million to settle an EEOC lawsuit that alleged the company had fired Black Haitian dishwashers who had complained about discrimination and replaced them with mostly light-skinned Hispanic workers. The EEOC also charged that their supervising chefs referred to the affected dishwashers as "f-----g Haitians," and "slaves" and reprimanded them for speaking Creole, even amongst themselves, while Hispanic employees were permitted to speak Spanish. ***EEOC v. SLS Hotel South Beach*, Case No. 1:17-cv-21446 (S.D. Fla. July xx, 2018).**

- In September 2016, Resource Employment Solutions, LLC, a temporary staffing agency, will pay $435,000 to settle a race and national origin discrimination lawsuit brought by the EEOC. The Commission claimed that the company illegally granted placement preferences to Hispanic temps over African American temps. Specifically, the company allegedly violated federal law by failing to place a class of African American workers into temporary shipping positions at a FedEx SmartPost location in Southaven, Mississippi. Instead, the staffing agency granted placement preferences to Hispanic workers and also retaliated against an African American employee who complained of the discrimination by refusing to place her and denying her a promotion. The 4-year consent decree also includes provisions requiring anti-discrimination training, reporting, and postings. ***EEOC v. Resource Employment Solutions, LLC*, No. 3:14-cv-00217-MPM-SAA (N.D. Miss. Aug. 29, 2016).**

- In July 2016, J&R Baker Farms LLC agreed to pay $205,000 and comply with the terms of a consent decree to settle an EEOC lawsuit alleging the Georgia farm favored foreign-born employees over African American and Caucasian domestic workers in employment. Specifically, the suit alleged that Baker Farms gave American-born workers fewer hours and tasks compared with the foreign-born workers and discharged U.S.-born White and African American employees based on their race or national origin. The lawsuit also alleged that Baker Farms segregated work crews by national origin and race. The U.S.-born employees were allegedly subjected to tougher production standards and sent home early on days in which the foreign-born workers continued to work. The settlement requires Baker Farms to stop discriminatory practices on the basis of national origin or race, refrain from automatically filling jobs with H-2A workers, or foreign nationals who receive a visa to fill temporary agricultural jobs, without first considering American workers and institute a formal anti-discrimination policy by Aug. 1, in addition to the monetary relief. The 2-year consent decree also requires the farm must hold interviews at the Georgia Department of Labor at least 1 day a week for 2 weeks "before the start of each H-2A season," and provide to the EEOC upon request a list of those people they hired, including their names, phone numbers, addresses, and national origin, in addition to applicants not hired and those whom they fired, including any claims of discrimination, with those same details. ***EEOC v. J&R Baker Farms LLC*, No. 7:14-cv-00136 (M.D. Ga. July 6, 2016).**

- In April 2016, Lawler Foods, a large local bakery, agreed to settle for $1 million an EEOC race and national origin discrimination class case. The EEOC alleged that Lawler violated Title VII by engaging in a pattern or practice of intentionally failing to hire Black and other non-Hispanic applicants for jobs, and by using hiring practices, including word-of-mouth recruiting and advertising a Spanish-language preference, that had an adverse disparate impact on Black and other non-Hispanic applicants without any business justification. In addition to the monetary claims fund, the 4-year consent decree provides for extensive injunctive relief, including recruiting and hiring of Blacks and non-Hispanic job applicants, and training for managers. Additionally, Lawler will seek to recruit and hire Black and other non-Hispanic job applicants for its production jobs; conduct an extensive self-assessment of its hiring to ensure non-discrimination and compliance with the terms of the consent decree; conduct employee training to further its non-discrimination commitment; and designate an internal leader to prioritize compliance with the requirements of the consent decree. ***EEOC v. Lawlor Foods*, Civil Action No. 4:14-cv-03588 (Apr. 26, 2016).**

- In July 2014, the EEOC filed a lawsuit against AutoZone alleging the company unjustly fired a Chicago man for refusing to be transferred because of his race. The complaint alleges that AutoZone attempted in 2012 to redistribute the non-Hispanic workers at its auto parts retail location at S. Kedzie Ave. and W. 49th Street in Gage Park. The EEOC claims that the company wanted to broaden the number of Hispanics at the store to better reflect its customer base. The EEOC said that when an African American sales manager was allegedly told to report to another store on the far South Side, he was fired for refusing the transfer. ***EEOC v. AutoZone, Inc.*, No. 1:14cv5579 (7th Cir. complaint filed July 22, 2014).**

- In December 2012, Hamilton Growers, Inc., doing business as Southern Valley Fruit and Vegetable, Inc., an agricultural farm in Norman Park, GA, agreed to pay $500,000 to a class of American seasonal workers—many of them African American—who, the EEOC alleged, were subjected to discrimination based on their national origin and/or race, the agency announced today. The agreement resolves a lawsuit filed by the EEOC in September 2011. The EEOC's suit had charged that the company unlawfully engaged in a pattern or practice of discrimination against American workers by firing virtually all American workers while retaining workers from Mexico during the 2009, 2010, and 2011 growing seasons. The agency also alleged that Hamilton Growers fired at least 16 African American workers in 2009 based on race and/or national origin as their termination was coupled with race-based comments by a management official. Additionally, the lawsuit charged that Hamilton Growers provided lesser job opportunities to American workers by assigning them to pick vegetables in fields which had already been picked by foreign workers, which resulted in Americans earning less pay than their Mexican counterparts. ***EEOC v. Hamilton Growers, Inc.*, No. 7:11-cv-134 (M.D. Ga. Consent decree entered Dec. 10, 2012).**

- In December 2012, EEOC and a North Carolina printing firm settled for $334,000 a lawsuit alleging the firm violated Title VII of the 1964 Civil Rights Act by not placing non-Hispanic workers in its "core group" of regular temporary workers who perform the company's light bindery production jobs and giving disproportionately more work hours to Hispanic workers. Under the proposed 2-year consent decree, PBM Graphics Inc. would place the settlement funds in escrow for distribution later among non-Hispanic workers identified by EEOC as victims of the alleged national origin discrimination. ***EEOC v. PBM Graphics Inc.*, No. 11-805 (M.D.N.C. proposed consent decree filed 12/10/12).**

- In October 2012, a Hampton Inn franchise in Craig, CO, agreed to pay $85,000 to resolve a race and national origin discrimination lawsuit regarding the terminations of three Caucasian and non-Latino employees. According to the lawsuit, the general manager of the hotel allegedly was told by the business owners "to hire more qualified maids, and that they preferred maids to be Hispanic because in their opinion Hispanics worked harder" and that White or non-Hispanic workers were indolent. ***EEOC v. Century Shree Corp. & Century Rama Inc.*, Case No. 11-cv-2558-REB-CBS (D. Colo. Oct. 2, 2012).**

- In September 2012, an Indianapolis hotel agreed to pay $355,000 to settle a job discrimination case with the EEOC. The Hampton Inn is accused of firing Black housekeepers because of their race and retaliating against those who had complained. According to the EEOC, the general manager of the Hampton Inn hotel advised her employees that she wanted to get "Mexicans" in who would clean better and complain less than her Black housekeeping staff, even if the Hispanic hires were equally or less qualified than Black candidates. In addition to the monetary relief, the hotel must offer three of those employees their next available housekeeping positions and train any employees involved in the hiring process. ***EEOC v. New Indianapolis Hotels, Inc.*, Case No. 1:10-cv-1234 (S.D. Ind. Sep. 21, 2010).**

- In September 2010, the EEOC sued an Indianapolis hotel for denying employment to Black housekeeping applicants, offering lower pay and hours to Black housekeeping staff, terminating Black housekeeping staff who complained of the less favorable treatment, and destroying employment records since at least September 2, 2008, because of the hotel's preference for Hispanic workers. According to the EEOC, the general manager of the Hampton Inn hotel located at 2311 North Shadeland Ave. advised her employees that she wanted to get "Mexicans" in who would clean better and complain less than her Black housekeeping staff. The EEOC's lawsuit seeks relief for a class of terminated housekeeping employees as well as a class of Black housekeeping applicants who sought employment at its Shadeland Avenue Hampton Inn facility between approximately September 2, 2008, and June 2009. ***EEOC v. New Indianapolis Hotels Inc.*, Case No. 1:10-cv-1234 (S.D. Ind. filed Sept. 30, 2010).**

- In August 2010, a judge refused to dismiss an EEOC lawsuit alleging that a freight management company hired Hispanic workers to the exclusion of equally or more qualified non-Hispanic employees for non-management positions at a Walmart distribution facility in Shelby, NC. The court rejected the company's claims that the EEOC had failed to state a claim in its complaint and that the suit was barred by laches. ***EEOC v. Propak Logistics Inc.*, No. 09-00311 (W.D.N.C. Aug. 6, 2010).**

- In August 2010, a temporary staffing agency with operations in five states admitted no wrongdoing but agreed to pay $585,000 to settle an EEOC suit alleging that the agency favored Hispanic workers over Black workers in hiring at a warehouse in Memphis, Tennessee. The Commission claimed that the agency selected Hispanics regardless of prior experience, place in line or availability. In addition to the monetary settlement, the staffing agency will create and publish a written hiring and placement policy prohibiting discrimination, post such policy at its Memphis facilities, and provide race and national origin discrimination awareness training for all recruiters, and onsite personnel. Further, to demonstrate its strong and clear commitment to a workplace free of race and national origin discrimination, the agency agreed that if it advertises, it will devote a portion of its advertising budget to placing ads in diverse media outlets. ***EEOC v. Paramount Staffing Inc.*, No. 2:06-02624 (W.D. Tenn. settled Aug. 23, 2010).**

- In August 2009, a Pinehurst, NC-based support services company for condominium complexes and resorts paid $44,700 and will furnish significant remedial relief to settle a race and national origin discrimination lawsuit, alleging the company unlawfully discharged six housekeepers because of their race (African American) and national origin (non-Hispanic) and immediately replaced them with Hispanic workers. ***EEOC v. Little River Golf, Inc.*, No. 1:08CV00546 (M.D.N.C. Aug. 6, 2009).**

- In May 2009, a Statesville, NC, grocery store agreed to settle for $30,000 a lawsuit alleging that it had fired a White, non-Hispanic meat cutter based on his race and national origin and replaced him with a less-qualified Hispanic employee. In addition, the store has agreed to distribute a formal, written anti-discrimination policy, train all employees on the policy and employment discrimination laws, and send reports to the EEOC on employees who are fired or resign. ***EEOC v. West Front Street Foods LLC*, d/b/a Compare Foods, No. 5:08-cv-102 (W.D.N.C. settled May 19, 2009).**

- In January 2008, a Charlotte, NC, supermarket chain paid $40,000 to settle an EEOC lawsuit alleging that the supermarket fired or forced long-term Caucasian and African American employees to resign and replaced them with Hispanic workers after it took over a particular facility. In addition to the monetary relief, the consent decree required the company to distribute a formal, written anti-discrimination policy; provide periodic training to all its employees on the policy and on Title VII's prohibition against national origin and race discrimination; send periodic reports to the EEOC concerning employees who are fired or resign; and post a "Notice to Employees" concerning this lawsuit. ***EEOC v. E&T Foods, LLC, d/b/a Compare Foods*, Civil Action No 3:06-cv-318 (W.D.N.C. settled Jan. 28, 2008).**

Job Segregation

- In December 2018, Maritime Autowash (later known as Phase 2 Investments, Inc.) paid $300,000 in monetary relief and furnished equitable relief to settle an EEOC race and national origin discrimination lawsuit. According to the EEOC's August 2017 lawsuit, Maritime violated Title VII of the Civil Rights Act of 1964 by segregating a class of Hispanic workers into lower-paying jobs as laborers or detailers at its former Edgewater, MD, facility. Maritime allegedly failed to offer them promotion or advancement opportunities to key employee or cashier positions, despite their tenure and outstanding job performance, and paid many class members only the minimum wage despite years of service, while paying non-Hispanic workers higher wages and promoting them. The EEOC also charged that Maritime discriminated against the Hispanic class members in their terms and conditions of employment, such as forcing them to perform other duties without additional compensation and denying them proper safety equipment or clothing. The EEOC said Maritime required Hispanic workers to perform personal tasks for the owner and managers, such as routinely assigning the female Hispanic class members to clean the houses of the owner or manager and assigning the male Hispanics to perform duties at their homes, such as landscaping, cleaning the pool, picking up dog excrement, painting, or helping with moves. The 3-year consent decree enjoins Maritime from retaliating in the future against any individual for asserting his or her rights under Title VII or otherwise engaging in protected activity. Should Maritime reopen and reactivate its Maryland facilities, it shall be enjoined from creating or maintaining a hostile work environment and inferior economic terms and conditions of employment on the basis of national origin or race. ***EEOC v. Phase 2 Investments, Inc.*, Civil Action No. 1:17-cv-02463 (D. Md. pre-trial settlement filed Dec. 2018).**

- In June 2017, the Seventh Circuit affirmed the district court's grant of summary judgment on the Commission's race segregation claim brought pursuant to 42 U.S.C. § 2000e-2(a)(2), Title VII's subsection prohibiting the limiting, classifying, or segregating of employees based on a protected trait. The court "assume[d] for the sake of argument" that the evidence created a material factual dispute about whether AutoZone intentionally segregated its Black employee Kevin Stuckey because of his race when it transferred him out of a predominantly Hispanic-staffed store. But it concluded that a jury would not find the lateral transfer had adversely affected Stuckey's employment since he suffered no reduction in pay, benefits, or responsibilities and it did not "alter his conditions of employment in a detrimental way." Nonetheless, the court rejected AutoZone's argument, accepted by the district court below, that the absence of an "adverse employment action" defeats a claim' under § 2000e-2(a)(2). It ruled that 42 U.S.C. § 2000e-2(a)(2) requires only that the transfer had a "tendency to deprive a person of employment opportunities," but concluded that there was "[n]o evidence" in the record to make the requisite showing in this case. Id. ***EEOC v. AutoZone, Inc.*, No. 15-3201 (7th Cir. June 20, 2017), *reh'g en banc denied* (7th Cir. Nov. 21, 2017).**

- In June 2013, the largest and oldest adult entertainment strip club in Jackson, MS, paid $50,000 to settle a lawsuit alleging that it discriminated against Black dancers when it maintained schedules only for Black women and forced them to compete for dancing slots on the "Black shift." The lawsuit also alleged that the club retaliated against the Black dancers after one of them filed a complaint with the EEOC, allegedly by reducing their work hours and subjecting them to fines, forcing one of them to quit. Under the consent decree, the club will implement new policies and practices designed to prevent racial discrimination and retaliation. It also will conduct supervisor and employee training on discrimination and retaliation laws and establish a confidential process for people to submit discrimination and retaliation complaints. The process will include employer protections of non-retaliation and requirements for a prompt, thorough, and impartial investigation. EEOC officials said Danny's will also post notices at the work site, including EEOC on new allegations of race discrimination and retaliation during the 2-year period. ***EEOC v. Danny's Cabaret*, No. 3:10-cv-00681 (S.D. Miss. consent decree filed June 28, 2013).**

- In May 2013, the EEOC sued Clarksdale's Stone Pony Pizza, alleging that the pizza place maintains a racially segregated workforce, and that it "hired only whites for front-of-the-house positions such as server, hostess, waitress, and bartender, and hired African Americans for back-of-the-house positions such as cook and dishwasher." ***EEOC v. Stone Pony Pizza, Inc.*, No. 4:13-cv-92(SA)(JMV) (N.D. Miss. reopened after dismissal due to bankruptcy Mar. 30, 2015).**

- In November 2011, a hospital on Chicago's South Side agreed to pay $80,000 to settle a class race, sex discrimination, and retaliation lawsuit filed by the EEOC. According to the Commission's lawsuit, the hospital allegedly subjected a class of Black female employees to different terms and conditions of employment and segregation in job assignments because of their race. The suit also alleged that at least one of the women was demoted in retaliation for opposing and complaining about unlawful employment practices. Further, the agency's administrative investigation revealed that numerous Black female medical technicians at the hospital appear to have been required to perform assignments that their male Asian-Indian counterparts were allegedly not required to perform. The 2-year consent decree resolving the case enjoins the hospital from engaging in further race and/or sex discrimination or retaliation. The consent decree also requires that the hospital provide training to all employees, including supervisory employees, in its Cardiopulmonary Department; that it submit periodic reports to the EEOC about any complaints of sex and/or race discrimination or retaliation; and that it post a notice at various locations within its facility regarding the outcome of this lawsuit. ***EEOC v. Jackson Park Hosp. & Med. Ctr.*, No. 11 C 04743 (N.D. Ill. Nov. 21, 2011).**

- In September 2010, the owner of a strip club settled for $95,000 a race discrimination lawsuit, alleging that two African American doormen were harassed, segregated, and provided different terms and conditions of employment because of their race. The managers of the club used racial slurs when speaking of and to the doormen, forced them to work in the back of the club instead of at the entrance, and complained that "black music makes the club look bad." In addition to the monetary damages, the 30-month consent decree provided injunctive relief, required the company to post a notice about the settlement, and obligated the company to conduct anti-discrimination training and to report race discrimination complaints. ***EEOC v. Papermoon-Stuart, Inc.*, No. 0:09-cv-14316 (S.D. Fla. settled September 28, 2010).**

- In September 2010, the EEOC commenced a lawsuit against a giant shipping and delivery service for subjecting a class of African American employees to different job assignments because of their race. The EEOC's administrative investigation found that African American drivers were assigned to predominately Black neighborhoods and White drivers to White neighborhoods. Furthermore, the investigation revealed that African American employees were assigned to more difficult and dangerous work than Caucasian employees. ***EEOC v. DHL Express (USA), Inc.*, No. 1:10-cv-06139 (N.D. Ill. filed Sept. 24, 2010).**

- In June 2010, the EEOC and an Atlanta home builder settled for $378,500 a suit alleging the company unlawfully discriminated by assigning Black sales employees to neighborhoods based on race, failing to promote African Americans or women to management, and harassing an employee who complained. ***EEOC v. John Wieland Homes and Neighborhoods Inc.*, No. 1-09-CV-1151 (N.D. Ga. consent decree approved June 22, 2010).**

- In September 2009, a supply company in Arizona agreed to pay $49,500 to settle an EEOC lawsuit that alleged the company assigned an African American employee and his Hispanic team member to less desirable, lower-paying jobs than their Caucasian counterparts because of the Black employee's race. Additionally, the lawsuit alleged that the supervisor responsible for determining job assignments used racial slurs such as "pinche negro," the n-word, and other racially derogatory comments to refer to the Black employee. The consent decree enjoins the company from engaging in racial discrimination. Additionally, the decree requires the company to implement and post written anti-discrimination policies and procedures, to provide training on race discrimination for all personnel and neutral references for the claimants, and to report to the EEOC any changes to its anti-discrimination policies and any future complaints alleging racial discrimination. ***EEOC v. L&W Supply Co.*, Case No. 2:07-cv-01364-JWS (D. Ariz. settled Sept. 2, 2009).**

- In June 2009, a federal district court granted summary judgment for a Michigan-based freight and trucking company on all race discrimination claims asserted by the EEOC and the claimant. The EEOC had alleged that the company refused to hire a Black female applicant for a part-time customer service position, even after she was designated best qualified and had passed the requisite drug test. According to the lawsuit, the company's regional manager vetoed her hire because he was concerned about a Black customer service representative working with customers and drivers in southeast Missouri. On September 22, 2010, the Eighth Circuit affirmed the district court on all federal law claims and remanded the claimant's state law claim. On January 7, 2011, the district court dismissed the claimant's state law claim without prejudice. ***EEOC v. Con-way Freight, Inc.*, No. 4:07-cv-01638 (E.D. Mo. June 17, 2009).**

- In May 2009, a North Carolina-based restaurant entered a 3-year consent decree to pay $14,700 and provide a positive letter of reference for the claimant. The EEOC had alleged that the restaurant refused to hire an African American employee for a bartender position because of his race. According to the complaint, the Black employee sought and was qualified for the bartender position, but the restaurant hired him as a server and refused to place him in the bartender position on several occasions when it became available. Evidence indicated that the restaurant had a practice of hiring only White people as bartenders. Eventually, the Black employee resigned because he believed he would never be placed in the bartender position. The consent decree enjoins the restaurant from discriminating based on race in hiring or promotion into the bartender position, requires the restaurant to adopt a written anti-discrimination policy, provide Title VII training to all managers and supervisors, keep records related to any future complaints alleging racial discrimination in hiring or promotion, and submit reports to the EEOC. The restaurant must also keep records on the hiring of and promotion into the bartender position. ***EEOC v. Chelda, Inc. and Charmike Holdings, LLC*, dba Ham's Restaurant, Civil Action No. 1:08-cv-00236 (W.D.N.C. May 12, 2009).**

- In March 2008, a national restaurant chain entered a consent decree agreeing to pay $30,000 to resolve an EEOC case charging that the company gave African American food servers inferior and lesser-paying job assignments by denying them assignments of larger parties with greater resulting tips and income, by denying them better paying assignments to banquets at the restaurant, and by failing on some occasions to give them assignments to any customers. The consent decree enjoins the restaurant from engaging in racial discrimination and requires the chain to post a remedial notice and amend and distribute its anti-discrimination and anti-harassment policies. The amended policies must state that prohibited racial discrimination in "all other employment decisions" includes, but is not limited to, making decisions and providing terms and conditions of employment such as pay, assignments, working conditions, and job duties; also, it must prohibit retaliation. In addition, the company must revise its complaint mechanism and clarify and expand its website and toll-free phone number for the reporting of incidents of employment discrimination. The consent decree also requires the restaurant to provide training in equal employment opportunity laws for all of its employees and to appoint an Equal Employment Office Coordinator, who will be responsible for investigating discrimination complaints. ***EEOC v. McCormick & Schmick's Restaurant Corp*, No. 06-cv-7806 (S.D.N.Y. March 17, 2008).**

- In January 2008, a bakery café franchise in Florida entered a 2-year consent decree that enjoined the company from engaging in racial discrimination or retaliation and required it to pay $101,000 to the claimants. The EEOC had alleged that the company segregated the Black employees from non-Black employees and illegally fired a class of Black employees in violation of Title VII. Under the consent decree, the principal of the company must attend an 8-hour training session on equal employment opportunity laws. The decree also mandated that if the company ever re-opens the franchise in question or any other store, it must distribute its anti-discrimination policy to all employees, post a remedial notice, and report any future complaints alleging race-based discrimination. ***EEOC v. Atlanta Bread Co., International and ARO Enterprise of Miami*, Inc., No. 06-cv-61484 (S.D. Fla. January 4, 2008).**

- In July 2007, the EEOC and Walgreens agreed to a proposed settlement of $20 million to resolve allegations that the Illinois-based national drug store chain engaged in systemic race discrimination against African American retail management and pharmacy employees in promotion, compensation, and assignment. In addition to the monetary relief for an estimated 10,000 class members, the consent decree prohibits store assignments based on race. ***EEOC v. Walgreen Co.*, No. 07-CV-172-GPM; *Tucker v. Walgreen Co.* No. 05-CV-440-GPM (S.D. Ill. July 12, 2007).**

- In March 2007, the owners of a Louisiana motel agreed to pay $140,000 to charging party and three other claimants who alleged that the motel would not hire them for front-desk positions because they are African American. The company also agreed not to exclude any African American employee or applicant for the front-desk day positions based on their race for any future businesses it may operate. The consent decree further requires it to maintain a complaint procedure to encourage employees to file internal good faith complaints regarding race discrimination and retaliation. ***United States v. Sunrise Hospitality BC-II LLC*, No. 5:06cv1684 (W.D. La., *consent decree entered* Mar. 27, 2007).**

- In April 2006, the EEOC obtained $450,000 to settle a race discrimination case in which a health-care provider explained its refusal to hire "Blacks or Jews" for a client in Oregon by arguing that it was protecting the safety of its employees, especially in areas where the KKK is active. ***EEOC v. Health Help, Inc.*, 03-1204 PHX RGS (D. Ariz. Apr. 2006).**

Terms and Conditions

- In February 2020, the EEOC's Office of Federal Operation (OFO) found that the Department of Veteran Affairs engaged in race and age discrimination when it did not select a Registered Nurse (RN) at the Murfreesboro VA Medical Center facility in Tennessee for the position of Nurse Manager, Specialty Clinics. According to the OFO, the Agency investigated the claim which produced evidence in support of the allegation. After screening qualified candidates using a "Best Qualified" (BQ) grid, the primary panel interviewed the five highest-scoring candidates, including Complainant. Selectee failed to pass the BQ screening and was not interviewed. After the interviews, the panel selected Complainant. Complainant had approximately 30 years' experience as an RN, supervisor, assistant director, and manager. Selectee possessed the basic qualifications and had served as Acting Nurse Manager for a few months. The Selection Official, however, rejected Complainant, noting she was the second-ranked candidate, and the top-ranked candidate, also an African American, and directed the panel to re-interview the candidates. The Associate Director emailed the panel chair and Selection Official, asking that the panel interview Selectee "as a professional courtesy." The BQ grid results were disregarded and all candidates were rated and ranked based solely on interview scores. Based on interview scores, Selectee was chosen. The OFO found that the elimination of objective "Best Qualified" criteria in favor of rating and ranking candidates based solely on interviews was the creation of a deliberately subjective selection process that was highly suggestive of pre-selection and unlawful discrimination. The OFO rejected the Agency's explanation that the BQ scoring grid failed to consider years of nursing experience within specialty care clinics, noting that Selectee was considerably less experienced than Complainant. The OFO found that the Agency's explanation was a pretext for its unlawful discrimination in the selection process and the Agency had failed to articulate a legitimate, nondiscriminatory reason for its actions. The OFO ordered the Agency to promote Complainant and pay back pay with interest and benefits, investigate and determine her entitlement to compensatory damages, and consider disciplining and provide EEO training to the responsible management officials. A posting notice and attorney's fees were also ordered. ***Arleen L. v. Dep't of Veterans Affairs (Veterans Health Administration)*, EEOC Appeal No. 2019002725 (February 4, 2020).**

- In January 2018, the EEOC reversed an agency's decision, holding on appeal that an African American Senior Officer Specialist (SOS), GS-8, at the Department of Justice's Low Security Correctional Institution (LSCI) in North Carolina had subjected the SOS to disparate treatment regarding promotions. According to evidence in the record, management denied the SOS the opportunity to attend the trainings necessary for promotion into a Security Officer Locksmith (SOL), citing budgetary reasons. Meanwhile, in the same time frame, management approved such training for two similarly situated White officers who were eventually promoted to SOL. The Commission noted that several witnesses subscribed to Complainant's view that management intentionally foreclosed minorities from career advancement. The EEOC did not find that the SOS had been subjected to a racially hostile work environment even though he averred that while he and another African American coworker were working, a Caucasian Officer reportedly said to them as they were walking away, "See you, boys," and said to Complainant on another occasion, "See you tomorrow boy." To remedy the discrimination, the Commission ordered the Agency to provide Complainant the trainings at issue, and to noncompetitively promote him in a similar fashion to the two cited Caucasian comparators. ***Nathan S. v. Dep't of Justice*, EEOC Appeal No. 0120151282 (Jan. 9, 2018).**

- In November 2017, the EEOC reversed the Department of Homeland Security's (Agency) finding of no race discrimination on the Complainant's allegation that the Agency discriminated against him based on race when it issued him Letters of Counseling for unprofessional conduct and missing a duty call. In reversing the Agency's decision finding no discrimination, the Commission found that the issuances of the disciplinary actions giving rise to these claims was motivated by discriminatory animus based on Complainant's race. Specifically, the Commission found that the discipline issued was disproportionate and lacked uniformity, and the record showed that other employees were not disciplined for engaging in similar conduct. The Agency was ordered, among other things, to rescind the Letters and remove them from Complainant's personnel record, as well as adjust any subsequent discipline that was based on the Letters. The Commission affirmed the Agency's finding of no discrimination with respect to other matters raised in the complaint. ***Erwin B. v. Dep't of Homeland Sec.*, EEOC Appeal No. 0120151276 (May 15, 2017), request for reconsideration denied EEOC Request No. 0520170446 (Nov. 3, 2017).**

- In August 2017, the EEOC affirmed an Administrative Judge's finding that the Department of Defense (Agency) had discriminated against Complainant when it did not select him for an Assistant Special Agent in Charge position. Following a hearing, the AJ found that the Agency failed to articulate a legitimate, nondiscriminatory reason for Complainant's non-selection. While the Agency asserted that Complainant was not promoted because he did not pass an annual physical fitness exam, Agency managers testified that the supervisory position would involve more administrative work than Complainant's position and there would not be a substantial change in the physical requirements. Further, the AJ noted that the selection criteria was changed for one candidate who did not meet the requirements but not for Complainant. Complainant also stated that the Director, who was extensively involved in the selection yet did not testify at the hearing, made several comments that revealed a discriminatory intent. The AJ questioned the Director's credibility, finding that there were considerable gaps in the Director's statements. The Commission affirmed the AJ's findings on appeal and noted that even if the Agency met its burden of providing a legitimate reason for Complainant's non-selection, the evidence supported a finding of pretext. Specifically, Complainant was considered the best candidate by his second-level supervisor, and the record showed that Complainant was better qualified than the selectee. The Agency was ordered, among other things, to place Complainant into the position or a similar position, with appropriate back pay and benefits, and pay him proven compensatory damages. ***Kenny C. v. Dep't of Def.*, EEOC Appeal No. 0720150030 (Aug. 29, 2017).**

- In March 2017, the EEOC settled its contempt action against Baby O's Restaurant, dba Danny's Downtown, a Jackson-based provider of adult entertainment services. The contempt action charged that Danny's breached the terms of an agreement it entered into with the EEOC to resolve a racial discrimination and retaliation lawsuit. According to the EEOC's lawsuit, Danny's subjected four African American females to unlawful race discrimination and retaliation. The EEOC charged that Black entertainers were subjected to a variety of less advantageous terms and conditions of employment than White ones. The misconduct included subjecting African American entertainers to arbitrary fees and fines, forcing them to work on less lucrative shifts, and excluding them from company advertisements, all because of their race. The EEOC also charged that Danny's retaliated against the entertainers by reducing their work hours when one of them engaged in activity protected by law, including filing a discrimination charge with the EEOC. The EEOC alleged the retaliation was so severe that one of the entertainers was forced to leave her employment. In June 2013, the company entered into a consent decree agreeing to pay $50,000 in relief to the Black females who had been subjected to the racial discrimination and retaliation. The decree also provided for significant injunctive relief, including revising the company's anti-discrimination policy; promulgating and disseminating it to employees; providing a copy of that policy to the EEOC; providing mandatory Title VII training to supervisory and non-supervisory employees and entertainers; making periodic reports of its compliance to the EEOC; and posting a notice of the policy in its workplace. After paying the $50,000, Danny's failed to comply with the rest of the decree. The Commission filed a contempt action, and on March 2, 2017, the court approved an amended consent decree that extended the injunctive requirements of the decree by one year. ***EEOC v. Baby O's Restaurant dba Danny's Downtown*, Civil Action No. 3:12-CV-681-DPF-FKB (SD. Miss. Mar. 2, 2017).**

- In December 2016, a south Alabama steel manufacturing plant agreed to pay $150,000 as part of a 3-year consent decree to resolve an EEOC lawsuit. In June 2015, the EEOC filed a lawsuit accusing Outokumpu Stainless USA, LLC of not promoting workers at its Calvert plant because of their race. The Commission said certain Black workers were highly qualified to become Team Leaders, but the company hired White applicants who were less qualified for the job. In addition to the $150,000 payment, Outokumpu agrees to take specified actions designed to prevent future discrimination, including implementing new policies and practices designed to prevent race discrimination in employment decisions, providing anti-discrimination training to employees, and the posting of anti-discrimination notices in its workplace. ***EEOC v. Outokumpu Stainless USA, LLC*, No. 1:13-cv-00473-WS-N (S.D. Ala. Dec. 2016).**

- In June 2015, Dollar General Corporation paid $32,500 and furnished other relief to settle a race discrimination lawsuit filed by the EEOC. In its lawsuit, the EEOC charged that Dollar General refused on at least three separate occasions to promote a Black employee to a vacant assistant store manager position at its Long Beach, MS, store because of her race. The EEOC alleged that she had expressed interest in promotion and had substantial qualifications, but Dollar General instead hired less-qualified White applicants. The suit further alleged that Dollar General subjected the Black employee to increasing hostility and discipline after she complained about the unequal treatment. The company denied the allegations in court. The court denied Dollar General's motion for summary judgment and the parties ultimately entered a 2-year consent decree requiring Dollar General to maintain effective anti-discrimination policies, distribute the policies to all newly hired employees, and provide management training on anti-discrimination laws and other injunctive relief to ensure discrimination complaints are promptly reported and investigated. ***EEOC v. Dolgencorp, LLC d/b/a Dollar General*, No. 1: 13-cv-00383-LG-JCG (S.D. Miss. June 11, 2015).**

- In July 2014, the apprenticeship school affiliated with a New Jersey construction trade union will pay $34,500 and provide substantial remedial relief to settle a discrimination claim by the EEOC, alleging that the Joint Apprenticeship and Training Committee of Sheet Metal Workers Local 25 discharged a Black apprentice because of his race just 2 weeks before he was to graduate from the 4-year apprenticeship program. The EEOC's findings arose from its investigation of the apprentice's appeal of his dismissal, which he filed with the court-appointed special master who monitors Local 25 and its JATC pursuant to past judicial findings of race and national origin discrimination. According to the EEOC, the JATC violated the court's previous orders by summarily discharging the apprentice for alleged poor performance just days before he was to complete the program and be promoted to journeyman status. The JATC imposed this severe sanction despite the apprentice satisfactorily completing virtually the entire eight-term program and despite his complaints about inadequate on-the-job training from biased contractors. ***EEOC v. Day & Zimmerman NPS, Inc.*, No. 1:71-cv-02877(LAK)(MHD) (S.D.N.Y. consent decree filed July 11, 2014).**

- In March 2012, the U.S. Court of Appeals for the Fifth Circuit ruled that the EEOC presented sufficient evidence that two African American railroad workers were disciplined more harshly for workplace rule violations than comparable White employees to raise a jury issue of race discrimination under Title VII. In a 2–1 decision partially overturning a federal trial court in Louisiana, the divided panel found that the EEOC established a prima facie case of "work-rule" discrimination against Kansas City Southern Railway Co. on behalf of two of the four claimants. In short, the appellate court found that a train engineer and a train conductor, both African American, were fired following separate incidents involving operational errors while White employees involved in the same incidents were not disciplined or were dismissed but reinstated despite committing comparable infractions. ***Turner v. Kansas City S. Ry. Co.*, No. 09-30558 (5th Cir. revised opinion Mar. 26, 2012).**

- In May 2011, a property and casualty insurance giant agreed to pay $110,000 to settle an EEOC lawsuit alleging that it unlawfully refused to promote an Asian employee in its Milwaukee underwriting office because of her race. The suit further asserted that the insurance company illegally retaliated against the employee by passing her over for job openings after she filed a discrimination charge with the EEOC. ***EEOC v. Fed. Ins. Co., d/b/a Chubb & Son,* Case No. 2:10-cv-00849 (E.D. Wis. *settled* May 3, 2011).**

- In November 2010, a company which transports saltwater from oil wells and has facilities in Quitman, AZ, settled for $75,000 the EEOC's lawsuit alleging that it subjected a Black truck driver and another Black employee at its Quitman location to racial harassment, which included racial jokes and racially derogatory language (e.g., "nigger"); gave them fewer work assignments than White employees because of their race; and further reduced the driver's work assignments because of his complaints about racial discrimination and suspended and discharged him because of his race and his complaints about racial discrimination. The driver complained about the racial jokes and language to management but was suspended for 4 days following a dispute about a work assignment and was discharged during the suspension. The 5-year consent decree, *inter alia*, enjoins the company from subjecting Black employees to disparate working assignments based on race and from suspending and terminating employees in retaliation for opposing practices unlawful under Title VII or for participating in Title VII proceedings. The company is also required to provide training for its employees on reporting and investigating race discrimination and race harassment complaints. ***EEOC v. Complete Vacuum and Rental, Inc.*, No. 1:09-cv-00049-SWW (E.D. Ark. Nov. 8, 2010).**

- In January 2012, a Henderson, NV-based chain of automotive dealerships agreed to pay $150,000 to two Black employees to settle a Title VII lawsuit alleging that the company violated federal law by engaging in discrimination, harassment, and retaliation. According to the EEOC, a parts department manager, who is White, allegedly used the "N-word" to refer to at least two Black employees and made racially derogatory comments and jokes on a near daily basis at the dealership. The same manager allegedly referred to one Black employee as "gorilla" while the employee was holding a banana. The EEOC contended that the manager also imposed stricter work-related rules upon the dealership's Black employees by disciplining them for conduct that non-Black employees were not disciplined for and giving them less favorable work assignments. Ultimately, both Black employees were terminated, but the EEOC asserted that one of the employees was discharged for an infraction for which non-Black employees were not disciplined, while the other was discharged after relaying his intention to file a charge of discrimination to the company. In addition to the monetary relief, the company agreed to distribute a revised discrimination and complaint policy and hire an employment consultant. ***EEOC v. Shack-Findlay Automotive, LLC d/b/a Findlay Honda and Findlay Automotive Group, Inc.*, Case No. 2:10-cv-01692-KJD-RJJ (D. Nev. Jan. 17, 2012).**

- In June 2010, a Warren, MI, automotive supplier paid $190,000 to settle a race discrimination and retaliation lawsuit in which the EEOC alleged that the supplier repeatedly overlooked qualified non-White employees, including a group of Black employees and a Bangladeshi employee, for promotions to the maintenance department. In addition, a White employee who opposed this type of race discrimination and complained that managers in the maintenance department were using racial slurs allegedly was fired shortly after the company learned of his complaints. ***EEOC v. Noble Metal Processing, Inc.*, No. 2:08-CV-14713 (E.D. Mich. press release filed June 8, 2010).**

- In March 2010, the EEOC upheld an Administrative Judge's determination that a federal agency discriminated against a Black employee on the basis of race when it terminated the complainant's participation in a training program. The record showed that complainant was not rated as "marginal" and that the Manager who made the decision to terminate complainant conceded that complainant passed all required tests. Further, the Manager did not consult with the instructors before making the decision, but instead relied upon one individual who was clearly hostile toward complainant and who the AJ found was not credible. Additionally, the environment was not favorable to Black recruits. Two witnesses testified that they heard someone remark "one down and two to go" when complainant turned in his equipment following his termination. At that time, there were only three Black students in the 31-person class. One week before the class was to graduate, the third and last Black student was removed from the program. The record also revealed that it was the agency's policy to afford remedial training and an opportunity to correct behavior before removing candidates from the training program. The record indicated that the policy was followed with respect to White comparatives, but was not followed in complainant's case. The agency was ordered to, among other things, offer complainant reinstatement into the next training program, with back pay. ***Thalamus Jones v. United States Department of Energy*, EEOC Appeal No. 0720090045 (March 5, 2010).**

- In January 2010, an international designer and manufacturer of medical devices agreed to pay $250,000 to settle the EEOC's Title VII lawsuit alleging race discrimination. The suit alleged that the manufacturer subjected a Black full-time sales representative to different terms and conditions of employment when it removed him from top accounts, assigned him to poorer producing accounts, and then terminated him even though he continued to perform successfully, while failing to discharge any of the poorer performing White sales executives. The 2-year consent decree also requires the manufacturer to rehire the Black sales rep in its North Texas District at a higher salary with 3% commissions and relocation expenses up to $15,000. ***EEOC v. Linvatech Corp. d/b/a Conmed Linvatech,*** **No. 09-2158 (N.D. Ill. Jan. 4, 2010).**

- In December 2009, a Tennessee company that processes nuclear waste agreed to settle claims by the EEOC that Black employees were subjected to higher levels of radiation than others. Specifically, the EEOC alleged that, in addition to paying them less and permitting a White manager to refer regularly to them with the N-word and other derogatory slurs, such as "boy," the company manipulated dosimeters of Black employees assigned to work with radioactive waste to show lower levels of radiation than the actual ones. Under the agreement, 23 Black employees will receive $650,000. ***EEOC v. Race, LLC, doing business as Studsvik, LLC,*** **Civil Action No. 2:07-cv-2620 (W.D. Tenn. Dec. 2009).**

- In June 2009, the EEOC overturned an AJ's finding of no discrimination in a Title VII race discrimination case. Complainant alleged he was discriminated against on the bases of race (African American) and retaliation when he was not selected for any of four vacant Risk Management Specialist positions. Complainant applied for the position, was rated as qualified, interviewed for the position, and was not selected. All four of the selectees were White. The agency found no discrimination and complainant appealed. The Commission found that the agency failed to provide a legitimate, non-discriminatory reason for the non-selection. The agency stated that the selectees were chosen because their skills and qualifications fit the agency's needs. The Commission found that the agency's reasons were not sufficiently clear so that complainant could be given a fair opportunity to rebut such reasons. The Commission also noted that the agency did not produce any rating sheets from the interview panel, and that complainant appeared to possess similar qualifications to the other selectees. Thus, the Commission found that the prima facie case and complainant's qualifications, combined with the agency's failure to provide a legitimate, nondiscriminatory reason for complainant's non-selection, warranted a finding of race discrimination. Because of this finding, the decision found it unnecessary to address the basis of retaliation. As remedies, the agency was ordered to place complainant into the Risk Management Specialist position with back pay and consideration of compensatory damages, EEO training to responsible agency officials, consideration of discipline for responsible agency officials, attorneys fees order, and posting notice. ***Frazier v. United States Department of Agriculture,*** **EEOC Appeals No. 0120083270 (June 4, 2009).**

- In August 2009, a Washington Park, IL, packaging and warehousing company agreed to pay $57,500 and provide training to settle a race discrimination and retaliation lawsuit alleging that the company failed to provide a Black employee the pay raise and health insurance coverage provided to his White coworkers, and then fired him in retaliation for filing a charge of race discrimination with the EEOC. ***EEOC v. Material Resources, LLC,* d/b/a Gateway Co-Packing Co., No. 3:08-245-MJR (S.D. Ill. August 14, 2009).**

- In January 2008, the EEOC settled a race and national origin discrimination case against a Nevada U-Haul company for $153,000. The EEOC had charged that the company subjected Hispanic and Asian/Filipino employees to derogatory comments and slurs based on their race and/or national origin. Hispanic employees also were subjected to comments such as "go back to Mexico." In addition, Filipino mechanics were denied promotions while less qualified White employees were promoted. The EEOC also charged that Hispanic and Filipino employees were told they had to be "White to get ahead" at the company. As part of the injunctive relief, U-Haul further agreed to provide training to all employees in its Nevada locations, and provide annual reports to the EEOC regarding its employment practices in its Nevada branches. ***EEOC v. U-Haul Company of Nevada,* Case No. 2:06-CV-01209-JCM-LRL(D.Nev. settled Jan. 28, 2008).**

- In May 2008, in New Capital Dimensions case the EEOC resolved a race discrimination and retaliation suit against a North Georgia restaurant chain for $135,000. The lawsuit alleged that a White male store manager ordered all the African American employees to be strip-searched in response to a White cashier's drawer turning up $100 short. When advised about the missing money by the store manager, the White cashier asserted she knew nothing about it and was permitted to leave without being searched. When the Black employees complained about the discriminatory treatment, the manager fired them. The consent decree also includes provisions for equal employment opportunity training, reporting, and posting of anti-discrimination notices. **EEOC v. New Capital Dimensions, Inc., dba Krystal Restaurant, 2:08-cv-00089-RWS (N.D. Ga. Settled May 21, 2008).**

- In September 2007, the Commission upheld an AJ's determination that complainant was discriminated against on the bases of race (Asian American), national origin (Japanese), sex (female), and/or in retaliation for prior EEO activity when: (1) she received an unsatisfactory interim performance rating; (2) she was demoted from her GS-14 Section Chief position; and (3) management's actions created and allowed a hostile work environment. The agency was ordered to restore leave; pay complainant $50,000.00 in non-pecuniary compensatory damages and $6,944.00 in pecuniary compensatory damages; and pay $45,517.50 in attorney's fees and $786.39 for costs. ***Sugawara-Adams v. EPA,* EEOC Appeal No. 0720070050 (Sep. 10, 2007).**

- In July 2007, the Sixth Circuit agreed in part with the EEOC's amicus argument that a district court improperly granted summary judgment against a Black rehabilitation aide because she presented sufficient evidence—whether categorized as "direct" or "circumstantial"—that race was a factor motivating her employer's decision not to promote her. This evidence included a White manager's statement that if the Black recommending official hired the Black aide based on the strength of her interview and her demonstrated ability to interact and work one-on-one with clients, "people are going to think" nonetheless that she was selected "because she was Black." The manager hired a White candidate with more seniority. On appeal, the circuit court decided that "the subject of race was improperly introduced into the selection process and used as a consideration in [the] hiring decision" and that the manager's decision was motivated by the aide's race and not the selectee's experience or seniority. The court then reversed summary judgment and remanded the case for trial. ***Brewer v. Cedar Lake Lodge, Inc.*,** **No. 06-6327 (6th Cir. July 31, 2007) (unpublished opinion).**

- In September 2006, the EEOC filed this Title VII lawsuit alleging that a nonprofit organization that provides rehabilitation services for people with disabilities discriminated against four African American employees because of their race (delayed promotion, unfair discipline, and termination) and retaliated against three of them for complaining about racially disparate working conditions, reduction of working hours, discipline, and termination. Under the 3-year consent decree, four Black employees will share $400,000 in monetary relief and the organization will increase one Black employee's hours to no less than 20 per week to restore her eligibility for various employment benefits. ***EEOC v. Richmond of New York d/b/a Richmond Children's Center*,** **No. 05-CV-8342 (SCR)(MDF) (S.D.N.Y. Sept. 11, 2006).**

- In February 2006, the Commission settled for $275,000 a Title VII lawsuit alleging that defendant, an aviation services company, subjected Charging Party to discriminatory terms and conditions of employment, discipline, and demotion based on race, Black. After 6 years as a line service technician, defendant promoted Charging Party to supervisor. Defendant did not announce the promotion until 2 months after Charging Party had begun the new job and did not issue Charging Party a cell telephone or a company email address during his tenure in the position. In contrast, defendant announced the promotion of Charging Party's White successor within 3 days and issued him a cell telephone and a company email address immediately. Just 4½ months after promoting Charging Party, defendant reprimanded him and demoted him. ***EEOC v. Signature Flight Support Corp.*,** **No. C 05 1101 CW (N.D. Cal. Feb. 23, 2006).**

- In May 2005, the EEOC obtained a $500,000 settlement against a nursing facility in Puyallup, WA, for alleged violations of Title VII, which included the all-White care management team preparing a care plan incorporating a White family's request that no "colored girls" work with the resident; tolerating frequent use of racial slurs, including reference to a Black nurse as a "slave"; assigning Black nurses to the night shift, while giving White nurses the more desirable day shifts; assigning Black and White employees to separate lunchtimes and lunchrooms; and twice denying a Black nurse a promotion to a staffing position for which she had several years of experience and was highly qualified. ***EEOC v. Central Park Lodges Long Term Care, Inc., d/b/a Linden Grove Health Care Center,*** **No. 04-5627 RBL (W.D. Wash. consent decree filed May 13, 2005).**

Compensation Disparity

- In January 2020, Jackson National Life Insurance paid Black female employees in Denver and Nashville $20.5 million to settle a racial and sexual discrimination case brought by the EEOC's Denver and Phoenix offices. Twenty-one employees filed an EEOC complaint about receiving less pay than their White colleagues, being passed over for promotions, being subjected to sexual harassment and referred to by slurs, including "lazy" and "streetwalkers." In addition to the payout, the deal requires Jackson to take steps to prevent future race- and sex-based harassment, including designating an internal compliance monitor and hiring a consultant to review its policies. ***EEOC v. Jackson National Life Insurance Company,*** **Civil Action No. 16-cv-02472-PAB-SKC (D. Colo. Jan. 9, 2020).**

- In May 2019, a Mississippi federal court jury returned a verdict in favor of the EEOC and five Black dancers who were subjected to egregious race discrimination while employed by Danny's of Jackson, LLC (Danny's), doing business as Danny's Downtown Cabaret, a Jackson, Mississippi, night club. The verdicts included $1.5 million in punitive damages, $1.68 million in compensatory damages, and $130,550 in back pay. According to the EEOC, Danny's, and its predecessor, Baby O's Restaurant, subjected Black dancers to discriminatory terms and conditions of employment for years, including limiting the number of shifts Black dancers could work, and subjecting them to racially offensive epithets. The jury found that Danny's also forced the dancers to work at a related club, Black Diamonds, even though they were subject to arrest there because they were not licensed to work at that club. The pay and working conditions at Black Diamonds were inferior to those at Danny's, and there was less security there. The dancers who refused to work at Black Diamonds were fined and sent home, and not allowed to work at Danny's. Despite at least 8 years of efforts by the EEOC, which included two EEOC charges, three prior lawsuits and contempt proceedings, and three consent decrees Danny's continued to discriminate against the dancers. ***EEOC v. Danny's Restaurant, LLC and Danny's of Jackson, LLC f/k/a Baby O's Restaurant, Inc. d/b/a Danny's Downtown Cabaret,*** **Civil Action No. 3:16-cv-00769-HTW-LRA (S.D. Miss. May 2019).**

- In August 2015, the district court denied a motion to dismiss by J&R Baker Farms LLC and J&R Baker Farms Partnership in a lawsuit brought by the EEOC. The EEOC had alleged that the Farms subjected American workers, most of whom were African American, to discrimination based on national origin and race at their Colquitt County location. According to the EEOC's lawsuit, the employer favored foreign-born workers or workers they believed to be foreign-born, while engaging in a pattern or practice of discrimination against White American and African American workers. The agency alleges that all American workers were discriminatorily discharged, subjected to different terms and conditions of employment, and provided fewer work opportunities, based on their national origin and/or race. Regarding the disparate terms and conditions, the agency alleges that work start times were habitually delayed for White American and African American workers, that they were sent home early while foreign workers continued to work, and that they were subjected to production standards not imposed on foreign-born workers. These practices led to all American workers receiving less pay than their foreign-born counterparts. ***EEOC v. J&R Baker Farms LLC, et al.*, No. 7:14-CV-136 (M.D. Ga. dismissal order filed Aug. 11, 2015).**

- In December 2012, Hamilton Growers, Inc., doing business as Southern Valley Fruit and Vegetable, Inc., an agricultural farm in Norman Park, GA, agreed to pay $500,000 to a class of American seasonal workers—many of them African American—who, the EEOC alleged, were subjected to discrimination based on their national origin and/or race, the agency announced. The agreement resolves a lawsuit filed by the EEOC in September 2011. The EEOC's suit had charged that the company unlawfully engaged in a pattern or practice of discrimination against American workers by firing virtually all American workers while retaining workers from Mexico during the 2009, 2010, and 2011 growing seasons. The agency also alleged that Hamilton Growers fired at least 16 African American workers in 2009 based on race and/or national origin as their termination was coupled with race-based comments by a management official; provided lesser job opportunities to American workers by assigning them to pick vegetables in fields which had already been picked by foreign workers, which resulted in Americans earning less pay than their Mexican counterparts; and regularly subjected American workers to different terms and conditions of employment, including delayed starting times and early stop times, or denied the opportunity to work at all, while Mexican workers were allowed to continue working. The settlement provides monetary relief to 19 persons who filed charges with the agency and other American workers harmed by the practices. Additionally, Hamilton Growers agreed to exercise good faith in hiring and retaining qualified workers of American national origin and African American workers for all farm work positions, including supervisory positions; will implement non-discriminatory hiring measures, which include targeted recruitment and advertising, appointment of a compliance official, and training for positive equal employment opportunity management practices; will create a termination appeal process; extend rehire offers to aggrieved individuals from the 2009–2012 growing seasons; provide transportation for American workers; and limit contact between the alleged discriminating management officials and American workers. The decree also provides for posting anti-discrimination notices, record-keeping, and reporting to the EEOC. ***EEOC v. Hamilton Growers, Inc.*, Civil Action No. 7:11-CV-00134-HL (N.D. Ga. settlement announced Dec. 13, 2012).**

- In August 2011, an Obion County producer of pork sausage products paid $60,000 and furnished other relief to settle a wage discrimination and racial harassment lawsuit filed by the EEOC. In its lawsuit, the EEOC charged that near Union City violated federal law by paying an African American maintenance worker less than White counterparts and subjecting him to a hostile work environment. The EEOC asserted that Williams Country Sausage gave raises and paid higher salaries to all maintenance department employees except the department's lone African American employee and allegedly allowed a supervisor to regularly use racially offensive language toward the employee because of racial animus. The 5-year consent decree enjoins the sausage company from engaging in future race discrimination, and requires annual Title VII training on employee rights, record-keeping of racial harassment complaints, and annual reports to the EEOC. The decree also requires the company to establish and enforce a written policy that will ensure that employees are protected from discrimination. ***EEOC v. Williams Country Sausage*, Civil Action No. 1:10-CV-01263 (W.D. Tenn. Aug. 11, 2011).**

- In April 2011, the EEOC and a Bedford, OH, auto dealership reached a $300,000 settlement of a case alleging that the dealership permitted a general manager to harass Black employees and also discriminated against Black sales employees with regard to pay. ***EEOC v. Ganley Lincoln of Bedford Inc.*, No. 1:07-cv-2829 (N.D. Ohio consent decree entered Apr. 19, 2011).**

- In March 2011, the EEOC filed a lawsuit alleging that a provider of preventive maintenance for residential and commercial heating and air conditioning systems, which has approximately 247 employees at 13 locations within Florida, Georgia, the District of Columbia, Northern Virginia, and Maryland, violated federal law by discriminating against non-Caucasian employees based on their race when it paid them less than their Caucasian colleagues. Additionally, the EEOC alleged that an African American telemarketer was paid less than a Caucasian telemarketer in a substantially similar job. Despite complaining to management, the African American employee's compensation remained the same until she resigned. ***EEOC v. United Air Temp / Air Conditioning & Heating, Inc.*, Civil Action No. 1:11-cv-281 (E.D. Va. filed Mar. 21, 2011).**

- In March 2011, a television station settled a race and sex discrimination case filed by the EEOC for $45,000 and additional consideration. From 1996 to 2007, an African American female reporter was paid lower wages than a comparable White female reporter and male reporters of all races. She was also subjected to unequal terms and conditions of employment. In addition to the damages, the station must post an anti-discrimination notice, publicize an anti-discrimination policy, and provide annual race and sex discrimination training to its employees. ***EEOC, et al. v. KOKH,*** **No. 5:07-cv-01043-D (W.D. Okla. March 4, 2011).**

- In September 2010, the EEOC filed a lawsuit against a Union City, TN, pork company, alleging that the company engaged in race discrimination by paying an African American maintenance worker less than non-Black employees, subjecting him to a hostile work environment, and forcing him out of his job. According to the EEOC's complaint, the company gave raises and paid higher salaries to all maintenance department employees except the department's lone African American employee because of racial animus and allowed a supervisor to regularly use racially offensive language toward the Black employee, causing the employee to quit his job to escape the abuse. ***EEOC v. Williams Country Sausage Co.,*** **Civil Action No. 1:10-cv-01263 (W.D. Tenn. filed Sept. 30, 2010).**

- In November 2009, a nationwide supplier of office products and services entered into an 18-month consent decree, agreeing to pay $80,000 to an African American account manager who the EEOC alleged was denied appropriate wages because of his race. According to the EEOC's lawsuit, the complainant was hired as a junior account manager in the supplier's Baton Rouge, LA, office with an annual salary of $32,500, plus commissions. At the time of his hire, complainant was told that after 6–8 months, he would be promoted to account manager with an increase in his base salary. The supplier promoted complainant, but did not increase his base salary. The salary of the complainant, the only African American account manager in his region, was never increased despite good performance or even when he assumed the accounts of two White employees who left the company. The complainant resigned and was replaced by a White junior account manager who earned a higher base salary than complainant had ever earned as an account manager. Under the decree, the supplier will provide web-based training to all employees at its Baton Rouge and Harahan, LA, offices on Title VII and defendant's antidiscrimination policies and complaint reporting procedures. The supplier also will maintain policies and procedures prohibiting race discrimination and wage disparities based on race, which will include investigation procedures and contact information for reporting complaints. Additionally, it will submit annual reports to the EEOC on complaints of race discrimination and harassment it receives at its Baton Rouge and Harahan offices and their resolution. ***EEOC v. Corporate Express Office Products, Inc.,*** **No. 3:09-cv-00516 (M.D. La. Nov. 23, 2009).**

- In September 2007, a federal district court in Arizona granted a motion to dismiss the EEOC's race discrimination case against a northern Arizona hospital. The EEOC had alleged that the hospital, which served parts of the Navaho Nation, paid its non-White doctors thousands of dollars less than a White American physician who performed the same work. The non-White physicians represented different races and national origins, including Asian, Native American, Nigerian, Puerto Rican, and Pakistani. When they, as well as a former medical director, sought redress of the wage difference and filed discrimination charges with the EEOC, the EEOC alleged that the hospital retaliated against them with threats of termination and threats of adverse changes to the terms and conditions of their employment. ***EEOC v. Navajo Health Foundation-Sage Memorial Hospital, Inc.*, No. 06-CV-2125-PHX-DGC (D. Ariz. Sept. 7, 2007).**

- In August 2009, a Washington Park, IL, packaging and warehousing company agreed to pay $57,500 and provide training to settle a race discrimination and retaliation lawsuit alleging that the company failed to provide a Black employee the pay raise and health insurance coverage provided to his White coworkers, and then fired him in retaliation for filing a charge of race discrimination with the EEOC. ***EEOC v. Material Resources, LLC,* d/b/a Gateway Co-Packing Co., No. 3:08-245-MJR (S.D. Ill. August 14, 2009).**

- In March 2007, the EEOC reached a $60,000 settlement in its Title VII lawsuit against Stock Building Supply d/b/a Stuart Lumber alleging that defendant did not give Charging Party a salary increase when he was promoted to a managerial position while White employees who were promoted were given salary increases. ***EEOC v. Stock Building Supply f/k/a Carolina Holdings, Inc. d/b/a Stuart Lumber Co.*, Civil Action No. 2:05-CV-306-FTM-29 (M.D. Fla. March 26, 2007).**

- In August 2006, the EEOC resolved this Title VII/Equal Pay Act case alleging that the largest electronic screen-based equity securities market in the United States failed to promote its only Black female into higher level Research Analyst positions in its Economic Research Department and paid her less than White male Research Analysts, on the basis of race and sex. The case settled for $75,000 and a raise in her annual salary. ***EEOC v. NASDAQ Stock Market, Inc.*, No. 06-1066-RWT (D. Md. Aug. 30, 2006).**

- In May 2006, Orkin, Inc. paid $75,000 to settle a race discrimination lawsuit filed by the EEOC, alleging that Orkin refused to reinstate a Black former employee to a service manager position at the Memphis location and paid him less when he held the position because of his race. ***EEOC v. Orkin, Inc.*, No. 05-2657-Ma/P (W.D. Tenn. May 26, 2006).**

Hostile Work Environment

- In March 2020, Baltimore County-based Bay Country Professional Concrete paid $74,000 and furnished significant equitable relief to settle two federal harassment and retaliation lawsuits by the EEOC. In the first lawsuit, the EEOC charged that Bay Country's owner repeatedly used racial slurs and fired a secretary in retaliation for her opposition to the racial harassment. In the second lawsuit, the EEOC said that Bay Country subjected a concrete finisher, who is male and African American, to racial and sexual harassment by a foreman and coworkers. The harassment included racial slurs, explicit sexual comments and gestures, and threats. The concrete finisher called the police to file charges after one coworker groped him and another intentionally poked him with a shovel handle, the EEOC said. According to the suit, the concrete finisher complained about the harassment and Bay Country fired him in retaliation the same day. ***EEOC v. Bay Country Professional Concrete LLC*, Civil Action No. 1:19-cv-02848-ELH (Mar. 31, 2020).**

- In March 2020, G.N.T, Inc., doing business as GNT Foods, a grocery store located in East Point, GA, paid $60,000 and furnished other relief to settle a racial harassment and retaliation lawsuit filed by the EEOC. Corey Bussey, Justin Jones, and Christopher Evans worked in the meat department at GNT Foods. According to the EEOC's lawsuit, the three African American men endured the store owner's daily use of racial slurs, one employee was slapped by the owner, and racially offensive posters of monkeys were prominently displayed in the workplace to humiliate the Black employees. The harassing behavior continued despite numerous complaints by all three employees. In addition to the monetary damages to the three men, the two-year consent decree requires GNT Foods to provide employment discrimination training to its employees, to post its policies and anti-discrimination notice, and to comply with reporting and monitoring requirements. ***EEOC v. GNT, Inc.*, Civil Action No. 1:17-CV-3545-MHC-LTW (N.D. Ga. Mar. 25, 2020).**

- In February 2020, an Illinois fencing company paid $25,000 to settle a race harassment case brought by the EEOC. According to the EEOC's lawsuit, the company's employees and warehouse manager verbally harassed an African American employee based on his race by calling him racial slurs and making offensive comments about Black people in his presence. When the Black employee complained, no action was taken, and the mistreatment continued. Additionally, two coworkers attempted to put his head in a noose that was hanging in the warehouse; the warehouse manager saw the noose and laughed despite company policies that obligated him to report the harassment. After the noose incident, the Black employee quit his job and filed a constructive discharge suit. The judge ruled in the EEOC's favor on summary judgment. Thereafter, the parties agreed to settle the matter. The 2-year consent decree requires the company to strengthen its discrimination complaint procedure and develop and implement investigation procedures. The decree also mandates training of employees and reporting to the EEOC any future complaints of race harassment. ***EEOC v. Driven Fence, Inc.*, Civil Action No. 17 C 6817 (N.D. Ill. Feb. 18, 2020).**

- In November 2019, On The Border Acquisitions, LLC, doing business as On The Border Mexican Grill & Cantina (OTB), paid $100,000 and provided other relief to settle an EEOC race harassment lawsuit. The EEOC alleged that OTB failed to act when several employees at its Holtsville, NY, location subjected an African American cook to harassment based on his race, including repeatedly calling him racial slurs. ***EEOC v. On The Border Acquisitions, LLC, d/b/a On The Border Mexican Grill & Cantina*, Civil Action No. 2:18-cv-05122 (E.D.N.Y. Nov. xx 2019).**

- In October 2019, a Phoenix-based moving company accused of "pervasive" racial harassment against a Black employee will pay $54,000 to settle an EEOC lawsuit. According to the EEOC's lawsuit, a supervisor at Arizona Discount Movers frequently made racist comments to an African American employee named Clinton Lee. The EEOC alleged that the supervisor also told Lee he could not enter the building because they were having a Ku Klux Klan meeting and put a statue of a jockey on his desk with a whip in the jockey's hand tied in a noose. He labeled the statue "Clint." According to the EEOC, the same supervisor hung a troll doll painted Black with a Post-it affixed to the doll that read, "Clint King." The doll was hung from a hook and displayed in the middle of the facility. The EEOC also alleged that Lee's supervisor pointed to the doll and said "Hey Clint look! That's you!" Lee complained to the owner, who told Lee to take the doll down if he did not like it. Lee felt he had to resign because of the harassment, and the EEOC further alleged that, since 2011, Arizona Discount Movers has required its employees sign a two-page "Rules and Employee Agreement," which included both "Negative attitudes, fighting, complainers will not be tolerated here" and "Drugs, fighting, foul language, racism, arguing will be tolerated." In addition to the monetary settlement, the company is required to write an apology letter and a positive letter of reference for its former employee. ***EEOC v. Arizona Discount Movers*, Civil Action No. 2:18-cv-01966-HRH (D. Ariz. Oct. 15, 2019).**

- In September 2019, the EEOC Office of Federal Operations reversed an agency finding of no discrimination. Complainant filed an EEO complaint alleging that the U.S. Department of Transportation discriminated against her on the bases of race (African American) and color (Black), when on November 11, 2016, she was subjected to harassment by a coworker. Complainant indicated that the coworker who also was the president of the local union sent her an email with the subject line "Asshole" and stated the following: "If [Complainant] wasn't such a N** who would run an[d] yell racism tomorrow. At work. I would love to answer her with this . . . Those people are pieces of shit and hopefully they try that with me so I can gun them down." The Agency found no discrimination. The appellate decision found that Complainant was subjected to harassment when she received the email from the coworker. The decision then determined that the Agency erred finding that it took prompt action. The decision noted that the Agency took 6 months to engage in an internal investigation and issue the coworker a proposed 30-day suspension. The Agency failed to inform the Commission what, if any, final disciplinary action was issued against the coworker. Accordingly, the decision held that the Agency failed to take prompt action to meet its affirmative defense. As such, the decision concluded that Complainant had been subjected to harassment based on her race and color. The decision remanded the matter to the Agency for a determination on Complainant's entitlement to compensatory damages, for training and reconsideration of discipline for the coworker, for training for management focusing on addressing harassment, and for consideration of disciplinary action against the management officials who failed to respond to Complainant's claims of harassment in a prompt manner. ***Sharon M. v. DOT*, EEOC Appeal No. 0120180192 (Sep. 25, 2019).**

- In September 2019, a tire, wheels, and auto service company agreed to pay $55,000 and furnish other relief to settle a racial harassment and retaliation lawsuit filed by the EEOC. According to the EEOC's lawsuit, the store manager of the Port Huron, MI, location made derogatory, race-based comments to the only African American employee. The remarks included calling the employee "cricket" and "dumb-dumb" and telling him that "blacks don't get Saturdays off." The comments were sometimes accompanied by demeaning physical contact, such as slapping the employee in the head or shoving him, the EEOC said. After the employee formally complained to human resources about the harassment, he was fired within 48 hours. The manager was given a written warning for "shop talk" and "horseplay." The 3-year consent decree provides that the company also will take meaningful steps toward ensuring a work environment that is free from harassment by redistributing its anti-discrimination policy and providing annual anti-harassment training for certain human resources professionals and managers. The decree also required the company to report future complaints of race harassment and any measures taken to investigate and remedy such complaints. ***EEOC v. Belle Tire Distributors, Inc.*, Case No. 2:18-cv-13795 (E.D. Mich. Sept. 24, 2019).**

- In June 2019, Aaron's Inc. paid $425,000 and provided anti-discrimination training to its New York City area workforce to settle a federal government lawsuit accusing it of racial harassment. The EEOC alleged in a December 2017 complaint that the rent-to-own furniture chain subjected Black employees at a Queens, NY, warehouse to racist name-calling by two managers. The same managers also regularly assigned Black employees to longer routes with heavier items to deliver than they assigned White employees, the EEOC alleged. The 4-year agreement requires the company to furnish semi-annual compliance reports to the EEOC, including regarding the whereabouts of the two managers accused of the alleged harassment. It must also place a notation in the personnel file of both managers stating that they were the subject of a racial harassment complaint. ***EEOC v. Aaron's, Inc.*, No. 1:17-cv-07273 (E.D.N.Y. consent decree entered 6/4/19).**

- In April 2019, A&F Fire Protection, Inc., a NY fire sprinkler and standpipe contractor, paid $407,500 to settle a race discrimination lawsuit in which the EEOC alleged that Black and Hispanic employees were frequently subjected to racial remarks by managers and coworkers and a supervisor who used gorilla sounds as a ringtone for a Black employee. A Hispanic employee said his supervisor called him an anti-Hispanic slur and referred to him as a "dumb-in-a-can" in reference to his Dominican national origin. A Black assistant superintendent said that his contact information was saved in his supervisor's cell phone contacts as "BBG" and when he called the phone would say "Big, Black gorilla is calling" and the ringtone would make gorilla sounds. A Puerto Rican employee reported that a coworker said that the company was starting to look like "an immigration camp" because of all the Black and Hispanic employees. ***EEOC v. A&F Fire Protection, Inc.*, No. 2:17-04745 (E.D.N.Y. consent decree filed Apr. 23, 2019).**

- In April 2019, a Jacksonville-based licensed sports merchandise company agreed to pay a Black former employee $57,050 in back pay and $265,000 in compensatory damages, a total of $322,050 as part of a consent decree to settle an EEOC lawsuit. The lawsuit alleged that a Black employee was asked if he could read because "a lot of you guys can't read," and that a general manager referred to Black employees as "monkeys" or "Africans" and many other accusations. The employee also claimed he was hit with a racial slur from a team leader on his first day of work and that after voicing complaints about what he saw as unfair treatment of Black employees, his supervisor "told him that he would never be promoted." ***EEOC v. Fanatics Retail Group, Inc.*, Civil Action No. 3:18-cv-900-J-32PDB (M.D. Fla. consent decree filed April 17, 2019).**

- In November 2018, a Texas-based oil and gas company operating in Tioga, ND, paid $50,000 and furnished other relief to settle an EEOC racial harassment lawsuit. The EEOC's lawsuit charged that Murex Petroleum Corp. violated federal law when it subjected an African American roustabout to racial harassment by his White coworkers. The harassment included the White coworkers calling the Black employee racial slurs such as "spook," "spade," and "Buckwheat." The coworkers also made racially derogatory comments including using the racially offensive term "n----r-rigged," which was witnessed by the employee's supervisor who took no action to stop it. According to the EEOC's lawsuit, another African American employee complained to a high-level executive at the company, but, again, no action was taken to stop or prevent the harassment. ***EEOC v. Murex Petroleum Corp.*, Civil Action No. 1:18-cv-00169-CSM (D.N.D. Nov. 19, 2018).**

- In October 2018, MPW Industrial Services, Inc., a Hebron, OH, industrial cleaning company, paid $170,000 to settle a race discrimination lawsuit filed by EEOC. According to the EEOC's lawsuit, MPW subjected two African American employees to racial harassment, including hangman's nooses, racial epithets, racist comments and jokes, and an alleged KKK meeting at the worksite. The parties reached an agreement and filed a joint motion to enter a consent decree. The motion was approved by the court and the consent decree was entered on Oct. 23. Under the decree, which settles the suit, MPW Industrial Services is required to pay $170,000 to the two former employees who experienced the racial harassment. The decree also provides for injunctive and equitable relief and, in particular, requires that MPW train supervisors and managers to spot and prevent racial harassment in the future. ***EEOC v. MPW Industrial Services, Inc.*, Case No. 1:18-cv-00063 (S.D. Ohio consent decree filed Oct. 23, 2018).**

- In October 2018, Floyd's Equipment Inc., a Sikeston, MO, contractor, paid $25,000 and furnished other relief to settle an employment discrimination lawsuit filed by the EEOC. The EEOC filed suit against the company in September 2017, charging that Floyd's had engaged in race discrimination when a Floyd foreman repeatedly used the slur "n----r." After an African American employee complained, the foreman angrily confronted him and rather than disciplining the harasser, the company transferred Woodall from his assignment as a backhoe operator to a less desirable job doing pick-and-shovel work in another state. Ultimately, Floyd's fired Woodall. ***EEOC v. Floyd's Equipment, Inc.*, Civil Action No. 1:17-cv-00175-SNLJ (E.D. Mo. Oct. 17, 2018).**

- In September 2018, Big 5 store in Oak Harbor, Island County settled a racial harassment and retaliation case for $165,000 and other remedial relief. According to the EEOC lawsuit, a management trainee who was the only African American employee at the store was subjected to a "litany of unremedied racial comments" including being called "spook," "boy," and "King Kong" and told that he had the "face of a janitor" from store management. Additionally, the EEOC alleged that an assistant store manager threatened to lynch him. The trainee, stressed by the harassment and retaliation after reporting the harassment to upper management, took leaves from work and was eventually fired. Pursuant to a 3-year consent decree, the store also is required to provide training and ensure that it has appropriate anti-harassment policies in place. ***EEOC v. Big 5 Sporting Goods Corp.*, Civil Number 2:17-CV-01098 (W.D. Wash. Sept. 2018).**

- In July 2018, a Texas-based oilfield service company operating in Williston, ND, paid $39,900 to an equipment operator who alleged that he was subjected to a racially hostile work environment because of his race, Asian, and then fired after he complained about it. According to the EEOC's lawsuit, the employee was racially harassed by his White supervisor. The racial harassment included the supervisor calling him "little Asian" and "Chow" based on the Asian character in the movie "Hangover." On one occasion, the supervisor physically assaulted the employee when he poured a bottle of water on Villanueva's head, grabbed his head, and pushed it down toward a table, the EEOC charged. Although the employee complained about the harassment to supervisors and reported the assault to the police, he was fired. ***EEOC v. Cudd Energy Services*, Civil Action No. 4:15-cv-00037-LLP-ARS (D.N.D. consent decree filed July 19, 2018).**

- In January 2018, a water and waste-water services company in Bear, DE, paid $150,000 to settle an EEOC lawsuit alleging racial harassment. According to the EEOC, an African American foreman repeatedly had racial slurs directed at him by a White superintendent and other White foremen. The Black foreman complained to company management about the slurs to which he and other African American employees were subjected, including epithets such as "n—-r," "monkey," and "boy." The company not only failed to stop the harassment, but in fact promoted one of the wrongdoers and assigned the Black foreman to work under his supervision on a project. In May 2016, the company fired him allegedly in retaliation for complaining about the racially hostile work environment. Under a 2-year consent decree, the company is prohibited from engaging in discrimination based on race or unlawful retaliation in the future and must provide training on federal anti-discrimination laws, including preventing harassment. The company also will implement and disseminate to all employees a revised anti-harassment policy and will also post a notice regarding the settlement. The company will also provide a neutral reference letter to the terminated employee. ***EEOC v. Aqua America Inc., dba Aqua Resources Inc.*, No. 2:17-cv-04346-JS (E.D. Pa. Jan. 23, 2018).**

- In October 2017, Reliable Inc., doing business as Reliable Nissan, agreed to settle charges of discrimination based on race, national origin, and religion, along with retaliation. The agreement follows conciliation between the EEOC and Reliable Nissan over claims that two Reliable Nissan Managers repeatedly used the "N-word" during a sales meeting, and referred to African, African American, Native American, Muslim, and Hispanic employees in a derogatory manner. Employees alleged that managers made offensive jokes about Muslim and Native American employees' religious practices and traditions and used racial epithets like "n----r," "drunken Indians," "red," and "redskins." Racially offensive pictures targeted against minority employees were also posted in the workplace. As part of the conciliation agreement, Reliable Nissan agreed to pay a total of $205,000 to three employees who filed discrimination charges with the EEOC and 11 other minority employees who were subjected to the hostile work environment. The company also agreed to provide annual training for 2 years for its employees, including managers and human resources employees. Additionally, Reliable Nissan agreed to review its policies and procedures to ensure that employees have a mechanism for reporting discrimination and to make certain that each complaint will be appropriately investigated.

- In September 2017, a Hugo, MN, construction company paid $125,000 to settle a racial harassment lawsuit filed by the EEOC. The EEOC's lawsuit charged that JL Schwieters Construction, Inc. violated federal law when it subjected two Black employees to a hostile work environment, including physical threats, based on their race. According to the EEOC's lawsuit, two Black carpenters were subjected to racial harassment during their employment by a White supervisor, who made racially derogatory comments including calling them "n----r." The supervisor also made a noose out of electrical wire and threatened to hang them, the EEOC charged. ***EEOC v. JL Schwieters Construction, Inc.*, Civil Action No. 16-cv-03823 WMW/FLN (D. Minn. Sep. 6, 2017).**

- In July 2017, the largest producer of farmed shellfish in the United States, paid $160,000 and implemented other relief to settle an EEOC lawsuit. According to the EEOC's suit, a Black maintenance mechanic at the Taylor Shellfish's Samish Bay Farm faced repeated demeaning comments about his race, including the use of the "N word," "spook," and "boy." His direct supervisor commented that his father used to run "your kind" out of town. When the mechanic reported this behavior to management, the supervisor retaliated against him and Taylor Shellfish simply advised him to "put his head down and do what he was told." After being wrongly accused and disciplined for insubordination, he felt he had no other choice but to quit his job. Under the consent decree resolving this case, Taylor Shellfish has agreed to implement new policies, conduct extensive training for employees and management, post an anti-discrimination notice at the workplace, and report compliance to the EEOC for a 3-year period. ***EEOC v. Taylor Shellfish Company, Inc.*, 2:16-CV-01517 (W.D. Wash. July 31, 2017).**

- In July 2016, the Fourth Circuit reversed summary judgment in an employment discrimination case alleging race, national origin, religion, and pregnancy discrimination, hostile work environment, and retaliation in violation of Title VII and 42 U.S.C. § 1981, in which the EEOC filed an amicus brief in support of the plaintiff. Plaintiff Monica Guessous is an Arab American Muslim woman from Morocco who worked for Fairview Property Investments, LLC until she was terminated from her position as a bookkeeping assistant by her supervisor, Greg Washenko, Fairview's Chief Financial Officer. During her work tenure, Washenko made several derogatory comments about Morrocans, Muslims, and Middle Easterns, often referring to them as "terrorists" and "crooks." Additionally, he complained about plaintiff's request for a 3-month maternity leave and refused to transfer back her job duties when she returned to work. By failing to address numerous comments that were open to a racially motivated interpretation, and by circumscribing its analysis to just one comment without reviewing the totality of the circumstances, the district court committed reversible error in its grant of summary judgment for Fairview on the discrimination and hostile work environment claims. The Fourth Circuit also decided that discriminatory discrete acts could support a hostile work environment claim even if it is separately actionable. ***Guessous v. Fairview Prop. Invest.*, No. 15-1055 (4th Cir. 7/6/2016).**

- In January 2015, Carolina Metal Finishing, LLC, a Bishopville, SC-based metal finishing company, paid $40,000 and furnished significant remedial relief to settle a race harassment lawsuit filed by the EEOC. According to the EEOC's complaint, a Black powder coater at the Bishopville plant was repeatedly subjected to racial slurs by two White employees. The comments included repeated use of the "N-word." The Black employee allegedly complained to company management, but the harassment continued. Within hours of his final complaint, the coater was fired, allegedly in retaliation for his complaints of racial harassment. In addition to paying $40,000 in monetary relief, the company must abide by the terms of a 2-year consent decree resolving the case. The consent decree enjoins Carolina Metal from engaging in future racial discrimination. The decree also requires the company to conduct anti-discrimination training at its Bishopville facility; post a notice about the settlement at that facility; implement a formal anti-discriminatory policy prohibiting racial discrimination; and report certain complaints of conduct that could constitute discrimination under Title VII to the EEOC for monitoring. ***EEOC v. Carolina Metal Finishing, LLC*, No. 3:14-cv-03815 (D.S.C. Jan. 8, 2015).**

- In December 2014, Swissport Fueling, Inc., which fuels aircraft at Phoenix Sky Harbor Airport, paid $250,000 and furnished other relief to settle a lawsuit for race and national origin harassment filed by the EEOC. The EEOC's lawsuit was brought to obtain relief for fuelers who were from various African nations, including Sudan, Nigeria, Ghana, and Sierra Leone. The lawsuit alleged that a Swissport manager routinely called the African fuelers "monkeys" in various degrading ways. A manager also made demeaning references to slavery to the fuelers, such as telling them: "You guys are lucky I pay you because way back then, you did not get paid"; "You are lucky to be paid. A long time ago Blacks were doing this for free"; "At one time, you people would not be paid"; and "Blacks work for free." The EEOC alleged that the African fuelers reported the harassment verbally and in writing, including by signing a written petition and delivering it to the office of Swissport's general manager at the Phoenix facility to try to stop the harassment, but the abuse continued. ***EEOC v. Swissport Fueling, Inc.*, No. 2:10-cv-02101(GMS) (D. Ariz. Nov. 25, 2014).**

- In August 2014, a Thomasville mattress company agreed to pay a combined $42,000 to two Black former workers to settle an EEOC complaint that alleged they were unlawfully fired. The complaint alleged that they complained to the company about racial comments that included the "N-word" made by a White employee between June and August 2012, but the harassment continued. The 3-year settlement includes the company's agreement to not permit or maintain a hostile work environment based on race, not to discriminate or retaliate against any employees because of opposition to any unlawful practice, a posting of procedures for reporting discrimination and harassment, the submission of a report to the EEOC regarding internal discrimination and harassment complaints, and the provision of a neutral letter of reference that states one of the affected employees left employment because he was laid off. ***EEOC v. Carolina Mattress Guild Inc.*, No. 1:13-cv-00706 (M.D.N.C. consent decree entered Aug. 1, 2014).**

- In March 2014, Titan Waste Services, Inc., a Milton, FL, waste disposal and recycling company, was ordered to pay $228,603 for violating federal law by harassing and then firing a truck driver because of his race. According to the EEOC's suit, Titan's highest-level managers subjected its sole Black driver, Michael Brooks, to discriminatory treatment during his employment, including assigning White drivers more favorable routes, requiring Brooks to perform degrading and unsafe work assignments. Brooks was also subjected to harassment such as racial slurs and racially derogatory insults, taunting, and racial stereotypes, including the use of the "N-word." According to the EEOC, shortly before the 2008 presidential election, Titan's facility manager terminated Brooks without cause after discussing the upcoming election with him. After Titan's attorney withdrew from the case, the court found Titan did not continue to assert its defenses and ignored several orders of the court, displaying a reckless and willful disregard for the judicial proceedings. As a result, a default judgment was entered by U.S. District Judge M. Casey Rodgers, based upon evidence submitted by the EEOC and Titan was ordered to pay lost wages and other damages suffered by Brooks. ***EEOC v. Titan Waste Services, Inc.*, No. 3:10-cv-00379 (N.D. Fla. Mar. 10, 2014).**

- In March 2014, Olympia Construction, Inc. paid $100,000 jointly to three former employees to resolve a race harassment and retaliation lawsuit filed by the EEOC. The EEOC's lawsuit charged that Olympia subjected Adrian Soles, Anthony Moorer, and George McWilliams to racial slurs and intimidation. The agency also said that Olympia terminated the victims because they complained to the EEOC. ***EEOC v. Olympia Constr.*, No. 2:13-cv-155 (S.D. Ala. Feb. 27, 2014).**

- In June 2013, a national food distributor paid $15,000 in compensatory damages to three former employees to resolve an EEOC race discrimination lawsuit alleging that its Mason City warehouse failed for months to remove racist graffiti in a men's restroom that included a swastika and references to the Ku Klux Klan, despite complaints from an African American employee. Specifically, an African American employee complained to management that he had seen graffiti reading "N*****s STINK" in a men's restroom. The EEOC alleged that the distributor's supervisors, including the Black employee's supervisor, used that restroom, yet the racist message remained for 30 days after he complained. The EEOC's suit also alleged that, about a week after the distributor finally removed the graffiti, a second message appeared, this time stating "KKK I hate N*****s." The EEOC alleged that this second message remained visible for over 3 months after the employee alerted the EEOC to the situation. In addition to the monetary relief, the consent decree requires the company to repaint the restrooms and train employees on race discrimination within 45 days. ***EEOC v. MBM Corp.*, No. 3:12-cv-3069(LTS) (N.D. Iowa consent decree granted June 24, 2013).**

- In May 2013, a Tyler, TX-based petroleum and gas industry equipment provider paid $150,000 and furnished other relief to settle an EEOC racial harassment and retaliation suit. According to the EEOC's suit, an African American employee of Torqued-Up assigned to a field crew in South Texas experienced racial harassment in the form of racial slurs and epithets from two employees who supervised him on the job. According to the EEOC, the employee, who had 30 years of experience in the oil industry, reported the racial harassment to Torqued-Up's management, but instead of putting a stop to it, the company unlawfully retaliated against him. The punishment included removing the man from his crew and assigning him to perform menial tasks such as washing trucks and sweeping, rather than the oil field work that he had been hired to perform, and reducing his work hours, thereby reducing his income. ***EEOC v. Torqued-Up Energy Services, Inc.*, No. 6:12-cv-00051 (S.D. Tex. May 28, 2013).**

- In April 2013, a Utah construction company paid three former employees $230,000 and improved its future employment practices to settle an EEOC race harassment and retaliation lawsuit. The EEOC filed suit against the company in September 2010, charging that the company subjected Antonio and Joby Bratcher and a class of African American employees to racial harassment and retaliation. In a ruling ,Judge Dale A. Kimball found that the Bratchers and class member James Buie were subjected to an objectively hostile work environment based on race. The court observed that the site superintendent, Paul E. Facer, referred to the African American employees as "n----rs" or a variation of that word almost every time he spoke to them. Other Holmes employees used the term "n----r-rigging" while working there, and racist graffiti was evident both inside and outside portable toilets on the work site. In addition to the monetary relief, Holmes also committed to implement several affirmative steps to prevent and address race-based conduct on the worksite. These measures include: a comprehensive training regimen on discrimination (including racial discrimination and harassment); discussions of harassment in work site meetings on a monthly basis; the provision of an external ombudsman to receive and investigate complaints of discrimination or retaliation; and a detailed review and revision of Holmes' policies and procedures concerning protected-class discrimination and retaliation. ***EEOC v. Holmes & Holmes Industrial, Inc.*, No. 2:10-CV-955 (D. Utah consent decree filed Apr. 12, 2013).**

- In March 2013, the EEOC and Day & Zimmerman NPS, a leading supplier of maintenance, labor, and construction services to the power industry, filed a consent decree resolving the EEOC's claims that Day & Zimmerman violated federal law by creating a hostile work environment for an African American laborer for $190,000. In the lawsuit, the EEOC alleged that Day & Zimmerman, through its foreman at the Poletti Power Plant in Astoria, Queens, NY, had subjected Carlos Hughes to physical and verbal racial harassment that included racial insults and derogatory stories referring to African Americans as stupid and incompetent, as well as frequently tripping Hughes, and once kicking him in the buttocks. The foreman also told racist jokes in the workplace, and made negative comments about African Americans; including that Sean Bell (shot by the police at a nightclub) deserved to be shot, and threatened that candidate Barack Obama would be shot before the country allowed a Black president. The EEOC alleged that Hughes complained to management many times for more than a year regarding the harassment, and that when Day & Zimmerman finally arranged a meeting in response, it disciplined Hughes less than an hour later, and then fired him that same day, citing a false safety violation as a reason. ***EEOC v. Day & Zimmerman NPS, Inc.*, No. 1:11-cv-04741 (E.D.N.Y. consent decree filed Mar. 12, 2013).**

- The Commission alleged that Whirlpool violated Title VII of the Civil Rights Act of 1964 when it did nothing to stop a White male coworker at a Whirlpool plant in LaVergne, TN, from harassing an African American female employee because of her race and sex. The abuse lasted for 2 months and escalated when the coworker physically assaulted the Black employee and inflicted serious permanent injuries. During a 4-day bench trial, the court heard evidence that the employee repeatedly reported offensive verbal conduct and gestures by the coworker to Whirlpool management before she was violently assaulted, without any corrective action by the company. The trial also established that the employee suffered devastating permanent mental injuries that will prevent her from working again as a result of the assault. At the conclusion of the bench trial, the judge entered a final judgment and awarded the employee a total of $1,073,261 in back pay, front pay and compensatory damages on December 21, 2009. Whirlpool filed a motion to alter or amend the judgment on January 15, 2010, which the district court denied on March 31, 2011. On April 26, 2011, Whirlpool appealed the judgment to the U.S. Court of Appeals for the Sixth Circuit. The company withdrew its appeal on June 11, 2012, and agreed to settle the case with the EEOC and plaintiff intervener for $1 million and court costs. The plant where the discrimination occurred had closed during the litigation period. ***EEOC v. Whirlpool Corp.*, No. 11-5508 (6th Cir. June 12, 2012) (granting joint motion to dismiss).**

- Ready Mix paid a total of $400,000 in compensatory damages to be apportioned among the seven class members to settle an EEOC lawsuit. The Commission had alleged Ready Mix USA LLC, doing business as Couch Ready Mix USA LLC, subjected a class of African American males at Ready Mix's Montgomery-area facilities to a racially hostile work environment. A noose was displayed in the worksite, derogatory racial language, including references to the Ku Klux Klan, was used by a direct supervisor and manager and that race-based name calling occurred. Ready Mix denies that racial harassment occurred at its worksites. The 2-year decree enjoins Ready Mix from engaging in further racial harassment or retaliation and requires that the company conduct EEO training. Ready Mix will be required to modify its policies to ensure that racial harassment is prohibited and a system for investigation of complaints is in place. The company must also report certain complaints of harassment or retaliation to the EEOC for monitoring. ***EEOC v. Ready Mix USA LLC*, No. 2:09-cv-00923 (M.D. Ala. Feb. 3, 2012).**

- In January 2013, a federal jury found that two Black employees of a North Carolina trucking company were subjected to a racially hostile work environment and awarded them $200,000 in damages. The jury also found that one employee was fired in retaliation for complaining about the hostile environment. In a complaint filed in June 2011, the EEOC alleged that, from at least May 2007 through June 2008, one Black employee was subjected to derogatory and threatening comments based on his race by his supervisor and coworkers, and that a coworker mechanic displayed a noose and asked him if he wanted to "hang from our family tree." The EEOC also alleged that the mechanic also repeatedly and regularly called the employee "nigger" and "Tyrone," a term the coworker used to refer to unknown Black individuals. Evidence also revealed that A.C. Widenhouse's general manager and the employee's supervisor also regularly made racial comments and used racial slurs, such as asking him if he would be the coon in a "coon hunt" and alerting him that if one of his daughters brought home a Black man, he would kill them both. The employee also frequently heard other coworkers use racial slurs such as "nigger" and "monkey" over the radio when communicating with each other. The second Black employee testified that, when he was hired in 2005, he was the company's only African American and was told he was the "token black." The general manager also talked about a noose and having "friends" visit in the middle of the night as threats to Floyd. Both employees reported the racial harassment, but company supervisors and officers failed to address the hostile work environment. The jury awarded the former employees $50,000 in compensatory damages and $75,000 each in punitive damages. ***EEOC v. A.C. Widenhouse Inc.*, No. 1:11-cv-498 (M.D.N.C. verdict filed Jan. 28, 2013).**

- In January 2013, Emmert International agreed to settle an employment discrimination lawsuit filed by the EEOC that charged the company harassed and retaliated against employees in violation of federal law. Specifically, the EEOC's lawsuit alleged that the company's foreman and other Emmert employees repeatedly harassed two employees, one African American and the other Caucasian, while working on the Odd Fellows Hall project in Salt Lake City. Emmert's foreman and employees regularly used the "n-word," called the Black employee "boy," called the White employee a "n---- lover," and made racial jokes and comments. The EEOC also alleged that Emmert International retaliated against the Black employee for complaining about the harassment. The 24-month consent decree requires the company to pay $180,000 to the two employees, provide training to its staff on unlawful employment discrimination, and to review and revise its policies on workplace discrimination. The decree also requires Emmert International to post notices explaining federal laws against workplace discrimination. ***EEOC v. Emmert Industrial Corp., d/b/a Emmert International*, No. 2:11-CV-00920CW (D. Ariz. Jan. 7, 2013).**

- In October 2012, a district court ruled that the EEOC proved that a construction site where a White supervisor regularly used racial slurs was objectively a hostile work environment for Black employees under Title VII of the 1964 Civil Rights Act. It also decided, however, that a jury must determine if the three Black plaintiffs found the workplace subjectively offensive because, although their repeated complaints indicate they were offended, a jury must resolve factual issues raised by some coworkers' testimony that the plaintiffs actually did not seem bothered by the harasser's conduct. Ruling on the EEOC's motion for partial summary judgment, the court said the company's admissions that site superintendent/project manager referred to three Black plaintiff-intervenors as "nigger" or "nigga" on a near-daily basis and told racial jokes using those terms and other offensive epithets establishes an objective racially hostile work environment. The court said the undisputed evidence also indicated that human resources manager told the company's employees during a safety meeting not to "nigger rig their jobs"; that company management was aware the worksite's portable toilets were covered with racist graffiti; and that other White supervisors and employees routinely used racial epithets, including an incident where a White supervisor commented regarding rap music being played in a van transporting employees to the worksite, "I'm not listening to this nigger jig." When confronted by a Black employee about the comment, the White supervisor allegedly replied: "I can see where your feelings were hurt, but there is a difference between niggers and blacks, Mexicans and spics. But I see you as a black man." ***EEOC v. Holmes & Holmes Indus. Inc.*, No. 10-955 (D. Utah Oct. 10, 2012).**

- In March 2012, the EEOC sued a restaurant in Menomonie, WI, because its managers allegedly posted images of a noose, a Klan hood, and other racist depictions, including a dollar bill that was defaced with a noose around the neck of a Black-faced George Washington, swastikas, and the image of a man in a Ku Klux Klan hood. A Black employee complained and then was fired. ***EEOC v. Northern Star Hospitality Inc.*, Civil Action No. 12-cv-214 (W.D. Wis. Mar. 27, 2012).**

- In February 2012, a major cement and concrete products company paid $400,000 and furnished other relief to settle an EEOC lawsuit alleging racial harassment. The EEOC charged in its lawsuit that a class of African American males at Ready Mix's Montgomery-area facilities was subjected to a racially hostile work environment. The EEOC said that a noose was displayed in the worksite, that derogatory racial language, including references to the Ku Klux Klan, was used by a direct supervisor and manager and that race-based name-calling occurred. Ready Mix denies that racial harassment occurred at its worksites. The 2-year decree also enjoins Ready Mix from engaging in further racial harassment or retaliation and requires that the company conduct EEO training. Ready Mix will be required to modify its policies to ensure that racial harassment is prohibited and a system for investigation of complaints is in place. The company must also report certain complaints of harassment or retaliation to the EEOC for monitoring. ***EEOC v. Ready Mix USA d/b/a Couch Ready Mix USA LLC*, No. 2:09-CV-923 (M.D. Ala. *consent decree announced* Feb. 21, 2012).**

- In August 2011, a federal district court entered a default judgment in favor of the EEOC in its lawsuit alleging that a pipeline construction company permitted several African American employees to be subjected to hanging nooses in the workplace even after they complained about the offensive displays. The company failed to retain counsel to prosecute the lawsuit. The court granted the EEOC's motion for a default judgment and awarded $50,000 to five claimants. The court also enjoined the company from discriminating on the basis of race or protected conduct in violation of Title VII. ***EEOC v. L.A. Pipeline Constr. Co.*, No. 2:08-CV-840 (S.D. Ohio Aug. 5, 2011).**

- In June 2011, Herzog Roofing, Inc., a Detroit Lakes, MN, roofing company, agreed in a pre-suit settlement to pay $71,500 to seven Black, Hispanic, and American Indian employees to settle racial harassment and retaliation charges, alleging that the targeted employees were frequently subjected to racial epithets, racial jokes, and hostile treatment by managers and coworkers and that complaints were ignored. The EEOC also had found that the company retaliated against the employee who brought the initial complaint by firing him after he reported the unlawful treatment. In addition to monetary relief, the company has agreed to provide anti-discrimination training to all of its employees and additional training on harassment and retaliation to all supervisors, managers, and owners. It also will redistribute its anti-harassment policies and procedures and monitor its supervisors' compliance with equal employment opportunity laws.

- In May 2011, an IT service company entered a consent decree to pay $60,000 to an African American employee who had allegedly been subjected to race discrimination and retaliation. In its lawsuit, the EEOC had alleged that the employee's supervisors subjected him to racial epithets and asked if he was a "black man or a n----r." The Commission further alleged that, following his complaints of racial discrimination, the company demoted and later discharged the employee. The consent decree enjoins the company from engaging in any racial discrimination or retaliation and requires the company to post a remedial notice for 2 years. In addition, the company must draft its non-discrimination, anti-harassment, and retaliation policies in simple, plain language and include a complaint procedure within these policies. The consent decree also bolsters supervisor accountability and requires training on the requirements of Title VII for all managers, supervisors, and Human Resources personnel. Finally, the company must keep records of each future complaint related to race, national origin, or retaliation and furnish written reports to the EEOC regarding any potential complaints. ***EEOC v. Eclipse Advantage, Inc.*, No. 1:10-cv-02001 (N.D. Ohio consent decree filed May 2, 2011).**

- In April 2011, an architectural sheet metal company settled a racial harassment case for $160,000 in which the EEOC alleged that a White supervisor regularly referred to African American employees with the epithet "n----r" and used other slurs and racial graffiti was on display in common areas and on company equipment. In addition to monetary relief, the 18-month consent decree settling the lawsuit provides for training on employee rights under Title VII, and requires the company to maintain records of racial harassment complaints, provide annual reports to the EEOC, and post a notice to employees about the lawsuit that includes the EEOC's contact information. ***EEOC v. Ralph Jones Sheet Metal, Inc.*, No. 2:09-cv-02636 (W.D. Tenn. settled Apr. 22, 2011).**

- In April 2011, the Fourth Circuit vacated in part the district court's judgment and remanded for trial part of the EEOC's racial harassment suit against Xerxes, a fiberglass company. The EEOC had alleged that the company's Hagerstown, MD, plant permitted its Black employees to be subjected to a racially hostile work environment despite repeated complaints about the harassment. The alleged harassment included name-calling such as "black Polack," "Buckwheat," and "boy"; White coworkers' frequent use of the N-word; and the discovery of a note in a Black employee's locker that said: "KKK plans could result in death, serious personal injury, Nigga Bernard." The district court dismissed the EEOC's case, ruling that Xerxes had "acted quickly and reasonably effectively to end" the harassment. On appeal, the Fourth Circuit decided that a reasonable jury could find that the complaints by two claimants prior to February 2006 "were sufficient to place Xerxes on actual notice of racial slurs and pranks in the plant and that Xerxes' response was unreasonable." The court affirmed the rest of the district court's judgment. ***EEOC v. Xerxes Corp.*, No. 10-1156 (4th Cir. Apr. 26, 2011).**

- In October 2010, a South Point, OH-based contractor that constructs and installs water and sewer lines entered into a 5-year consent decree to settle claims that it violated Title VII when it failed to stop a White foreman and employees from racially harassing and retaliating against a Black laborer working at defendant's sewer installation site in White Sulphur Springs, WV. The alleged harassment included directing threatening language and conduct at the Black laborer, such as saying that President Obama would be assassinated and showing him a swastika that a White coworker had spray-painted on company equipment. The contractor fired the Black laborer allegedly because he refused to drop his complaint after the superintendent told him that he could not guarantee the laborer's safety and that he could not return to work while he continued to press his complaint. The consent decree awards the laborer $87,205 in monetary relief, $47,205 as back pay and $40,000 as punitive damages (paid in four quarterly $10,000 installments), all personally guaranteed by the owner, as well as a written offer of reinstatement. The decree also permanently enjoins race discrimination, racial harassment, and retaliation, and requires the contractor to implement antidiscrimination policies, complaint procedures with multiple avenues for complaining about discrimination, harassment, and retaliation, guidelines for prompt and thorough investigation of each such complaint or report (whether verbal or written), procedures for compiling and maintaining an investigative file, and EEO training for all managers, supervisors, and other employees. ***EEOC v. Mike Enyart & Sons*, No. 5:10-cv-00921 (S.D.W.Va. settled Oct. 6, 2010)**.

- In September 2010, the EEOC sued the largest private university in the United States and one of New York City's ten biggest employers for allegedly violating federal law by creating a hostile work environment for an African-born employee that included degrading verbal harassment based on national origin and race. According to the EEOC's suit, the supervisor of the mailroom in NYU's Elmer Holmes Bobst Library regularly subjected his assistant, who is a native of Ghana, to slurs such as "monkey" and "gorilla," and made comments such as "go back to your cage," "go back to the jungle," and "do you want a banana?" The supervisor also frequently mocked the assistant's accented English, deriding it as "gibberish," and expressed hostility toward immigrants generally and Africans specifically. Although the assistant complained repeatedly to NYU management and human resources personnel, NYU took months to investigate and then took virtually no action to curb the supervisor's conduct. Even after the assistant alerted NYU that the supervisor had retaliated against him for complaining, such as by fabricating grounds for disciplining him, the university did not stop the harassment. ***EEOC v. New York Univ.*, No. 10-CV-7399 (S.D.N.Y. filed Sept. 27, 2010)**.

- In September 2010, the largest uniform manufacturer in North America and provider of specialized services agreed to pay $152,500 to settle a racial harassment claim. A class of African American employees was subjected to racial harassment by coworkers when workers in a specific division were referred to as the "ghetto division," and were called derivations of "chocolate" or "chocolate delicious," conduct that went uncorrected. In addition to monetary relief, a consent decree enjoins the company from engaging in either sexual or racial harassment or retaliation. Furthermore, the company must conduct training on federal antidiscrimination laws, report on company responses to complaints, and post a remedial notice. ***EEOC v. Cintas Corp.*, No. 1:09-cv-04449 (E.D. Pa. settled Sept. 27, 2010)**.

- In September 2010, the EEOC filed a racial harassment lawsuit against a cell phone installation and testing company, asserting that the company violated federal anti-discrimination laws when it subjected an African American employee to severe and repeated harassment. According to the complaint, a foreman regularly subjected the employee to racially driven comments, gestures, and threats, including calling him "boy," telling him that "whites run things," and threatening to physically harm the employee. Furthermore, the foreman, who wore a swastika on his arm, stated that he had "cut an African from the belly to the neck" and that he "likes killing blacks and Mexicans." The foreman also said about Black people, "just hang them and burn a cross on the homes." The harassment continued even after the employee reported the conduct. Because the employee feared for his safety, he resigned. ***EEOC v. Towersite Services, LLC*, No. 1:10-cv-02997 (N.D. Ga. Sept. 20, 2010)**.

- In August 2010, an aircraft services company settled for $600,000 the EEOC's suit claiming the company permitted the unlawful harassment of Black, Filipino, and Guatemalan employees at a Burbank, CA, airport. Under a 2-year consent decree, Mercury Air Centers Inc. agreed to pay the settlement amount to at least seven employees who were allegedly subjected to "a barrage of harassing comments" by a Salvadoran coworker at Bob Hope Airport. Rather than respond to the employees' complaints about the alleged harasser, the company promoted the alleged harasser to supervisor, the Commission alleged. ***EEOC v. Mercury Air Centers Inc.*, No. 08-6332 (C.D. Cal. consent decree filed Aug. 9, 2010)**.

- In April 2010, a Houston-area construction company paid $122,500 and will provide additional remedial relief to resolve a federal lawsuit alleging race, national origin, and religious discrimination. The EEOC's lawsuit alleged that the company discriminated against Mohammad Kaleemuddin because he is of the Islamic faith and of East Indian descent, and against 13 other employees because they are Black or Hispanic when a supervisor referred to Kaleemuddin as "terrorist," "Taliban," "Osama," and "Al-Qaeda"; to the Black employees as "n----s"; and to Hispanics as "f-----g Mexicans." In addition to monetary relief, the consent decree required the owner to provide a signed letter of apology to Kaleemuddin and that the alleged harassing manager be prohibited from ever working again for the company. The company will also provide employee training designed to prevent future discrimination and harassment on the job. ***EEOC v. Pace Services, L.P.*, No. 4:08cv2886 (S.D. Tex. Apr. 2010)**.

- In April 2010, the EEOC settled its lawsuit against Professional Building Systems for $118,000 and significant non-monetary relief after it had identified at least 12 Black employees who had been subjected to racial harassment there. According to the EEOC's complaint, at various times between mid-2005 and 2008, Black employees were subjected to racial harassment that involved the creation and display of nooses; references to Black employees as "boy" and by the "N-word"; and racially offensive pictures such as a picture that depicted the Ku Klux Klan looking down a well at a Black man. In its complaint, the EEOC alleged that the managers of the company not only knew about the harassment and took no action to stop or prevent it, but also that a manager was one of the perpetrators of the harassment. ***EEOC v. Professional Building Systems of North Carolina, LLC,*** **Civil Action No. 1:09-cv-00617) (M.D.N.C. April 2010).**

- In February 2010, Big Lots paid $400,000 to settle a race harassment and discrimination lawsuit in which the EEOC alleged that the company took no corrective action to stop an immediate supervisor and coworkers, all Hispanic, from subjecting a Black maintenance mechanic and other Black employees to racially derogatory jokes, comments, slurs, and epithets, including the use of the words "n----r" and "monkey," at its California distribution center. ***EEOC v. Big Lots, Inc.,*** **CV-08-06355-GW(CTx) (C.D. Cal. Feb. 2010).**

- In January 2010, the Sixth Circuit affirmed in part and reversed in part a district court's decision granting summary judgment to defendant Whirlpool Corporation in a racial hostile work environment case in which the EEOC participated as amicus curiae. The alleged racial harassment largely involved a serial harasser who continually used racial slurs, including various permutations on "nigger," made references to the Ku Klux Klan openly and on a daily basis, and left a threatening message on a coworker's husband's answering machine. Other racially hostile incidents included White coworkers displaying the Confederate flag on their clothing and tow motors, threatening racial violence, making repeated references to the KKK and the n-word, telling of racist jokes, remarking that they wished they had a "James Earl Ray Day" as a holiday, and "laughing and talking about the Black guy that got drugged [sic] behind a truck in Texas[,] ... saying he probably deserved it." Several of the Black plaintiffs also testified about the presence of racial graffiti in the plant bearing similar messages, including "KKK everywhere," "go home sand niggers," and "Jesus suffered, so the niggers must suffer too, or ... Blacks must suffer, too." ***Armstrong v. Whirlpool Corp.,*** **No. 08-6376 (6th Cir. Jan. 26, 2010).**

- In January 2010, a Georgia car dealership agreed to pay $140,000 to settle a race discrimination suit. In this case, the EEOC alleged that a White consultant visited the car dealership three to four times a week and never missed an opportunity to make racially derogatory comments toward the Black sales manager and almost always in the presence of other people. After the Black sales manager complained about the derogatory comments, two White managers asked the consultant to stop his discriminatory behavior. The consultant ignored their requests to cease and continued to make the derogatory comments at every opportunity. The dealership denied any liability or wrongdoing but will provide equal employment opportunity training, make reports, and post anti-discrimination notices. ***EEOC v. S&H Thomson, Inc., dba Stokes-Hodges Chevrolet Cadillac Buick Pontiac GMC,*** **(S.D. Ga. Consent decree filed Jan. 14, 2010).**

- In September 2009, a Phoenix credit card processing company agreed to pay $415,000 and furnish significant remedial relief to settle a race harassment lawsuit, in which the EEOC charged that the company subjected a group of African American workers to racial slurs and epithets. According to one discrimination victim:

> "My supervisors often referred to my fellow African American employees and me as 'n—rs' and 'porch monkeys' and forced us to play so-called 'Civil War games' where employees were divided into North and South. They also referred to Black children or mixed-race children as 'porch monkeys' or 'Oreo babies.' On several occasions, I was told to turn off my 'jigaboo music."

> ***EEOC v. NPMG, Acquisition Sub, LLC.*, No. CV 08-01790-PHX-SRB (D. Ariz. Sep. 16, 2009).**

- In August 2009, a Mississippi-based drilling company agreed to pay $50,000 to settle a Title VII lawsuit, alleging that four employees, three White and one Black, experienced racial harassment and retaliation while assigned to a remote drilling rig in Texas. The harassment included being subjected to racial taunts and mistreatment from Hispanic employees and supervisors and having their safety threatened because the supervisors conducted safety meetings in Spanish only and refused to interpret for them in English. Told that they needed to learn Spanish because they were in South Texas, the employees said that instead of addressing their complaints of discrimination, they were fired. The company agreed to establish an effective anti-discrimination policy and to provide anti-discrimination training to its employees. ***EEOC v. E&D Services, Inc.*, No. SA-08-CA-0714-NSN (W.D. Tex. Aug. 2009).**

- In May 2009, a masonry company agreed to pay $500,000 to settle a Title VII lawsuit alleging race and national origin harassment of Hispanic employees. The suit charged that the foremen and former superintendent referred to the company's Latino employees with derogatory terms such as "f---ing Mexicans," "pork chop," "Julio," "spics," "chico," and "wetback." In addition, former employees alleged that Hispanic workers were routinely exposed to racist graffiti, which the company never addressed. The 3-year decree enjoins the company from future discrimination and retaliation on the basis of race or national origin and mandates anti-discrimination and investigation training for all of its employees and supervisors. ***EEOC v. Ceisel Masonry*, No. 06 C 2075 (N.D. Ill. May 22, 2009); *Ramirez v. Ceisel Masonry*, No. 06 C 2084 (N.D. Ill. May 2009).**

- In April 2009, high-end retailer Nordstrom settled an EEOC lawsuit alleging that it permitted the harassment despite complaints by Hispanic and Black employees about a department manager who said she "hated Hispanics" and that they were "lazy" and "ignorant" and that she didn't like Blacks and told one employee, "You're Black, you stink." Under the terms of the settlement, Nordstrom will pay $292,000, distribute copies of its anti-discrimination policy to its employees, and provide anti-harassment training. ***EEOC v. Nordstrom, Inc.*, No. 07-80894-CIV-RYSKAMP/VITUNAC (S.D. Fla. April 2009).**

- In July 2008, the largest independent tire companies in the nation agreed to pay $185,000 and furnish other corrective measures to settle a racial harassment lawsuit. In the lawsuit, the EEOC alleged that the company subjected a Native American employee to continuous race-based harassment, which included coworkers calling him derogatory names and making insulting jokes about Native Americans over a period of years and then fired him when he continued to complain about the mistreatment. ***EEOC v. Les Schwab Tire Centers of Montana, Inc.*, No. 06-149-M-DWM (D. Mont. July 1, 2008).**

- In June 2008, a San Jose-based manufacturer of semiconductor production equipment agreed to pay $168,000 to settle EEOC claims that it failed to stop the racial harassment of an African American assembly technician who was forced to listen to a Vietnamese coworker play and rap aloud to rap music with racially offensive lyrics and then fired the Black employee after he repeatedly complained about his work conditions. The manufacturer also agreed to amend its harassment policy to refer specifically to harassment through the playing of music, and to include offensive musical lyrics in its examples of racial harassment. ***EEOC v. Novellus Systems, Inc.*, C-07-4787 RS (N.D. Cal. settled June 24, 2008).**

- In June 2008, a landmark New York City restaurant in Central Park settled an EEOC Title VII lawsuit filed on behalf of female, Hispanic, and Black employees for $2.2 million. The EEOC had alleged that for the past 8 years the restaurant engaged in racial and sexual harassment. The alleged harassment included a manager's regular use of the "n-word" to refer to the Black employees and "sp*c" or "ignorant immigrants" to refer to the Hispanic employees. Additionally, the manager asked a Black hostess to "touch and suck his penis" and inappropriately grabbed her buttocks and breasts. Pursuant to the settlement agreement, the restaurant will establish a telephone hotline which employees may use to raise any discrimination complaints, distribute a revised policy against discrimination and retaliation, and provide training to all employees against discrimination and retaliation. ***EEOC v. Tavern on the Green*, Civil Action No. 07- CV-8256 (S.D.N.Y. settled June 2, 2008).**

- In May 2008, the Sixth Circuit ruled that two Black male dockworkers had been subjected to a racially hostile work environment in violation of Title VII. The harassment in this case, in which the EEOC filed an amicus brief in support of the victims, centered on the frequent use of the term "boy" to refer to the Black male employees. The term was spray-painted on walls and doors, written in Black marker or spray painted in the locker rooms, equipment, and on a calendar in the break room over Martin Luther King's birthday, etched into bathroom walls in the terminal, and written in dust on dock surfaces, even after the employer held a sensitivity session to explain the term's racial and derogatory implications. ***Bailey v. USF Holland, Inc.*, 526 F.3d 880 (6th Cir. 2008).**

- In April 2008, the Tenth Circuit Court of Appeals vacated the district court's decision granting summary judgment to the defendant on the plaintiff's Title VII claim alleging that he was subjected to a racially hostile work environment. The racial hostility manifested as racist graffiti, racial epithets, and the hanging of a noose at a Salt Lake City rail yard. Agreeing with the position taken by the EEOC as amicus curiae, the court of appeals held that nearly all of the racially hostile acts alleged by the plaintiff could be considered as a single hostile work environment under *National Railroad Passenger Corp. v. Morgan*, 536 U.S. 101 (2002), and that the plaintiff could obtain relief for the entire period of the hostile work environment at issue notwithstanding the fact that he failed to file suit after receiving a notice of right to sue on an earlier Title VII charge challenging the racial harassment. ***Tademy v. Union Pacific Corp.*, 520 F.3d 1149 (10th Cir. Apr. 1, 2008).**

- In March 2008, the Commission affirmed the AJ's finding of race (Native American) and national origin (Cherokee Nation) discrimination, where complainant had his life threatened by a client and the agency never took necessary actions to stop the harassment. The AJ found that a customer continually harassed complainant by, among other actions, referring to complainant as a "worthless Indian, dumb Indian, and stupid." The Commission affirmed the award of $50,000 in non-pecuniary damages due to complainant's emotional suffering, restoration of leave, payment of costs, and mileage. The Commission also ordered training of responsible officials, consideration of discipline, and the posting of a notice but rejected the AJ's award of $6,903.87 in closing costs for complainant's sale of his house as being too speculative to connect to the discriminatory conduct. ***Hern v. Department of Agriculture*, EEOC Appeal No. 0720060012 (March 10, 2008).**

- In January 2008, a Lockheed Martin facility in Hawaii settled a Title VII lawsuit for $2.5 million, the largest amount ever obtained by the EEOC for a single person in a race discrimination case. The EEOC asserted that the military contractor engaged in racial harassment and retaliation after it allegedly permitted a Latino supervisor and White coworkers to subject an African American electrician to racial jokes, slurs, and threats daily for a year. Additionally, the employees allegedly told the Black electrician it would have been better if the South had won the Civil War and talked regularly about lynching and slavery. After the electrician complained about the harassment, he was terminated. In addition to the monetary settlement, the company agreed to terminate the harassers and make significant policy changes to address any future discrimination. ***EEOC v. Lockheed Martin*, Civil No. 05-00479 SPK (D. Haw. settled Jan. 2, 2008).**

- In October 2007, the EEOC obtained $290,000 from an Oklahoma-based oil drilling contractor for seven African American men who alleged that, while on an oil rig, they were subjected to a hostile work environment, which included the display of hangman nooses, derogatory racial language, and race-based name calling. ***EEOC v. Helmerich & Payne Int'l Drilling Co.*, No. 3:05-cv-691 (D. Miss. 2007).**

- In October 2007, the Commission decided that a federal agency had improperly dismissed a Black employee's racial harassment complaint for failure to state a claim. The employee had alleged she was subjected to a hostile work environment because the agency had rehired a former employee who had been charged with discrimination after he made a noose and hung it up in the proximity of an African American employee. The Commission decided that the employee's allegations, if true, were sufficiently severe to state a hostile work environment claim in violation of Title VII since an employer is responsible for preventing discriminatory work environments when it is aware of such danger. The case was reinstated and remanded to the agency for an investigation. ***Juergensen v. Dep't of Commerce*, EEOC Appeal No. 0120073331 (Oct. 5, 2007).**

- In April 2007, the Commission decided that a Caucasian complainant, was subjected to racial harassment over a period of 2 years by both managers and coworkers who used various racially derogatory terms when referring to complainant. Evidence showed that management generally condoned racially related comments made by African American supervisors and coworkers who frequently voiced a "Black versus White" mentality at the workplace. The Commission ordered the agency to pay complainant $10,000.00 in compensatory damages and to provide training to all management and staff at the facility. **See *Brown v. United States Postal Service*, EEOC Appeal No. 0720060042 (April 11, 2007).**

- In April 2007, the EEOC reached a $900,000 settlement in a lawsuit alleging that a geriatric center subjected 29 Black, Haitian, and Jamaican employees to harassing comments because of race and national origin. The employees were also prohibited from speaking Creole and were retaliated against by being subjected to discipline when they complained about their treatment. ***EEOC v. Flushing Manor Geriatric Center, Inc. d/b/a William O. Benenson Rehabilitation Pavilion*, No. 05-4061 (E.D.N.Y. Apr. 23, 2007).**

- In January 2007, the EEOC settled a racial harassment lawsuit against AK Steel Corporation, a Fortune 500 company, for $600,000. The evidence in that case was both severe and pervasive because the workplace featured Nazi symbols, racially graphic and threatening graffiti with messages to kill Black people, displays of nooses and swastikas in work areas open to Black employees, racial slurs and epithets, an open display of KKK videos in the employee lounge areas, and circulation of political literature by David Duke, a known KKK leader. ***EEOC v. AK Steel Corp.* (Jan. 31, 2007).**

- In November 2006, the EEOC resolved a Title VII lawsuit alleging that defendant, a nationwide meat processing company, discriminated against Black maintenance department employees at its chicken processing plant in Ashland, AL, by subjecting them to a racially hostile work environment, which included a "Whites Only" sign on a bathroom in the maintenance department and a padlock on the bathroom door to which only White employees were given keys. The complaint also alleged that the two Charging Parties were retaliated against when they were suspended for minor issues within a few months of complaining about racial conditions at the plant. Thirteen Black employees intervened in the Commission action alleging violations of Title VII, 42 U.S.C. § 1981, and various state law provisions. Pursuant to a 3-year consent decree, 13 complainants would receive $871,000 and attorneys' fees and costs. ***EEOC v. Tyson Foods, Inc.*, cv-05-BE-1704-E (N.D. Ala. Nov. 7, 2006).**

- In July 2006, Home Depot paid $125,000 to settle a race discrimination and retaliation lawsuit. The suit alleged that a Black former night crew lumberman/forklift operator was subjected to a racially hostile work environment because management condoned racial remarks by his supervisors who called him "Black dog," "Black boy," a "worthless [racial epithet]," and told him that the Supreme Court had found Black people to be "inferior." ***EEOC v. Home Depot USA,* Inc., No. 05-11921 (D. Mass. July 13, 2006).**

- In March 2006, a commercial coating company agreed to pay $1 million to settle an EEOC case that alleged that a Black employee was subjected to a racially hostile environment that included frequent verbal and physical abuse that culminated in him being choked by a noose in the company bathroom until he lost consciousness. ***EEOC v. Commercial Coating Serv., Inc.*, No. H-03-3984 (S.D. Tex. Mar. 2006).**

- In February 2006, the Commission affirmed an AJ's finding that complainant had been subjected to hostile work environment discrimination based on race (African American) when a noose was placed in his work area. Although based on a single incident, the noose was a sufficiently severe racial symbol with violent implications that equates to a death threat. As such, the incident altered the condition of complainant's employment. Complainant was awarded $35,000.00 in non-pecuniary compensatory damages, restoration of annual and sick leave, and $34,505.87 in attorney's fees. The agency was ordered to provide racial harassment training to all employees at the federal workplace. ***Tootle v. Navy,* EEOC Appeal No. 07A40127 (Feb. 10, 2006).**

- In March 2005, the Commission found that a federal employee's supervisor subjected him to hostile work environment harassment when he used a historically-offensive racist slur (n-word) in the employee's presence and at least once in reference to him; treated him less favorably than he did White employees; verbally abused him; and subjected him to hazardous working conditions because of complainant's race (African American). The

EEOC also found that the supervisor violated the anti-retaliation provisions of Title VII when, standing behind the federal employee, he informed all employees that if they wanted to file an EEO complaint, they had to discuss it with him first. The EEOC ordered the agency to determine complainant's entitlement to compensatory damages; train the supervisor with regard to his obligations to eliminate discrimination in the federal workplace; and consider taking disciplinary action against the supervisor. ***Whidbee v. Department of the Navy,*** **EEOC Appeal No. 01A40193 (March 31, 2005).**

- In November 2004, in a case against an upstate New York computer parts manufacturer, the EEOC alleged that Native American employees were subjected to frequent name-calling, war whoops, and other derogatory statements (comments about being "on the warpath" and about scalpings, alcohol abuse, and living in tepees). The employees complained to several supervisors and the Human Resources Department, and the offending employees were occasionally warned, but the hostile environment continued. A consent decree required the company to pay $200,000 to the victims and enjoined future discrimination; to actively recruit Native Americans for available positions; to implement and publish a policy and procedure for addressing harassment and retaliation that includes an effective complaint procedure, and to report to EEOC on complaints of retaliation and harassment based on Native American heritage. ***EEOC v. Dielectric Labs, Inc.*** **(N.D.N.Y. Nov. 14, 2007), available at** *http://www.eeoc.gov/litigation/05annrpt/index.html#IID2.*

- In November 2004, the Commission decided that, although racially charged comments were only made on one day, the nature of the comments, which included several racial slurs, was sufficiently severe to render the work environment hostile. ***Nicholas v. Department of Agriculture,*** **EEOC Appeal No. 01A43603 (November 4, 2004).**

- In September 2004, the Commission affirmed an AJ's finding that a Caucasian registered nurse had been subjected to racial harassment and constructive discharge. The AJ found that for approximately 2½ years Black Health Technicians refused to comply with her orders while following the orders of African American nurses; that one Health Technician told complainant that she would not take orders from a White nurse; and that Technicians screamed, banged on doors, blocked complainant's exit when complainant asked for assistance. The AJ found that the harassment ultimately led to proposed disciplinary action and complainant's constructive discharge. The agency was ordered to reinstate complainant to a Registered Nurse position in a different work area, with back pay and benefits, pay complainant $10,000 in compensatory damages, and provide training to her former unit. ***Menard v. Department of Veterans Affairs,*** **EEOC Appeal No. 07A40004 (September 29, 2004), request for reconsideration denied, EEOC Request No. 05A50175 (January 18, 2005);** *http://www.eeoc.gov/decisions/05a50175.txt.*

Retaliation

- In October 2019, Eagle United Truck Wash, LLC, which operates truck washing facilities at truck stop locations around the United States, paid $40,000 and furnished significant equitable relief to settle a racial harassment, discrimination, and retaliation lawsuit. According to the suit, supervisors and employees subjected an African American truck washer, the only Black employee at the Milton facility for most of his employment, to racial epithets and insults despite the truck washer's complaints to management and then the company fired him on the same day that he complained. The 3-year consent decree enjoins the company from engaging in or condoning race-based harassment and retaliation; requires the provision of training on federal anti-discrimination laws with an emphasis on preventing race-based harassment; and mandates reporting to the EEOC on how it handles internal complaints of race-based discrimination and the posting of a notice regarding the settlement. ***EEOC v. Eagle United Truck Wash, LLC*, Civil Action No. 4:18-cv-1856 (M.D. Pa. Oct. 29, 2019).**

- In September 2019, the owner of a wedding event space in Kansas City agreed to pay $15,000 to a former part-time employee whom the EEOC alleged was the subject of a "campaign of intimidation and threats" for supporting a coworker's racial discrimination claim. The EEOC lawsuit accused the owner of 28 Event Space of retaliating against an African American employee who was a witness in an earlier race discrimination claim against Profile Cabinet and Design. The wedding event owner was a part owner of the custom cabinet maker. The EEOC alleged that initially the owner offered the Black employee money and the use of a limousine if the employee agreed not to testify in the discrimination case. When he refused, the EEOC claimed the owner threatened the employee's job and reduced his work hours. As part of the 3-year consent decree, the company also is required to create clear, understandable anti-discrimination policies, require training for the owner and employees, and provide regular reports to the EEOC for the next 3 years. ***EEOC v. 28 Event Space, LLC*, Civil Action No. 4:18-cv-889 (W.D. Mo. Nov. 9, 2018).**

- In June 2016, DHD Ventures Management Company Inc. will pay a total of $40,000 to settle allegations of racial harassment and retaliation. The EEOC charged that the company, a New York-based real estate management company, allowed Charles Lesine and Marlin Ware to be harassed from late 2007 to November 2011 at Grandeagle Apartments, a residential complex in Greenville, SC, that DHD managed. According to the lawsuit, Lesine and Ware allegedly were subjected to unwelcome derogatory racial comments and slurs made by a White coworker, including the repeated use of the "n" word. The two employees complained to management, but the harassment allegedly continued. ***EEOC v. DHD Ventures Mgmt. Co.*, Case No. 6:15-cv-00102-TMC-KFM (D.S.C. 2016).**

- In June 2016, a Minnesota-based Regis Corporation, which does business as Smart Style Family Hair Salon, paid $90,000 to resolve allegations of retaliation discrimination. According to the EEOC complaint, two employees at one of the company's North Carolina salons were allegedly fired for opposing what they reasonably believed was an unlawful employment practice. They alleged a soon-to-be salon manager told them that she did not want African Americans working in the salon. The two employees then told an African American candidate for an open position at the salon they believed the manager would not hire her due to her race. The company then purportedly fired the two employees, stating they had lied. The 2-year consent decree requires Regis to report the action it takes in response to any employee's complaint about discrimination and to post a notice to employees concerning their rights under federal, anti-discrimination laws. ***EEOC v. Regis Corp.*, Civil Action No. 7:15-CV-00151-F (E.D. N.C. June 2016).**

- In May 2016, American Casing & Equipment Inc., a Williston-based oil field service company, paid $250,000 to a Filipino worker it fired after he complained of harassment to settle a discrimination and retaliation lawsuit filed by the EEOC. The lawsuit alleged that since November 2012, a White manager harassed the worker of Filipino heritage by directing racial slurs ("non-white m----f----r," "non-white guy," "spic," "n----r," "monkey," and "ape") at him, jabbing him with a finger in the stomach and chest, and once urinating on his leg while he worked under a truck. No supervisor made any attempt to stop the abuse. The employee ultimately was fired after he complained to the company's safety manager about the harassment. ***EEOC v. for American Casing & Equipment Inc.*, Civil Action No. 4:15-cv-00066 (DLH-CSM) (D.N.D. May 24, 2016).**

- In September 2014, Izza Bending Tube & Wire agreed to pay $45,000 to settle an EEOC suit alleging that the company retaliated against employee Myrna Peltonen when it demoted her and reduced her salary after she refused to discriminate against an African American employee. The Commission lawsuit charged that Izza's manager instructed Peltonen not to hire the Black employee, who was working as a temporary employee, to a permanent position, and told her to get rid of him because of his race. The EEOC's lawsuit further alleged that after Peltonen filed a discrimination charge with the EEOC, she was laid off and then terminated in retaliation. The consent decree requires other equitable relief, including reporting and training. ***EEOC v. Izza Bending Tube & Wire, Inc.*, No. 0:13-cv-02570 (D. Minn. Sep. 19, 2014).**

- In March 2014, a federal district court upheld a jury verdict in favor of the EEOC and ruled that Sparx Restaurant of Menomonie, WI, must provide back pay with interest of more than $41,000 in addition to the jury's award of damages of $15,000 to a former employee who was fired in retaliation for complaining about a racist display in the workplace. The display included a dollar bill with a noose around George Washington's neck and drawings of a man on horseback and a hooded figure with "KKK" written on his hood. After the EEOC filed its case, Sparx Restaurant closed and was replaced by a Denny's franchise. The district court decided that the companies were a single employer. The court also entered a 3-year injunction, enjoining the defendants from: discharging employees in retaliation for complaints about racially offensive postings in their workplace; failing to adopt policies that explicitly prohibit actions made unlawful under Title VII; failing to adopt an investigative process with regard to discrimination claims; and failing to provide annual training regarding Title VII to Chris Brekken, who owns all interests in the three corporate defendants, and other managers. On appeal, the Seventh Circuit affirmed the district court's judgment and held for the first time held that a tax-offset award was appropriate in a Title VII claim when the lump-sum award place the employee in a higher tax bracket. The court also held that the new entity operating as a Denny's franchise was liable as a successor. ***EEOC v. Northern Star Hospitality, Inc.*, No. 3:12-cv-00214 (E.D. Wis. Judgment filed Feb. 25, 2014), aff'dl, *EEOC v. Northern Star Hospitality, Inc.*, 777 F.3d 898 (7th Circ. 2015).**

- In December 2012, an office and technology supply store paid $85,000 and target recruitment of African Americans and Hispanics to settle a retaliation lawsuit filed by the EEOC. The EEOC's lawsuit charged that OfficeMax violated federal law when its store manager retaliated against a sales associate after the associate complained that he had been terminated because he is Hispanic. The store manager was required to immediately reinstate the sales associate, but then engaged in a series of retaliatory actions designed to generate reasons to terminate him again and/or force the sales associate to resign, the agency alleged. In addition to the monetary settlement, the 4-year consent decree contained injunctive relief: OfficeMax agreed to target additional recruitment efforts in the Sarasota/Bradenton area to reach more African American and Hispanic applicants, provide training for its management and human resource personnel in three locations in the Bradenton/Sarasota area on racial harassment and retaliation, and will report future internal discrimination complaints to the EEOC. ***EEOC v. OfficeMax North America*, Case No. 8:12-cv-00643-EAK-MAP (M.D. Fla. Dec. x, 2012).**

- In April 2012, a real estate company in Little Rock agreed to pay $600,000 to former employees and a class of applicants to settle a race discrimination and retaliation lawsuit filed by the EEOC. The EEOC's suit alleged that the company excluded Black applicants for jobs at the company's Little Rock location based upon their race. The EEOC also alleged that the company retaliated against other employees and former employees for opposing or testifying about the race discrimination, by demoting and forcing one out of her job and by suing others in state court. In addition to the monetary relief, the 3-year consent decree requires the company to provide mandatory annual 3-hour training on race discrimination and retaliation under Title VII; have its president or another officer appear at the training to address the company's non-discrimination policy and the consequences for discriminating in the workplace; maintain records of race discrimination and retaliation complaints; and provide annual reports to the EEOC. ***EEOC v. Bankers Asset Management, Inc.*, No. 4:10-CV-002070-SWW (E.D. Ark. Apr. 18, 2012).**

- In March 2012, a northern Nevada company agreed to pay $50,000 to a Black driver to settle an EEOC lawsuit alleging racial harassment and retaliation. In its complaint, the EEOC said the driver was subjected to racial slurs by a supervisor and taunts by White employees. In one instance, the EEOC says a coworker flaunted a swastika tattoo and talked about keeping the White race "pure." The lawsuit alleged that the driver was fired after complaining twice in one month about the treatment. ***EEOC v. Sierra Restroom Solutions, LLC*, Civ. No. 3:09-CV-00537 (D. Nev. Mar. 20, 2012).**

- In March 2012, a Warren, MI-based painting company which does business in several states, will pay $65,000 to settle a retaliation lawsuit filed by the EEOC. The EEOC had charged that the company unlawfully retaliated against an employee for objecting to race discrimination. In its lawsuit, the EEOC said that Atsalis retaliated against a journeyman painter, who complained about the use of the "N-word" by his foreman, by not bringing him back to work for the 2008 work season. In addition to the monetary award, the decree requires the company to provide ongoing anti-discrimination training to all of the company's officers, managers, supervisors, and human resources personnel; create a new anti-discrimination policy; institute new procedures for handling discrimination complaints; and file reports with the EEOC regarding compliance with the decree's requirements. ***EEOC v. Atsalis Bros. Painting Co.*, Civil Action No. 11-cv-11296 (E.D. Mich. Mar. 9, 2012).**

- In November 2011, a furniture company operating in several locations in Puerto Rico, agreed to pay $40,000 and furnish other relief to settle a charge of retaliation at a worksite in San Juan. According to the EEOC's lawsuit, a Puerto Rican store manager allegedly harassed a dark-complexioned Puerto Rican sales associate because of his skin color (e.g., taunting him about his color and asking why he was "so Black") and then fired him for complaining. In addition to requiring a payment of damages, the consent decree settling the suit prohibits the furniture company from further retaliating against employees who complain about discrimination and requires the company to amend its current anti-discrimination policy to conform to EEOC policy and to provide 4 hours of anti-discrimination training to all Koper employees, including management personnel, on a biannual basis. ***EEOC v. Koper Furniture, Inc.*, Case No. 09-1563 (JAG) (D.P.R. *consent decree approved* Nov. 7, 2011).**

- In April 2011, a long-term care facility located approximately 4 miles from Little Rock, AR, agreed to pay $22,000 in back pay and compensatory damages to settle an EEOC retaliation case. The EEOC charged that the facility violated Title VII when it fired a housekeeping supervisor allegedly because she had complained that she found certain comments by her supervisor racist and that she believed a watermelon-eating contest in the workplace had racist overtones. The EEOC further alleged that, shortly after she complained, she was discharged for supposedly making "false, defamatory, and malicious statements" about a supervisor. Under the 2-year consent decree, the company is enjoined from engaging in retaliation, must instate a new policy on retaliation, and provide 2 hours of Title VII (including retaliation) training to all personnel in Little Rock. In addition, the company must submit two written reports to the EEOC regarding any future retaliation complaints and all pertinent information related to potential complaints. The consent decree also requires the company to post a remedial notice for one year and to notify any potential successors of the consent decree. ***EEOC v. StoneRidge Health and Rehab Center, LLC,*** **Civil Action No. 4:10-cv-1414 JMM (E.D. Ark. consent decree filed April 25, 2011).**

- In February 2011, the EEOC settled a suit against a Portland-based seafood processor and distributor for $85,000 on behalf of a warehouse worker. The lawsuit asserts that, after the warehouse worker spoke to management about race discrimination because a non-Hispanic coworker received a larger raise, he was told that if he was going to accuse the company of discrimination, they "should part ways." According to the terms of the settlement, the seafood distributor agreed to pay the employee $85,000 and redraft its policies on discrimination and retaliation as well as provide employee training on workplace discrimination. ***EEOC v. Pacific Seafood Co., Inc.,*** **No. cv-08-1143-ST (D. Or. settled Feb. 3, 2011).**

- In November 2010, a nationwide provider of engineering and janitorial services to commercial clients entered into a 4-year consent decree paying $90,000 in back pay and compensatory damages to settle the EEOC's claim that it discharged a building services engineer at a mall in Bethesda, MD, in retaliation for complaining of race and sex discrimination. The EEOC alleged that the engineer reported to his supervisor that the mall's operations manager was engaging in race discrimination and sexual harassment; the supervisor told the engineer to ignore the operations manager's conduct and offered to relocate the engineer. The EEOC also alleged that when the engineer declined to relocate, the provider discharged him. The decree also requires the provider to draft and distribute written policies against employment discrimination in English and Spanish, which provide for effective complaint and investigation procedures, including a toll-free number and email address for complaints, to all employees and independent contractors who work for defendant in Washington, DC, Maryland, and Virginia. The company will name an EEO officer to receive complaints of discrimination and retaliation, and starting in January 2011, and every 6 months thereafter, will report to the EEOC and to defendant's vice president of national operations on complaints of discrimination and retaliation received from applicants and employees in Washington, DC, Maryland, and Virginia and the outcome. Lastly, the company will provide discrimination and retaliation training of at least 2 hours to supervisors and managers in Washington, DC, Maryland, and Virginia. ***EEOC v. Crown Energy Services, Inc.,*** **No. PJM 8:09-CV-2572 (D. Md. Nov. 30, 2010).**

- In September 2010, the EEOC sued an oil well servicing contractor for terminating an African American employee allegedly because of his race and for complaining about racial discrimination. After being subjected to racial slurs and witnessing a supervisor display a noose with a black stuffed animal hanging from it, the employee complained. Subsequent to the complaints, the employee was fired. ***EEOC v. Basic Energy Services LP,*** **No. 5:10-cv-01497 (W.D. La. filed Sept. 28, 2010).**

- In September 2010, the EEOC filed suit against a Roanoke-based hair salon chain for allegedly firing an African American hair stylist for complaining about an assistant manager's racist comments. According to the EEOC's complaint, the assistant manager subjected the Black stylist to racist slurs in two separate incidents occurring in March and April 2008. In each incident, the assistant manager made references to African Americans using the N-word. On April 24, 2008, the Black stylist met with her operations manager and salon manager and complained to both supervisors about the assistant manager's offensive remarks. The EEOC alleges that several weeks later, on May 17, 2008, the salon manager discharged the stylist in retaliation for her race-related complaint. **EEOC v. Tomlin Hair Care, Inc., dba Cost Cutters Family Hair Care, Civil Action No. 4:10-cv-43 (W.D. Va. filed Sept. 23, 2010).**

- In August 2010, a North Carolina poultry processor entered a 2-year consent decree agreeing to pay $40,000 to resolve an EEOC case alleging that the company engaged in unlawful retaliation. The EEOC had asserted that the company gave an African American employee an unjustifiably negative performance evaluation shortly after she filed two internal complaints with management about her White supervisor's use of racially offensive language about her and in her presence and when it discharged her 2 weeks after she filed an EEOC charge because of her dissatisfaction with the company's response to her discrimination complaints. In accordance with the consent decree, the company must adopt, implement, and post a formal, written anti-discrimination policy, provide annual Title VII training for all managers and supervisors, and report to the EEOC semi-annually on any instances where employees opposed unlawful employer practices. ***EEOC v. Mountaire Farms of North Carolina Corp.*, Civil Action No. 7:09-CV-00147 (E.D.N.C. August 6, 2010).**

- In October 2007, the Commission obtained $2 million for approximately 50 claimants in this Title VII lawsuit alleging that defendant subjected employees in its three Illinois restaurant/gift stores to sex and race discrimination and retaliation, causing the constructive discharge of some employees. Female employees were subjected to offensive sexual comments and touching by managers and coworkers; Black employees to racially derogatory language, and directives to wait on customers that White employees refused to serve and to work in the smoking section; and a White employee to racially offensive language because of her association with a Black employee. The 2-year consent decree prohibits the company from engaging in sex and race discrimination and retaliation at the three stores. ***EEOC v. David Maus Toyota*, Civil Action No. 6:05cv-1452-ORL-28-KRS (M.D. Fla. Oct. 30, 2007).**

- In July 2006, the EEOC reached a $100,000 settlement in its Title VII lawsuit against a Springfield, MO, grocery chain alleging that a Black assistant manager was subjected to racially derogatory comments and epithets and was permanently suspended in retaliation for complaining about his store manager's racial harassment of him and the manager's sexual harassment of another worker. ***EEOC v. Roswil, Inc. d/b/a Price Cutters Supermarket*, No. 06-3287-CV-S-WAK (W.D. Mo. July 27, 2006).**

- In November 2005, the EEOC obtained a $317,000 settlement in a Title VII case alleging that an extended stay hotel business discharged and otherwise retaliated against a district manager (DM) for six properties in Georgia, Alabama, and Virginia because she complained about race discrimination. The DM, a White female, emailed Defendant's Chief Operating Officer in September 2001 expressing her concerns about the exclusion of African Americans and other racial minorities from management positions. Despite being considered a stellar performer, following her email, the DM was reprimanded, threatened with a PIP, accused of being disloyal to the company, and terminated. The 24-month consent decree applies to all of Defendant's facilities in Georgia and includes requirements that Defendant create and institute a nonretaliation policy, advise all employees that it will not retaliate against them for complaining about discrimination, and instruct all management and supervisory personnel about the terms of the decree and provide them with annual training on Title VII's equal employment obligations, including nonretaliation. ***EEOC v. InTown Suites Management, Inc.*, No. 1:03-CV-1494-RLV (N.D. Ga. Nov. 21, 2005).**
- In February 2005, the EEOC settled a retaliation case against Burger King for $65,000, on behalf of a Caucasian manager who was terminated after refusing to comply with a Black customer's preference that a "White boy" not make her sandwich. ***EEOC v. Star City LLC d/b/a Burger King*, No. 6:03-cv-00077 (W.D. Va. consent decree filed Feb. 11, 2005).**

Discharge

- In December 2019, DSW Shoe Warehouse Inc., a nationwide shoe retailer headquartered in Columbus, OH, paid $40,000 and furnished equitable relief throughout the stores in its Midwest Great Lakes Region (including Michigan and Ohio) to resolve a race discrimination lawsuit filed by the EEOC. The EEOC alleged that DSW intentionally discriminated against a former assistant manager at the company's Warrensville Heights, OH, retail store because she is Black when it terminated the assistant manager after she had been subjected to race-based discipline and unequal terms and conditions of employment. The 18-month consent decree enjoined DSW from future race discrimination and unlawful retaliation; required that DSW will provide training on federal laws and store policies prohibiting discrimination and retaliation and reporting regarding any internal complaints of alleged race discrimination or retaliation. ***EEOC v. DSW Shoe Warehouse, Inc.*, Civil Action No. 2:18-cv-01122 (S.D. Ohio consent decree filed Dec. 4, 2019).**
- In September 2019, a commercial truck washing facility paid $40,000 to settle an EEOC lawsuit accusing the owner of firing an employee because he is Black and had reported that he had been subjected to a racially hostile work environment. According to the lawsuit, the employee who was the only African American worker at the site was daily subjected to racial slurs by coworkers which management refused to address. Along with a monetary

settlement, the 3-year consent decree requires the company to disseminate and post a modified anti-discrimination policy; designate specific individuals to whom race-based discrimination complaints should be directed; provide at least 3 hours of anti-discrimination training by a compliance specialist for all management and supervisory personnel; and submit a written report to the EEOC after 1 year identifying all race-based discrimination complaints. ***EEOC v. Eagle United Truck Wash, LLC,*** **Civil Action No. 4:18-cv-1856 (M.D. Pa. Sep. 20, 2019).**

- In January 2017, Hospman LLC paid $35,000 and furnished other relief to settle a race discrimination lawsuit filed by the EEOC. According to the EEOC's suit, Hospman fired several Black employees in August 2012 after taking over management responsibility of a Fort Myers hotel. The EEOC charged that Hospman's former chief executive officer ordered the housekeeping supervisor to terminate all of the housekeepers—all but one of whom were Black—because he did not work with "those kind of people." He also asked the housekeeping supervisor about her race and, upon learning that she was Black, fired her as well. The only Black front desk attendant also was terminated, while other non-Black front desk workers were allowed to continue their employment. Under the consent decree resolving the EEOC's claims, Hospman also will revise policies regarding race discrimination complaints as set forth in its employee handbook; conduct annual training of its managers and supervisors on the requirements of Title VII; post a notice about the lawsuit for its employees; and report to the EEOC regarding complaints of race discrimination and the company's employment practices. ***EEOC v. Hospman, LLC,*** **Case No. 2:15-cv-00419-JES-CM (M.D. Fla. Jan. 27, 2017).**

- In September 2016, SFI of Tennessee LLC agreed to pay $210,000 to settle allegations of race discrimination. The EEOC charged SFI, a fabricator and supplier of heavy-gauge steel and value-added products, with discharging three Black employees on the same day because of their race. The three employees worked in the supply chain department at SFI and allegedly had no performance issues before their discharges. According to the EEOC, SFI replaced the Black employees with White employees. The agency alleges these actions were motivated by race. Purported conduct of this nature violates Title VII of the 1964 Civil Rights Act. In addition to monetary relief, the company must provide race discrimination training to all employees. ***EEOC v. SFI of Tenn. LLC,*** **No. 2:14-cv-02740 (W.D. Tenn. Sep. 7, 2016).**

- In June 2016, Bloom at Belfair, a nursing home in Bluffton, SC, paid $40,000 to settle an EEOC lawsuit alleging that the company discriminated against an African American activities director when it fired her in September 2014 because of her race. The EEOC charged that the director's firing followed the termination of other African American managers at the facility and was part of a company plan to eliminate African Americans from management. In addition to the monetary relief, the EEOC consent decree requires the company to provide EEO training and to post a notice about the lawsuit in the workplace. ***EEOC v. Bloom at Belfair,*** **No. 9:15-cv-04047-CWH-BM (D.S.C. June 9, 2016).**

- In April 2016, the Eleventh Circuit reversed the district court in an employment discrimination case alleging race and age discrimination in violation of Title VII and the ADEA, respectively. The EEOC filed an amicus brief in the case on behalf of the pro se plaintiff, a 65-year-old White female front desk clerk, who repeatedly had been told she was "too old" and "the wrong color" by the hotel general manager who terminated her. The Commission argued that, contrary to the district court's requirement that the plaintiff needed to identify comparators or a replacement to establish a prima facie case, the discriminatory comments were direct evidence of animus and sufficient to establish a prima facie case of discrimination as well as raise triable issues of pretext sufficient to overcome summary judgment. The Eleventh Circuit essentially agreed and concluded that the discriminatory comments constituted circumstantial evidence of discrimination sufficient to defeat summary judgment. ***Kilgore v. Trussville Dev.*, No. 15-11850 (11th Cir. Mar. 24, 2016).**

- In August 2015, the EEOC won a judgment of more than $365,000 against the Bliss Cabaret strip club and its parent company this week after a Black bartender was allegedly fired based on her race. In its lawsuit, the EEOC said the Clearwater strip club and its successor corporation, Executive Gentlemen's Club, fired a bartender because its owner said he didn't want a Black bartender working at the club. The EEOC claimed that the former manager who hired her was suspended and then fired after he refused to comply with the owner's request. The awarded relief included punitive damages, compensatory damages, back pay, interest, and tax-penalty offsets. ***EEOC v. AJ 3860, LLC, d/b/a The Executive Gentlemen's Club, and Southeast Showclubs, LLC,* Civ. No. 8:14-cv-1621-T-33TGW (M.D. Fla. default judgment filed Aug. 11, 2015).**

- Chapman University, a private university in Orange, CA, paid $75,000 and furnished other relief to settle an EEOC race discrimination. The EEOC had charged that Chapman's George L. Argyros School of Business & Economics (ASBE) discriminated against Stephanie Dellande, an assistant professor of marketing, because of her race. The EEOC contended that Dellande was denied both tenure and promotion to associate professor in 2006 because she is African American, despite strong recommendations in her favor by many professional peers. The university discharged her in June 2008 upon a denial of her tenure appeal. According to the EEOC's suit, Dellande was the first Black professor to have been allowed to apply for tenure at the ASBE and was subjected to a higher standard for obtaining tenure and promotion than her non-Black peers. ***EEOC v. Chapman Univ.*, No. 8:10-cv-1419(JAK) (C.D. Cal. June 20, 2014).**

- In September 2012, a Rosemont, IL-based food product distributor paid $165,000 and furnished other relief to settle a race discrimination lawsuit filed by the EEOC. In its lawsuit, the EEOC charged that the food distributor violated federal law by firing an African American employee who worked at its Memphis facility because of his race. Specifically, the EEOC said, the company discharged the Black employee after he failed to stop a Caucasian driver who reported to work under the influence of alcohol from making deliveries on his route. US Foods did not terminate the Caucasian driver for being under the influence, or another Caucasian safety specialist who saw the driver at the first stop on his route. Instead, the company discharged the White driver later for an unrelated matter. ***EEOC v. US Foods, Inc. fka U.S. Foodservice, Inc.*, Civil Action No. 2:11-cv-02861 (W.D. Tenn. Sep. 12, 2012).**

- In April 2012, the Fifth Circuit ruled that Kansas City Southern Railway Company (KCSR) violated Title VII when it engaged in race discrimination by terminating two Black employees because of work rule violations and retaining their similarly-situated White co-drivers who were involved in the same incidents leading to Black employees' dismissals. The Court also took issue with KCSR's failure to document the reasons for the terminations and inability to identify the decision-maker. The Court cautioned: "KCSR is no stranger to Title VII employment discrimination litigation, and it would behoove KCSR to discharge its burden with greater acuity." ***EEOC v. KCSR*, No. 09-30558 (5th Cir. 2012).**

- In July 2011, a global manufacturer and seller of chemical products in El Dorado, AR, will pay $80,000 and furnish other relief to settle an EEOC lawsuit alleging the company engaged in race discrimination when it terminated Black employees based upon discriminatory and subjective evaluations. In addition to the monetary relief, the consent decree settling the suit enjoins the company from terminating employees in its El Dorado central location's Inorganic Bromine Unit on the basis of race. The company also must provide race and color discrimination training to all supervisory and management personnel in its IOB Unit and post a notice reinforcing the company's policies on Title VII. ***EEOC v. Great Lakes Chemical Corp.*, Civil Action No. 1:09-CV-01042 (W.D. Ark. July 12, 2011).**

- In February 2011, the EEOC filed suit against an electric company alleging race discrimination. According to the lawsuit, the company's allegations that the Black journeyman electrician was in charge of a crew that damaged light fixtures is a pretext. The EEOC contends that the company's superintendent and foreman, both White, were actually in charge of the crew that caused the damage. The agency maintains that neither they nor the non-Black employees who actually caused the damage to the light fixture were terminated. ***EEOC v. Salem Electric Co.*, Civil Action No. 1-11-cv-00119 (M.D.N.C. Feb. 14, 2011).**

- In December 2010, a cosmetic laboratory settled an EEOC lawsuit charging discrimination based on race, color, national origin, and retaliation against a Black employee for $30,000. The laboratory hired the employee, a British subject born in Zimbabwe, for a full-time internship. Upon arrival, her employer realized she was Black and her supervisors gave her no direction and very few assignments despite her requests for work. The company's other two interns, who were White, participated in projects and worked closely with supervisors. When the Black intern raised concerns about unequal treatment with management, she was fired. In addition to the damages payment, the settlement requires that the laboratory adopt a non-discrimination policy and complaint procedure and conduct anti-discrimination training for its staff. ***EEOC v. Northwest Cosmetic Labs LLC,* Civil Action No. 10-608-CWD (D. Idaho Dec. 29, 2010).**

- In May 2009, the federal district court in Minnesota dismissed the EEOC's lawsuit alleging that a Minneapolis-based company provided contract human resources services to more than 37,000 entities, allegedly disciplined and fired a PhD social worker because of his race (African American) and his complaints about race discrimination. According to the EEOC, the 6-year employee had his work scrutinized more critically than non-Black employees, was placed on a performance improvement plan because of his race, and was fired when he complained despite his excellent performance history and numerous awards. ***EEOC v. Ceridian Corp.,* Civil Action No. 07-cv-4086 (D. Minn. May 26, 2009).**

- In February 2008, the Commission upheld an AJ's finding of race and color discrimination where a probationary employee was terminated from his position of Part-Time Flexible Letter Carrier. Although complainant was a probationary employee, the record reflected that he worked at the same level or better than other full-time carriers. The Commission found that, as no other probationary employee was available as a comparator, complainant established a prima facie case of discrimination by creating an inference of race and color discrimination. Further, the Commission found that the agency failed to provide a legitimate, nondiscriminatory reason for terminating complainant because the responsible management official failed to specify a standard to which complainant was compared when he determined that complainant was not performing at an acceptable level. Complainant was reinstated to his position with back pay. ***Artis v. United States Postal Service,* EEOC Appeal No. 0720070032 (February 4, 2008).**

- In October 2007, a trial court determined that the EEOC is entitled to a trial on its claim that a Toyota car dealership engaged in a wholesale elimination of Blacks in management when it demoted and ultimately terminated all of its African American managers because of their race. ***See EEOC v. David Maus Toyota,* Civil Action No. 6:05cv-1452-ORL-28-KRS (M.D. Fla. Oct. 30, 2007).**

- In July 2007, the EEOC received a favorable jury verdict in its Title VII lawsuit against the Great Atlantic & Pacific Tea Company (A&P) alleging that a Black senior manager terminated a White manager because of his race. The jury concluded the White manager was discharged solely because of his race and awarded approximately $85,000 in monetary relief. ***EEOC v. Great Atlantic & Pacific Tea Co.,* C.A. No. 1:05-cv-01211-JFM (D.Md. verdict filed July 30, 2007).**

- In December 2005, the Commission resolved for $145,000 this Title VII case alleging that a global company discharged a traffic clerk in a Colorado warehouse, based on his race (Black) and in retaliation for complaining about discrimination. The traffic clerk asserted that, prior to his discharge, his coworker, a White woman, expounded on her view that African Americans are more athletic than Whites because they were inbred as slaves and have an extra muscle in their legs, that she was afraid to be around certain people of color, and that a customer was entitled to use the "n-word" in reference to the clerk based on freedom of speech. The clerk told her she should take her hood off and not burn a cross on his lawn. Defendant investigated the racial incidents, but failed to interview two Black employee witnesses and fired the clerk in part for the hood and cross comment he made. Neither the White coworker nor the supervisors who witnessed the racial incidents were disciplined. The 3-year consent decree enjoins defendant's Golden, Colorado, facility from discriminating on the basis of race and from retaliation. `**No. 04-CV-2005-RPM-BNB (D. Col. Dec. 20, 2005).**

TABLE 3.3 Educating Racism and Colorism from Employment (E-RACE), 2002–2020

Types of Race/Color Discrimination

Category	**Financial Costs**
Color Discrimination	$467,500
Reverse Discrimination	526,500
Same Sex Discrimination	237,197
Intersectional Discrimination Harassment	
▸ Race/Age	737,500
▸ Race/Disability	297,250
▸ Race/Gender	1,658,261
▸ Race/National Origin	1,877,000
▸ Race/Pregnancy	110,600
▸ Race/Religion	806,000
▸ Race/Sex	0
Associational Discrimination	975,000
Biracial Discrimination	72,500
Code Words	3,241,470
Total	**$11,006.778**

NOTE. U.S. Equal Employment Opportunity Commission. https://www.eeoc.gov/initiatives/e-race/significant-eeoc-racecolor-casescovering-private-and-federal-sectors

Types of Race/Color Discrimination

Color Discrimination

- In June 2015, a Laughlin hotel has agreed to pay $150,000 to six Latino or brown-skinned workers who were "subjected to a barrage of highly offensive and derogatory comments about their national origin and/or skin color since 2006." A federal lawsuit filed by the EEOC alleged that supervisors and coworkers were "constantly" targeted with slurs such as "taco bell," "bean burrito," and "f____ aliens." The lawsuit also said workers were told not to speak Spanish on break, at least one employee lost his job after complaining about the treatment, and the company failed to correct the problems. In addition to monetary relief, the 4-year consent decree required Pioneer Hotel must hire a consultant to help implement policies, procedures, and training for all workers to prevent discrimination, harassment, and retaliation. The company also will receive additional training on its responsibilities under Title VII, will have to immediately report complaints to the human resources department, and must create a centralized system to track complaints. ***EEOC v. Pioneer Hotel, Inc. d/b/a Pioneer Hotel and Gambling Hall,* Case No. 2:11-cv-01588-LRH-GWF (D. Nev. June 17, 2015).**

- In June 2015, Pioneer Hotel, Inc. in Laughlin, NV, agreed to pay $150,000 and furnish other relief to settle a national origin and color discrimination lawsuit filed by the EEOC. The EEOC charged that a class of Latino and/or brown-skinned workers was subjected to a barrage of highly offensive and derogatory comments about their national origin and/or skin color since at least 2006. Housekeeping and security department staffers in particular were constantly the targets of slurs by several supervisors and coworkers. In addition, the EEOC asserted that Latino/brown-skinned workers were told not to speak Spanish during their break times. Pioneer failed to stop and rectify the harassment and discrimination despite repeated complaints by the Latino/brown-skinned workers. Pioneer entered into a 4-year consent decree that prohibits Pioneer from creating, facilitating, or permitting a hostile work environment for employees who are Latino or darker-skinned. Additionally, the hotel agreed to hire an outside equal employment opportunity consultant to ensure that the company implements effective policies, procedures, and training for all employees to prevent discrimination, harassment, and retaliation. Pioneer management will receive additional training on its responsibilities under Title VII; be required to immediately report complaints to the human resources department; create a centralized system to track complaints; and be held accountable for failing to take appropriate action. Notice of consent decree will be visibly posted at the hotel. ***EEOC v. Pioneer Hotel, Inc. d/b/a Pioneer Hotel and Gambling Hall,* Case No. 2:11-cv-01588-LRH-GWF (D. Nev. settlement June 18, 2015).**

- In March 2012, a Fairfax County, VA-based stone contracting company agreed to pay $40,000 and furnish other significant relief to settle an EEOC lawsuit alleging national origin, religion, and color discrimination. According to the EEOC's suit, an estimator and assistant project manager was subjected to derogatory comments from his supervisors, project manager, and the company's owner on the basis of his national origin (Pakistani), religion (Islam), and color (brown). The lawsuit indicated that the comments occurred almost daily and included things like telling the estimator he was the same color as human feces. The lawsuit also alleged that the estimator was told that his religion (Islam), was "f---ing backwards," and "f---ing crazy," and was asked why Muslims are such "monkeys." Pursuant to the 3-year consent decree enjoining the company from engaging in any further discrimination against any person on the basis of color, national origin, or religion, the contracting company also agreed to redistribute the company's anti-harassment policy to each of its current employees; post its anti-harassment policies in all of its facilities and work sites; provide anti-harassment training to its managers, supervisors, and employees; and post a notice about the settlement. ***EEOC v. Rugo Stone, LLC*, Civil Action No. 1:11-cv-915 (E.D. Va. Mar. 7, 2012).**

- In April 2011, the EEOC found that the transportation department engaged in race and color discrimination when it failed to select the Complainant, the Acting Division Secretary, for the position of Division Secretary. The EEOC found the Agency's explanation to be "so fraught with contradiction as not to be credible," and thus, a pretext for discrimination. The EEOC noted that Complainant discussed her experience as Acting Division Secretary in her KSA responses, and, contrary to the Agency's assertion, made numerous references to acting as a Division Secretary in her application. The EEOC ordered the placement of Complainant into the Division Secretary position, with appropriate back pay and benefits, and payment of attorney's fees and costs. ***Bowers v. Dep't of Transp.*, EEOC Appeal No. 0720100034 (Apr. 15, 2011).**

- In February 2009, a discount retail chain agreed to pay $7,500 to resolve an EEOC lawsuit alleging that Title VII was violated when a light skinned Black female manager subjected darker skinned African American employees to a hostile and abusive work environment because of their color. The lawsuit alleged that the manager told one employee she looked as "Black as charcoal" and repeatedly called her "charcoal" until she quit. The parties entered a consent decree that enjoins the company from engaging in color discrimination or retaliation. Pursuant to the consent decree, the retail chain's store manager and assistant managers must receive training on color discrimination, the chain must keep records on any complaint of color discrimination and all information related to the complaint, and it must submit reports on these matters to the EEOC. ***EEOC v. Family Dollar Stores, Inc.*, No. 1:07-cv-06996 (N.D. Ill. settled Feb. 17, 2009).**

- In April 2008, a national video store entered a consent decree to pay $80,000 and to provide neutral references for the claimant in resolution of the EEOC's Title VII lawsuit against it. The EEOC alleged that the store engaged in color discrimination when a Bangladeshi employee who was assigned to be store manager of a Staten Island location allegedly was told by her district supervisor that Staten Island was a predominantly White neighborhood and that she should change her dark skin color if she wanted to work in the area. The EEOC asserted that the supervisor also allegedly told her that she really should be working in Harlem with her dark skin color and threatened to terminate her if she did not accept a demotion and a transfer to the Harlem store. The employee also was subjected to national origin discrimination based on her name and accent when the district supervisor allegedly excluded the employee from staff meetings because he said the other employees could not understand her accent and asked her to change her name because the customers could not pronounce it. The consent decree enjoins the video store from discriminating on the basis of race, color, or national origin and requires the store to post a remedial notice in the store in question and the EEO poster in all locations across the country. ***EEOC v. Blockbuster, Inc.*, C.A. No. 1:07-cv-02221 (S.D.N.Y. filed *settled* Apr. 7, 2008)**.

- In May 2006, the Commission won a Title VII case filed on behalf of Asian Indian legal aliens who were victims of human trafficking, enslavement, and job segregation because of their race, national origin, and dark-skinned color. ***Chellen & EEOC v. John Pickle Co., Inc.*, 434 F.Supp.2d 1069 (N.D. Okl. 2006).**

- In August 2003, the EEOC obtained a $40,000 settlement on behalf of an African American former employee who was discriminated against based on his dark skin color by a light skinned African American manager and terminated when he complained to corporate headquarters. ***EEOC v. Applebee's Int'l Inc.*, No. 1:02-CV-829 (D. Ga. Aug. 7, 2003).**

Reverse Discrimination

- In June 2015, the EEOC filed an amicus brief in support of a pro se plaintiff whose race and age discrimination case was dismissed for failure to establish a prima facie case. The Commission argued in this appeal that the district court erred in dismissing the case because the general manager's repeated references to the plaintiff's race and age, such as "you're the wrong color" and "you're too old" along with plaintiff's supervisor's comment to her, "old white bi..." shortly before the general manager and supervisor terminated plaintiff were sufficient to establish a prima facie case and to provide evidence of pretext. ***Kilgore v. Trussville Develop., LLC*, No. 15-11850 (11th Cir. brief filed June 22, 2015).**

- In September 2012, the County of Kauai in Hawaii paid $120,000 to settle a federal charge of race harassment filed with the EEOC. A former attorney for the County of Kauai's Office of the Prosecuting Attorney, who is Caucasian, alleged that she was harassed due to her race by a top-level manager. The manager allegedly made continually disparaging comments to the former attorney, saying that she needed to assimilate more into the local culture and break up with her boyfriend at the time, also White, in favor of a local boy. The EEOC ultimately found reasonable cause to believe that the county violated Title VII of the Civil Rights Act of 1964 for the harassment to which the former attorney was subjected. Following the determination, the County of Kauai entered into an over 2-year conciliation agreement with the EEOC and the alleged victim. Aside from the monetary relief, the county agreed to establish policies and complaint procedures dealing with discrimination and harassment in the workplace and to provide live EEO training to all managers and supervisors. The county further agreed to post notices on the matter on all bulletin boards throughout the county and to permit the disclosure of the settlement.

- In September 2012, the County of Kauai in Hawaii agreed to pay $120,000 to settle an EEOC charge of race harassment, alleging that a Caucasian former attorney for the County's Office of the Prosecuting Attorney was subjected to racially disparaging comments by a top-level manager. The manager allegedly referred to the Caucasian attorney as haole and advised the former attorney that she needed to assimilate more into the local culture and break up with her boyfriend at the time, also White, in favor of a local boy. Aside from the monetary relief, the county agreed to establish policies and complaint procedures dealing with discrimination and harassment in the workplace and to provide live EEO training to all managers and supervisors. The county further agreed to post notices on the matter on all bulletin boards throughout the county and to permit the disclosure of the settlement.

- In June 2011, a national women's off-priced clothing retailer agreed to pay $246,500 and furnish other relief to 32 class members to settle a race discrimination lawsuit filed by the EEOC. The EEOC had alleged that the retailer denied employment to Caucasian applicants since early 2007. During that time, the EEOC contended, the retailer regularly hired Black entry-level applicants for sales positions, but excluded White applicants who were equally or better qualified. The store manager allegedly told one applicant that the store "does not hire White people." ***EEOC v. Dots, LLC,* No. 2:10-cv-00318-JVB-APR (N.D. Ind. June 3, 2011)**.

- In July 2010, the Seventh Circuit affirmed the EEOC's rulings on race discrimination and retaliation claims in a case brought by a White "policymaking level" employee under the Government Employee Rights Act. John Linehan contested his removal as chief deputy coroner by the elected coroner, who is African American. Among other reasons for removal, the coroner testified that he disagreed with Linehan's attempts to discipline certain subordinate employees. The Court decided that there was substantial evidence to support the Commission's determination that the coroner's reasons for Linehan's demotion and subsequent termination were pretextual. In its view, the coroner's "lack of credibility, combined with his stated preference for employing African Americans and his actions taken in furtherance of that goal, was sufficient for the EEOC to find that Linehan was subjected to race discrimination." However, the court vacated the $200,000 compensatory damages award as excessive and ruled that the EEOC and Linehan either could accept the remitted amount of $20,000 or hold a new hearing on the issue. ***Marion County v. EEOC & Linehan*, No. 09-3595 (7th Cir. July 27, 2010).**

- In May 2009, the fast-food giant Jack in the Box has agreed to pay $20,000 to settle a lawsuit alleging that the company did not take prompt action after a White hostess at its Nashville restaurant complained she was being harassed by Black coworkers who called her racial epithets and insulted her when they learned she was pregnant with a mixed-race child. ***EEOC v. Jack in the Box*, No. 3:08-cv-009663 (M.D. Tenn. settled May 19, 2009).**

- In April 2009, a private historically Black college located in Columbia, SC, agreed to settle a Title VII lawsuit alleging that it discriminated against three White faculty members because of their race when it failed to renew their teaching contracts for the 2005–2006 school year, effectively terminating them. ***EEOC v. Benedict College*, No. 3:09-cv-00905-JFA-JRM (D.S.C. April 8, 2009).**

Same Race Discrimination

- In November 2007, the district court ruled in favor of the EEOC in its Title VII suit alleging that a Texas transportation shuttle service discriminated against African American drivers in favor of native African drivers by denying them the more profitable routes, sending them to destinations where no passengers awaited pickup, and misappropriating tips earned by the Black American drivers and instead giving them to the African drivers. The judgment prohibits Ethio Express's President, Berhane T. Tesfamariam, and his business partner, Mohammed Bedru, from engaging in other discriminatory practices in the future. The judgment also assessed $37,197.00 in monetary damages against Ethio Express. ***EEOC v. Ethio Express Shuttle Service, Inc. dba Texans Super Shuttle*, No. H-06-1096 (S.D. Tex. judgment entered Nov. 2007).**

- In July 2006, the EEOC settled a Title VII action against a Dallas-based HIV service agency, in which four Black employees were allegedly racially harassed by the center's founder and former Executive Director, who is also African American. The persistent same-race harassment—which was reported to management and the Board of Directors—included graphic language, racial slurs, and pejorative insults. Although it ceased operations, the agency agreed to pay $200,000 to the aggrieved employees. ***EEOC v. Renaissance III*, No. 3:05-1063-B (N.D. Tex. July 19, 2006).**

- In September 1998, an EEOC AJ properly decided that a Black male hospital director who abused all employees was not insulated from liability for racially harassing an African American female where evidence showed that she was the target of more egregious and public abuse than other employees. Evidence revealed that the director told her he only hired her because she is a Black woman, he often used profanity toward her, referred to her by race and gender slurs, singled her out for verbal abuse in front of other employees, told plaintiff to "get your Black ass out of here," and told her and other Black managers they better not file EEO complaints. **Veterans Admin., EEOC No. 140-97-8374x-RNS (Sept. 21, 1998).**

Intersectional Discrimination/Harassment

Race/Age

- In December 2016, the EEOC affirmed the Administrative Judge's (AJ) finding of race and age discrimination involving a 47-year-old Black applicant. Following a hearing, the AJ found that the U.S. Department of Agriculture (Agency) discriminated against Complainant on the bases of race and age when it did not select him for a Contracting Officer position. The AJ determined that Complainant's qualifications were plainly superior to the Selectee's qualifications in that Complainant had more years of contracting experience, had contracting experience involving more complex matters and higher monetary amounts, and had more years of supervisory experience. The AJ also found that the Selecting Official's testimony about the Selectee's qualifications was not credible and was not supported by the documentation in the record. On appeal, the Commission concluded that the AJ's finding was supported by substantial evidence, and agreed with the AJ that the Agency's legitimate, nondiscriminatory reason for not selecting Complainant was a pretext for race and age discrimination. While the Agency asserted that the Selecting Official's selection history precluded a finding of discrimination, the Commission stated that selection history is not controlling, and the AJ reasonably relied upon Complainant's prior performance appraisal as an indicator of his performance. Further, the AJ was entitled to draw a reasonable inference from the fact that the Selecting Official did not contact Complainant's supervisor despite having contacted the Selectee's most recent supervisor. The Agency was ordered, among other things, to offer Complainant the position, pay him appropriate back pay and benefits, and pay him $5,000 in proven compensatory damages. ***Neil M. v. Dep't of Agric.*, EEOC Appeal No. 0720140005 (Dec. 9, 2016).**

- In March 2012, a financial services company formerly located in various cities in Michigan agreed to settle for $55,000 an age and race discrimination suit brought by the EEOC. The EEOC lawsuit alleged that Wells Fargo Financial failed to promote a highly qualified 47-year-old African American loan processor on the basis of age and race. The loan processor applied for a promotion but was passed over for five lesser qualified Caucasian women aged between 23 and 30 who were based in various other branch offices, even though the processor had the best combination of relevant, objective scores that measured productivity, was "loan processor of the year" for 2007, the year immediately preceding the promotion decision, worked at one of the largest and most profitable offices in the relevant district, and was the "go-to person" for the district on loan processing. ***EEOC v. Wells Fargo Financial Michigan, Inc.*, Case No. 2:10-CV-13517 (E.D. Mich. Mar. 22, 2012).**

- In November 2011, one of the nation's largest retailers will pay $100,000 and furnish other relief to settle the EEOC's race, sex, and age discrimination and retaliation lawsuit. According to the EEOC lawsuit, an over 40, African American female employee who worked in loss prevention at several Sears stores in the Oklahoma City area, from 1982 until her termination in March of 2010, was passed over for promotion to supervisor several times beginning in 2007 in favor of younger, less experienced, White males. Sears allegedly retaliated against Johnson for her initial EEOC discrimination charge in September 2007 by subjecting her to worsening terms and conditions at work. In addition to the $100,000 payment, Sears has agreed to take specified actions designed to prevent future discrimination, including the posting of anti-discrimination notices to employees, dissemination of its anti-discrimination policy, and providing anti-discrimination training to employees. ***EEOC v. Sears, Roebuck & Co.*, No. 5:10-cv-01068-R (W.D. Okla. Nov. 4, 2011).**

- In October 2010, defendants, a Spring, TX, new and used car dealership and its general partner, agreed to pay $160,000 and provide neutral references indicating their eligibility for rehire to a 50-year-old White male used car salesperson (Robinson) and a 50-year-old African American male used car salesperson (Cotton). The EEOC alleged that an African American male sales supervisor subjected Cotton to derogatory comments about his age and made sexual advances toward him. The supervisor also allegedly threatened Robinson, that he would "get back at" him for the "terrible things whites had done to blacks" in the past and allegedly berated him for being "too old" for the job and "washed up" in the industry. Robinson reported the misconduct to several managers, but rather than taking corrective action, the director of used cars joined in the harassing conduct. Robinson later transferred to a lower-paid sales position to avoid the sales supervisor, but the sales supervisor ultimately transferred to a position in finance where he was responsible for approving paperwork on all sales, and he refused to process any of Robinson's sales transactions, causing Robinson to resign the same month. The 2-year consent decree enjoins sex and race harassment and discrimination and retaliation in violation of Title VII and age discrimination under the ADEA. Annually, defendants must provide copies of the decree to all supervisors and managers and obtain signed statements that they have read the decree and agree to be bound by its terms. ***EEOC v. Autotainment Partners Ltd., P'ship d/b/a Planet Ford and Worldwide Autotainmentt, Inc.*, No. 4:09-CV-03096 (S.D. Tex. Oct. 12, 2010).**

- In June 2010, the Equal Employment Opportunity Commission and a Kansas-based national employment staffing firm settled for $125,000 a case on behalf of a White, 55-year-old former employee who allegedly was treated less favorably than younger Black colleagues and fired when she complained. According to the Commission's lawsuit, the staffing company unlawfully discriminated against a senior functional analyst, who was the oldest employee and only Caucasian in the department, because of her race and age in violation of Title VII and the ADEA when a young, African American supervisor subjected her to different treatment and terminated her when she complained. ***EEOC v. Spencer Reed Group,*** **No. 1:09-CV-2228 (N.D. Ga. consent decree approved 6/8/10).**

- In August 2006, a Pennsylvania health-care company agreed to pay $16,000 to two older workers who allegedly were denied promotions based on their race (Black) and their ages (50 and 53), despite their extensive relevant experience of 13+ years. The EEOC alleged that, instead of promoting one older Black employee, the company promoted a 28-year-old Caucasian employee with 7 months of experience and who did not meet the stated criteria for the position. In the 2-year consent decree, the company states it will avoid engaging in racial discrimination or retaliation and must post a remedial notice and provide Title VII training to all supervisors and managers. In addition, the company must provide training in its policies on hiring, promotion, transfer, and co-employment. ***EEOC v. Mainline Health Care,*** **No. 05-cv-4092(CN) (E.D. Pa. settled Aug. 25, 2006).**

- In October 2007, the EEOC resolved a discrimination lawsuit alleging race and age discrimination for $48,000. The EEOC had charged that a South Carolina beauty salon violated federal law by refusing to promote a 51-year-old African American stylist. Between June and September 2006, three employees resigned from the salon manager position and in filling the salon manager position all three times, the salon selected a succession of three White employees from other salons whose ages ranged from late teens to early 20s even though the Black stylist was more than qualified to fill the position. ***EEOC v. Regis Corporation d/b/a SmartStyle,*** **Civil Action No. 7:06-cv-02734 (D.S.C. settled October 5, 2007).**

- In June 2007, the Commission affirmed its decision that complainant, a 48-year-old Black male Supervisory Deputy with the U.S. Marshals Service, was not selected for the position of Assistant Chief Deputy U.S. Marshal because of race, gender, and age discrimination when the agency's Career Board selected a 34-year-old Caucasian female based on her academy achievement, work experience, and interview. The Commission found that the record showed that complainant's qualifications were observably superior to those of the selectee and concluded that the agency's stated reasons for not selecting complainant for the position in question were a pretext for discrimination. The agency was ordered to appoint complainant to the position of Assistant Chief Deputy U.S. Marshal, with back pay and benefits, and pay complainant $50,000.00 and attorney's fees. ***Washington v. Department of Justice,*** **EEOC Appeal No. 0720060092 (February 8, 2007),** ***request for reconsideration denied,*** **EEOC Request No. 0520070324 (June 15, 2007).**

- In November 2006, the EEOC affirmed an AJ's findings that a federal employee complainant was not selected for promotion to Team Leader based on race (African American), sex (female), and age (DOB 2/14/54), notwithstanding her qualifications, and that she was subjected to discriminatory harassment by the same management official. The decision awarded complainant a retroactive promotion with back pay, $150,000 in compensatory damages and attorney's fees and costs. ***Goodridge v. SSA,* EEOC Appeal No. 0720050026 (November 15, 2006).**

- In June 2006, a Newark port facility paid $28,500 to settle a race and age discrimination lawsuit brought by the EEOC, which alleged that the facility's new manager mistreated and then fired a 56-year-old African American customer service representative, who was the only Black and oldest of seven employees, because of her race and age. ***EEOC v. Port Elizabeth Terminal & Warehouse,* Civil Action 05-cv-4828 (WJM) (D.N.J. June 22, 2006).**

Race/Disability

- In December 2009, a telemarketing company agreed to pay $60,000 to a Black former employee who the EEOC alleged was immediately terminated following a diabetic episode at work in violation of Title VII and the ADA. The consent decree enjoins the company from engaging in racial discrimination and requires it to post a remedial notice and arrange training in racial discrimination for its managers and supervisors. The company also must submit reports to the EEOC on its compliance with the consent decree. See ***EEOC v. RMG Communications,* LLC, Civil Action No. 1:08-cv-0947-JDT-TAB (S.D. Ind. settled Dec. 16, 2009).**

- In November 2007, the Commission upheld an Administrative Judge's finding of discrimination on the bases of race (African American), sex (female), and disability (cervical strain/sprain) when complainant was not accommodated with a high back chair. The agency was ordered to provide complainant with back pay for the period she was out of work due to the failure to accommodate, and complainant was awarded $2,250 in compensatory damages. ***Jones v. United States Postal Service,* EEOC Appeal No. 0720070069 (November 8, 2007).**
  - An EEOC Administrative Judge's finding that a blanket policy excluding employees with Type I and II Diabetes adversely impacted African Americans and Native Americans resulted in a settlement and change in policy.

- In June 2005, an AJ found direct evidence of retaliation and circumstantial evidence of race discrimination where the agency's managers did not act on the Black complainant's plea for mail handling assistance for many months before the complainant injured himself. The managers told him that he should have thought of this [that he might need future assistance from them] before he filed his [previous] EEO complaint. They also treated him differently than non-Black employees. The complainant suffered debilitating and career-ending shoulder, neck, arm, and back injuries and lapsed into a major depression. The AJ awarded 28 months of back pay and 24 months of from pay; lost benefits; compensatory damages of $120,000 for physical and mental pain and suffering; and approximately $40,000 in attorney's fees and costs. **See USPS, EEOC Hearing No. 370-2004-00099X (June 21, 2005).**

- In April 2004, a letter carrier prevailed in part on his federal sector complaint alleging employment discrimination based on race/national origin (Asian), disability (PTSD), and retaliation. The allegations included that the Postal facility forced him to remain in a plywood shack for hours each day; disabled postal workers were routinely assigned to "the Box," as it was called, while non-disabled workers were never assigned to "the Box"; employees consigned to "the Box" did not have a telephone, radio, computer, or any other equipment with which to perform any work and were not given any work assignments; and the disabled employees were required to knock on a little window in "the Box" when they needed to use to the restroom. AJ found that the Agency discriminated against this letter carrier on the basis of disability when it forced him to remain in the plywood shack, and when it denied him leave, but decided the remaining claims in the favor of the agency. The Commission affirmed the AJ's decision awarding $75,000.00 in non-pecuniary compensatory damages, restoration of sick leave, payment of attorney's fees and other expenses, and the dismantling of "the Box." **See *USPS,* EEOC Hearing No. 270-2003-090077X (April 20, 2004).**

Race/Gender

- In July 2012, hotel groups Pacific Hospitality and Seasons Hotel agreed to pay $365,000 and provide preventative measures to settle a federal harassment lawsuit by the EEOC. The EEOC charged in its lawsuit that the general manager who worked at both the Best Western Evergreen Inn (formerly La Quinta Federal Way) and Best Western Tacoma Dome persistently harassed and denigrated women, including those who were minorities and had strong religious beliefs, in violation of federal law. According to the EEOC, female employees were subjected to the constant use of racial slurs and derogatory sex-based and racial comments, yelling, and physical intimidation. One employee had a stapler thrown at her head while another was told she was nothing but a "welfare mother" and should abort her pregnancy. The EEOC also alleged that the general manager also illegally fired five women after they revealed they were pregnant. Further, the EEOC alleged that the harasser belittled the various religious beliefs of employees, including calling a professed Christian "weak-minded" and allegedly telling another employee that she should have an abortion because she already had a child, and that she was her own God and could control her own destiny. ***EEOC v. Pacific Hospitality LLC d/b/a La Quinta Inn Federal Way*, No. 3:10-CV-5175 (W.D. Wash. consent decree entered July 3, 2012).**

- In May 2011, the nation's second-largest pharmacy chain, a new owner of Longs Drugs, agreed to pay $55,000 to settle an EEOC race and sex discrimination lawsuit alleging that Longs subjected an African American female product buyer to a hostile environment after hiring her in January 2007, and firing her in May 2008 in retaliation for her complaint to company managers. The suit claimed that the buyer was given more difficult tasks and less assistance than her colleagues who were not Black and female, was unfairly disciplined for performance scores that were higher than those of her White female coworkers who did not face any disciplinary action, and that the supervisor gave her White coworkers permission for vacation days but ignored the Black buyer's earlier requests for the same days. The suit further alleged that within a few months after the Black female buyer complained to the human resources department about the differential treatment, she was discharged from her position. Although all of the alleged events occurred before the chain purchased Longs, the chain has agreed to institute new anti-discrimination staff training procedures. ***EEOC v. Longs Drugs & CVS Caremark*, Civ No. 3:10-CV-04384-RS (May 31, 2011).**

- In April 2011, a federal district court in Tennessee reaffirmed a court judgment of $1,073,261 when it denied the world's leading manufacturer and marketer of major home appliances' motion to reduce the victim's front and back pay awards. In December 2009, the EEOC won the $1 million judgment in a race and sex discrimination suit following a 4-day trial. The evidence showed that a Black female employee reported escalating offensive verbal conduct and gestures by her White male coworker over a period of 2 months before he physically assaulted her at the Tennessee-based facility; four levels of Whirlpool's management were aware of the escalating harassment; Whirlpool failed to take effective steps to stop the harassment; and the employee suffered devastating permanent mental injuries that will prevent her from working again as a result of the assault and Whirlpool's failure to protect her. On January 15, 2011, the corporation asked that the damages be reduced because, inter alia, the plant where the victim had worked had closed. The court denied the request. ***EEOC v. Whirlpool Corp.*, Civil Action No. 3:06-0593 (M.D. Tenn. Apr. 1, 2011).** Whirlpool appealed. On June 11, 2012, Whirlpool Corporation agreed to pay one million dollars and court costs to settle the lawsuit, drawing to a close 6 years of litigation.

- In March 2011, the Ninth Circuit affirmed the judgment of the district court against a major auto parts chain because it had permitted an African American female customer service representative (rep) to be sexually harassed by her Hispanic store manager. The manager's harassment included "humping" her from behind, grabbing her head, demanding that she perform oral sex on him, telling customers that she had AIDS "because it was proven that 83 percent of African American women had AIDS," calling her a slut, and slapping her in the face with his penis. The jury awarded $15,000 in compensatory damages and $50,000 in punitive damages to the rep. The Ninth Circuit ruled that the jurors could have reasonably determined that the district manager and regional human resources manager failed to exercise reasonable care to correct promptly "the obscene and harassing behavior" of the store since management did not check the video cameras that were in parts of the store where the rep was assaulted, the investigation was not confidential, certain employees were never interviewed, the harassment was not reported to the corporate office, critical corroborating evidence was lost, and the rep had complained to management "immediately and repeatedly." The Court also affirmed the punitive damages award because a reasonable juror could conclude that the company had not acted in good faith to comply with Title VII when the human resources manager threatened to terminate the rep for hitting the store manager while defending herself against the sexual assault. ***AutoZone, Inc. v. EEOC,* 2011 WL 883658 (9th Cir. Mar. 15, 2011).**

- In March 2007, the EEOC upheld an AJ's finding that complainant was subjected to a hostile work environment on the bases of her race (African American) and sex (female) when management: yelled at complainant; refused to communicate with her on work matters; failed to assist her; interfered with her work; removed her space leasing duties and responsibilities which fundamentally changed the nature of her position; and engaged in an effort to get her off the leasing team. Remedial relief included back pay, benefits including reimbursement of leave, compensatory damages and attorney's fees, posting of a notice, training, and recommended disciplinary action against the responsible management officials. ***Burton v. Department of the Interior,* EEOC Appeal No. 0720050066 (March 6, 2007).**

- In December 2004, the Commission affirmed an AJ's finding that a Black female complainant was subjected to discrimination on the basis of her race and sex with regard to the processing and approval of her application for telecommuting and her request for advanced sick leave. The Commission noted that, while complainant was asked to provide additional information concerning child care and told that she would have to submit to a home inspection, a White male employee who also had children at home was not asked to do so. The agency was ordered to pay complainant $100,000.00 in compensatory damages, expunge any derogatory materials relating to complainant's performance, and pay attorney's fees and costs. ***Ellis-Balone v. Department of Energy,* EEOC Appeal No. 07A30125 (December 29, 2004).**

- In September 2004, an AJ determined that a Black male complainant was subjected to race discrimination when he was not selected for an EEO Specialist (Mediator) position despite having performed the duties of the position in the area in which he applied. Testimony in the record showed that the approving official was biased against those of complainant's race, particularly males. In addition, it was suspected that none of the seven members of complainant's race who had been performing the Mediator duties were selected for the position, while the one individual outside of complainant's race was chosen. **See *McMillian v. Department of Transportation,* EEOC Appeal No. 07A40088 (September 28, 2004), *requests for reconsideration denied,* EEOC Request No. 05A50171 (December 13, 2004), & EEOC Request No. 05A50361 (April 25, 2005).**

Race/National Origin

- In March 2017, an Illinois sheet metal and HVAC company paid $325,000 to settle EEOC charges that it subjected a Black Puerto Rican worker to national origin, race, and color harassment that culminated in a brutal physical assault. The harassment by White employees of King-Lar Co. directed at the employee included calling him "Mexican nigger," "wet-back," and "nigger slave," the Commission alleged in a lawsuit filed in August 2015. Under a 30-month consent decree, the company must designate an EEOC-approved individual to conduct independent investigations into future complaints of workplace harassment and determine what, if any, disciplinary and corrective action needs to be taken in response to a harassment complaint. King-Lar's policies and training materials also must reference the name and contact information for the designated employee as well as an 800 number and website that employees can use to make anonymous complaints. The company also agreed to fulfill notice-posting, training, and reporting requirements. ***EEOC v. King-Lar Co.*, No. 3:15-cv-03238 (C.D. Ill. consent decree filed 3/29/17).**

- In December 2012, an agricultural farm in Norman Park, GA, agreed to pay $500,000 to a class of American seasonal workers—many of them African American—who, the EEOC alleged, were subjected to discrimination based on their national origin and/or race. The EEOC's suit had charged that the company unlawfully engaged in a pattern or practice of discrimination against American workers by firing virtually all American workers while retaining workers from Mexico during the 2009, 2010, and 2011 growing seasons. The agency also alleged that Hamilton Growers fired at least 16 African American workers in 2009 based on race and/or national origin as their termination was coupled with race-based comments by a management official. Additionally, the lawsuit charged that Hamilton Growers provided lesser job opportunities to American workers by assigning them to pick vegetables in fields which had already been picked by foreign workers, which resulted in Americans earning less pay than their Mexican counterparts. Pursuant to the consent decree settling the suit, the Hamilton Growers will exercise good faith in hiring and retaining qualified workers of American national origin and African American workers for all farm work positions, including supervisory positions. Hamilton Growers will also implement non-discriminatory hiring measures, which include targeted recruitment and advertising, appointment of a compliance official, and training for positive equal employment opportunity management practices. The company has also pledged, among other things, to create a termination appeal process; extend rehire offers to aggrieved individuals from the 2009–2012 growing seasons; provide transportation for American workers which is essential to viable employment in that part of the country; and limit contact between the alleged discriminating management officials and American workers. The decree also provides for posting anti-discrimination notices, record-keeping and reporting to the EEOC. ***EEOC v. Hamilton Growers, Inc. d/b/a Southern Valley Fruit and Vegetable, Inc.*, No. 11-cv-134 (M.D. Ga. consent decree filed 12/10/12).**

- In August 2011, New York University agreed to pay $210,000 in lost wages and compensatory damages to settle a racial and national origin harassment lawsuit by the EEOC, alleging that an African NYU Library employee from Ghana was subjected to racial slurs, such as "monkey" and "gorilla" and insults such as "do you want a banana," "go back to the jungle," and "go back to your cage" by his mailroom supervisor. Pursuant to a 3-year consent decree, the university also will improve and implement university-wide enhanced policies and complaint procedures; designate an EEO coordinator to monitor NYU's compliance with federal anti-discrimination laws; conduct in-person, comprehensive EEO training sessions for employees, supervisors, and HR staff; and maintain records of its responses to future employee complaints of discrimination, harassment, and retaliation. ***EEOC v. NYU*, No. 10-CV-7399 (S.D.N.Y. Aug. 16, 2011).**

- In June 2011, a leading provider of advanced office technology and innovative document imaging products, services, and software agreed to pay $125,000 and to provide substantial affirmative relief to settle a Title VII case alleging race, national origin, and retaliation claims. The EEOC had charged the company with subjecting a Black Liberian employee to harassment because of his race and national origin and two Hispanic employees, one Colombian and the other Puerto Rican, to harassment based on national origin at one of its work sites in Greensboro, NC. The lawsuit further charged that the company suspended and then fired all three employees for complaining about the harassment. The alleged unlawful conduct included the site manager commenting to the three employees that she "hated Puerto Ricans," that "Hispanics are so stupid," that "Colombians are good for nothing except drugs," and that "damn, f-----g Africans . . . ain't worth s--t." In addition to providing monetary relief, the company agreed to conduct employee training on its anti-harassment policy and make the policy available to all employees. The company also will report all harassment complaints of race or national origin harassment to the EEOC for the next two years. ***EEOC v. Ricoh Americas Corporation*, Civil Action No. 1:10-cv-00743 (M.D.N.C. settled June 15, 2011).**

- In April 2011, a provider of operational support software and back office services deployed by cable and broadband operators worldwide agreed to pay $60,000 to settle a race and national origin discrimination lawsuit. In September 2010, the EEOC had filed the lawsuit alleging that the company fired a Black Tanzanian network operations analyst because of her race and national origin. The analyst was terminated allegedly because she left work 30 minutes early to beat the traffic. However, the employer did not fire a Caucasian employee who left 2 hours early on 2 different days because he was tired. The consent decree also includes provisions for equal employment opportunity training, reporting, and posting of anti-discrimination notices. ***EEOC v. Integrated Broadband Services*, No. 1:10-03106 (N.D. Ga. settled Apr. 5, 2011).**

- In November 2008, a popular pizzeria based in Ferndale, MI, agreed to pay $20,000 to resolve an EEOC lawsuit alleging that the pizzeria violated federal law when it told two qualified Black job seekers for waitress positions, one of whom is African and spoke with an accent, on two separate occasions that it had run out of applications but hired a White applicant as a waitress later the same day without requiring her to fill out an application. In the consent decree, the pizzeria agreed to provide equal employment and hiring opportunities in all positions and Title VII training for supervisors, managers, and owners. The consent decree also requires the pizzeria to keep records on information relevant to whether unlawful practices have been committed and its hiring data, and to submit reports to the EEOC on this information. ***EEOC v. Como's of Ferndale*, Case No. 2:07-cv-14091 (E.D. Mich. Nov. 24, 2008).**

- In February 2008, a restaurant agreed to pay $165,000 to resolve a Title VII lawsuit the EEOC brought on behalf of a dining manager who was Arab and Moroccan because he and an Arab waiter from Tunisia allegedly had been subjected to customer harassment based on race and national origin and then the manager was fired in retaliation for opposing the harassment. According to the EEOC's investigation, when the dining manager complained, the customer turned on him, saying, "If you don't like it, why don't you go back to your country?" and "I fought two wars to get rid of people like you!" The parties entered a 3-year consent decree which enjoins the restaurant from engaging in race and national origin discrimination or retaliation. The restaurant also must revise its discrimination complaint and investigation policies and disseminate them when they are approved by the EEOC as well as create a complaint procedure that is designed to encourage employees to come forward with incidents of racial discrimination. Additionally, the restaurant must train its employees in anti-discrimination laws and policies and impose appropriate disciplinary measures against supervisors who engage in discrimination. ***EEOC v. Albion River Inn*, No. C-06-5356 SI (N.D. Cal. settled Feb. 27, 2008).**

- In December 2007, a convenience store distributor paid $100,000 to resolve an EEOC lawsuit alleging race, color, and national origin discrimination. The EEOC alleged that a Black employee from West Guinea, Africa, was subjected to verbal and physical harassment and then fired when he complained. The consent decree requires the company to implement a policy prohibiting race, color, and national origin harassment. The company also must submit reports to the EEOC demonstrating its compliance with the consent decree. ***EEOC v. Eby-Brown, LLC*, No. 1:06-CV-1083-SEB-VSS (S.D. Ind. Dec. 20, 2007).**

- In November 2007, a high-end suburban Illinois retirement facility agreed to pay $125,000 to settle a discrimination lawsuit alleging that it terminated its director of nursing, because of her national origin (Filipino) and race (Asian). The federal district court approved a 2-year consent decree requiring the facility to provide training regarding anti-discrimination laws to all its employees; post a notice informing its employees of the consent decree; report to the EEOC any complaints of discrimination made by its employees; and take affirmative steps to recruit Asian nurses. ***EEOC v. Presbyterian Homes,*** **Case No. 07 C 5443 (N.D. Ill. Nov. 28, 2007).**

- In March 2007, MBNA-America agreed to pay $147,000 to settle a Title VII lawsuit alleging discrimination and harassment based on race and national origin. According to the lawsuit, an Asian Indian employee was subjected to ethnic taunts, such as being called "dot-head" and "Osama Bin Laden," was physically attacked by a coworker with a learning disability who believed he was Osama's brother, and was denied training and promotional opportunities afforded to his White coworkers. ***EEOC v. MBNA-America*** **(E.D. Pa. Mar. 2007).**

- In December 2006, a New York apple farm agreed to pay $100,000 to Jamaican migrant workers holding H-2B worker's visas who were allegedly subjected to different terms and conditions of employment on the basis of their race (African-Caribbean), color (Black), and national origin (Jamaican). EEOC asserted in the lawsuit that the farm harassed Jamaican migrant workers and forced them to pay rent while permitting non-Jamaicans to live in housing rent-free in violation of Title VII. ***EEOC v. Porpiglia Farms,*** **Civil Action No. 06-cv-1124 (N.D.N.Y. Dec. 22, 2006).**

- In January 2006, the Commission settled for $200,000 a case against Bally North America filed on behalf of a former manager of its Honolulu store who was harassed and fired due to her Asian race and Chinese national origin. ***EEOC v. Bally North America, Inc.,*** **No. 05-000631 (D. Haw. Jan. 2006).**

Race/Pregnancy

- In July 2008, a Florida laundry services company agreed to pay $80,000 and furnish other remedial relief to settle an EEOC discrimination lawsuit. The EEOC had charged that a Black Haitian laundry worker at Sodexho Laundry Services, Inc. lost her job because of her race, national origin, and pregnancy. The employee had developed complications early in her pregnancy, obtained a light duty assignment, but was not permitted to continue her light duty assignment after her doctor imposed lifting restrictions even though Hispanic managers routinely assigned pregnant Hispanic women to light duty work at the same time she was being denied the same opportunity. ***EEOC v. Sodexho Laundry Services, Inc.*** **(S.D. Fla. settled July 2008).**

- In October 2006, the EEOC obtained a $30,600 settlement in Title VII suit, alleging that a California-based office equipment supplier had fired an accounts payable specialist because she was African American and because she had been pregnant, when it told her that after she returned from maternity leave, her assignment was complete and there were no other positions in the accounting department, permanently placed a non-Black, non-pregnant female who she had trained to fill in during her maternity leave in her former position, and a week later hired a non-Black male to work in another accounting position in the same department. ***EEOC v. Taylor Made Digital Systems, Inc.*, No. C-05-3952 JCS (N.D. Cal. Oct. 25, 2006).**

Race/Religion

- In March 2013, a not-for-profit developer of real estate, offices, and facilities around Grand Central Terminal in New York City paid $135,000 to settle a lawsuit filed by the EEOC. The EEOC's lawsuit asserted that a non-Rastafarian security officer threatened to shoot a group of Rastafarian officers. When the Rastafarians complained, a White security supervisor made light of the physical threat and implied the Rastafarians were at fault. One Rastafarian security officer objected to the supervisor's reaction and complained that he heard the supervisor had referred to the Rastafarians by the "N-word." The Rastafarian security officer immediately contacted the EEOC about the incident. The EEOC had previously sued the developer for failing to accommodate the religious beliefs of four Rastafarian employees who needed modifications to its dress code. That lawsuit was resolved by a 2009 consent decree which prohibited Grand Central Partnership from retaliating against Rastafarian security officers for their participation in the lawsuit, but the developer's current conduct constituted a breach of the earlier consent decree. In addition to the monetary relief, the new consent decree requires the developer to conduct extensive training on investigating discrimination complaints, including methods for proper documentation and unbiased assessment of witness credibility. The decree also requires developer to regularly report to the EEOC about any further complaints of religious discrimination or retaliation. ***EEOC v. Grand Central Partnership, Inc.*, No. 1:11-cv-09682 (S.D.N.Y. Mar. 1, 2013).**

- In June 2011, a district court ruled that the EEOC could proceed with its two Title VII cases alleging race, national origin, and religious discrimination by a meatpacking firm against a class of Black Somali Muslim workers at its facilities in Greeley, CO, and Grand Island, NE, even though the relevant union local is not a party to the suit. The EEOC alleged that the company failed to accommodate the Muslim workers' religious beliefs by hindering their prayer breaks and Ramadan observances, and that supervisors and coworkers harassed the Somali workers by uttering vulgar epithets and throwing bones, meat, and blood at them. In September 2008, the company locked out, suspended, and ultimately fired Somali Muslim employees in Greeley who had walked outside the plant to break their Ramadan fasts, the EEOC alleged. The company claimed the entire case should be dismissed either because the EEOC failed to join the relevant local union, which the company believed was a necessary party to the litigation, the EEOC failed to conciliate the discrimination charges, and the plaintiff-intervenors failed to exhaust their administrative remedies. The court rejected the first two arguments, and issued a mixed ruling on whether the intervenors' claims had been exhausted. ***EEOC v. JBS USA LLC d/b/a JBS Swift & Co.*, No. 10-cv-02103 (D. Colo. June 9, 2011).**

- In January 2009, a cocktail lounge agreed to pay $41,000 to settle an EEOC lawsuit alleging that the lounge engaged in race and religious discrimination when it refused to promote an African American employee who wears a headscarf in observance of her Muslim faith to be a cocktail server because the owner said she was looking only for what she termed "hot, White girls." In accordance with the 5-year consent decree, the company is enjoined from engaging in racial and religious discrimination or retaliation and must implement and enforce anti-discrimination policies, procedures, and training for all employees. The consent decree also requires the owner/manager to attend individual training on EEO issues and the company must report to the EEOC on its compliance with the consent decree. ***EEOC v. Starlight Lounge*, No. 2:06-cv-03075 (E.D. Wash. Jan. 13, 2009).**

- In July 2008, an Oregon video company paid $630,000 to resolve an EEOC lawsuit alleging that two employees, an African American who was converting to Judaism and a Hispanic with some Jewish ancestry, were forced to endure repeated racial, religious, and national origin jokes, slurs, and derogatory comments made by employees and upper management since the beginning of their employment in 2005. The EEOC also charged that the company then engaged in a series of acts designed to punish the victims for complaining and to ridicule those who corroborated the complaints. The parties entered a 3-year consent decree on July 30, 2008, which enjoins the company from engaging in racial discrimination or retaliation and requires the company to institute an equal employment opportunity policy and distribute this new policy to its employees. The consent decree also requires 4 hours of Title VII training for all Video Only employees. ***EEOC v. Video Only*, No. 3:06-cv-01362 (D. Or. July 30, 2008).**

Race/Sex

- In October 2019, the EEOC's Office of Federal Operation found that the U.S. Bureau of Prison's (BOP) Devens Federal Medical Center in Ayer, MA, discriminated against a Hispanic female former Health Information Technician on the basis of race and sex when a supervisor gave her an unwarranted negative reference which cost her the job. The employee was required to get a reference from her supervisor when she applied for a job to become a U.S. Public Health Service officer at the prison. The prison officer job would have meant the Hispanic employee would have had as much or greater authority as her current supervisor. The EEOC found that the employee's supervisor, an Asian woman, "intentionally sabotaged" complainant because she did not want a Hispanic woman "to potentially serve as her supervisor." The complainant also alleged that the supervisor only wanted to promote Caucasian employees. The EEOC ordered the BOP, among other things, to consider disciplinary action against the supervisor and to pay the job seeker damages. ***Thomasina B. v. U.S. Bureau of Prisons*, EEOC Appeal No. (Oct. 2019).**

- In June 2017, the EEOC reversed the Administrative Judge's finding of no discrimination by summary judgment, which the Department of Homeland Security (Agency) adopted, regarding Complainant's claim that the Agency discriminated against her, an African American woman, when it failed to select her for a promotion. The Commission instead found that summary judgment in favor of Complainant was appropriate. The Selecting Official stated that she did not select Complainant for the position because Complainant did not demonstrate experience relevant to the job description, while the Selectee did demonstrate relevant experience and received the highest interview score. The record, however, showed that Complainant specifically listed relevant experience in all areas identified by the Selecting Official, and that the Selectee's application failed to establish relevant experience in two areas. In addition, one of the individuals on the interview panel stated that the Selectee was not completely qualified for the position. The Agency also appeared to have violated its Merit Promotion Plan by having a lower-level employee participate in the interview panel. Therefore, the Commission found that Complainant established that the Agency's stated reasons for her non-selection were a pretext for race and sex discrimination. The Agency was ordered, among other things, to offer Complainant the position or a substantially similar position, and pay her appropriate back pay, interest, and benefits. ***Shayna P. v. Dep't of Homeland Sec.*, EEOC Appeal No. 0120141506 (June 2, 2017).**

Associational Discrimination

- In February 2011, a family-owned restaurant agreed to pay $25,000 to settle an EEOC case alleging that it violated Title VII when it demoted and discharged an African American employee because of his race, and then discharged a Caucasian employee because of her association with him. The EEOC complaint stated that the African American employee was subjected to derogatory remarks, such as use of the N-word, from both the restaurant's co-owner and customers. The Caucasian employee also was called derogatory names, such as "N-lover," when she turned down customers for dates. These customers also threatened to get her fired because of her association with the African American employee. The restaurant also allegedly failed to display information regarding federal anti-discrimination laws. The consent decree enjoins the company from engaging in racial discrimination or retaliation and requires the company to post the EEO poster in an area visible to all employees. In addition, the company must also create and post an anti-discrimination policy in the restaurant, train its employees annually on Title VII requirements, and submit written reports regarding any future complaints alleging discrimination to the EEOC. ***EEOC v. Marvin's Fresh Farmhouse, Inc.*, No. 1:10-cv-00818 (M.D.N.C. consent decree filed February 24, 2011).**

- In May 2010, an apartment management company paid $90,000 in monetary relief and agreed to provide affirmative relief to settle an EEOC lawsuit alleging that the company violated Title VII by firing a White manager in retaliation for hiring a Black employee in contravention of a directive by one of the owners to maintain a "certain look" in the office, which did not include African Americans. Pursuant to the 3-year consent decree, the company is enjoined from engaging in retaliation or racial discrimination and required to implement a written anti-discrimination policy. The company also must provide equal employment opportunity training for all of its employees and post a remedial notice. **EEOC v. Management Solutions, Inc., No. SA09CA0655XR (W.D. Tex. May 7, 2010).**

- In June 2009, a restaurant, which was accused of creating a hostile work environment for Black, White, and female employees, settled an EEOC lawsuit for $500,000 and specific relief. According to the lawsuit, White employees were harassed because of their association with Black coworkers and family members, including being referred to as "n----r lovers" and "race traitors" by White managers. Additionally, Black workers were terminated because of their race, female workers were subjected to a sex-based hostile work environment, which included male managers making sexual advances and calling them gender-related epithets such as "b-----s," and all complainants suffered retaliation for reporting the discrimination. ***EEOC v. Fire Mountain Restaurants LLC, d/b/a Ryan's Family Steakhouse,*** **No. 5:08-cv-00160-TBR (W.D. Ky. June 15, 2009).**

- In February 2009, the Sixth Circuit published a favorable decision in a Title VII associational discrimination case in which the EEOC participated as amicus curiae. According to the lawsuit, three White workers at the Whirlpool plant in LaVergne, TN, witnessed numerous instances of racial hostility and slurs directed at their Black coworkers. Because they maintained friendly relationships with, and engaged in various acts of advocacy on behalf of, their Black coworkers, they became targets of various threats and harassment by other White employees who were responsible for the racial hostility directed against their Black colleagues. The hostile conduct ranged from "cold shoulder" type behavior to the use of the term "nigger lover," references to the KKK, and direct threats on their lives, as well as being told to "stay with their own kind." The Sixth Circuit Court of Appeals affirmed in part, reversed in part, and remanded the district court's decision granting summary judgment to the defendant on the White plaintiffs' Title VII claims alleging that they were subjected to a racially hostile work environment based on their association with their Black coworkers. Agreeing with the position taken by the Commission as amicus curiae, the court of appeals held that there is no prerequisite degree or type of association between two individuals of different races in order to state a claim for associational discrimination or harassment, so long as the plaintiff can show that she was discriminated against because of her association with a person of a different race. The court of appeals also held that no particular degree or type of advocacy on behalf of individuals of a different race is required to state an associational discrimination claim based on this theory, again, so long as a plaintiff can show that she was discriminated against based on her advocacy on behalf of such individuals. ***Barrett v. Whirlpool Corp.*, No. 556 F.3d 502, 515 (6th Cir. 2009).**

- In March 2008, a wholesaler book company settled an EEOC lawsuit alleging that it violated Title VII when the owner verbally harassed a White female employee after he learned she had biracial children such as stating that they were "too dark to be hers." The suit also alleged that the owner made sex- and race-based insults to a class of other employees and retaliated against them when they complained or cooperated with the EEOC's investigation. The settlement included a donation of $10,000 value of books or 1,000 books relevant to the EEOC's mission, which will be given to a nonprofit organization with an after-school program. ***EEOC v. Books for Less,* C.A. No. 06-4577 (E.D.N.Y. Mar. 10, 2008).**
- In July 2007, the EEOC sued a steakhouse restaurant chain for permitting its customers to harass a White employee because of her association with persons of a different race. The case settled for $75,000 and injunctive relief which included mandatory EEO training for managers, supervisors, and employees. ***EEOC v. Ponderosa Steakhouse,* No. 1:06-cv-142-JDT-TAB (S.D. Ind. settled July 3, 2007).**
- In May 2006, the EEOC settled a hostile work environment case against a retail furniture store chain for $275,000. The store manager allegedly made racially and sexually offensive remarks to a Black employee, referred to the African Americans as "you people" and interracial couples as "Oreos" or "Zebras," and disparaged the employee for marrying a Caucasian man. ***EEOC v. R.T.G. Furniture Corp.,* No. 8:04-cv-T24-TBM (M.D. Fla. May 16, 2006).**
- In April 2006, the Commission resolved a race discrimination lawsuit challenging the termination of a White female employee who worked without incident for a hotel and conference center until management saw her biracial children. ***EEOC v. Jax Inn's/ Spindrifter Hotel,* No. 3:04-cv-978-J-16-MMH (M.D. Fla. April 2006).**
- In January 2004, the Commission affirmed an AJ's finding that complainant was subjected to associational race discrimination (African American who associates with White employees). The record showed that complainant had a close working relationship with White managers, which the selecting official held against her because of her race. The record evidence showed that the selecting official's actions in not choosing complainant for the position were intended to show the White managers that they were not running the region, and that he had a philosophy of rewarding African American employees who aligned themselves with him instead of those, like complainant, who aligned themselves with White managers. ***Wiggins v. Social Security Administration,* EEOC Appeal No. 07A30048 (January 22, 2004).**

Biracial Discrimination

- In April 2007, a Virginia steel contractor settled for $27,500 a Title VII lawsuit, charging that it subjected a biracial (Black/White) employee to harassment based on race and color and then retaliated against him when he complained. ***EEOC v. Bolling Steel Co.*, Civ. Action No. 7:06-000586 (W.D. Va. April 25, 2007).**

- In March 2004, the EEOC settled a hostile work environment case in which a Caucasian-looking employee, who had a White mother and Black father, was repeatedly subjected to racially offensive comments about Black people after a White coworker learned she was biracial. When the employee complained, she was told to "pray about it" or "leave" by the owner; the employee resigned. The company agreed to pay $45,000 to the biracial employee, to create a policy on racial harassment, and to train the owner, managers, and employees about how to prevent and address race discrimination in the workplace. ***EEOC v. Jefferson Pain & Rehabilitation Center*, No. 03-cv-1329 (W.D. Pa. settled March 10, 2004).**

Code Words

- In January 2017, Gonnella Baking Co. of Chicago, an established bread and rolls manufacturer, agreed to pay $30,000 to settle an EEOC lawsuit alleging racial harassment at the company's Aurora, IL, facility. According to the EEOC's complaint, Gonnella violated federal law by allegedly failing to respond adequately to a Black employee's complaints that he endured a pervasive pattern of disparaging racial comments made by his coworkers. Examples of the harassing conduct included persistent coded references to Black employees as "you people," as well as offensive statements such as, "Black people are lazy," and "I better watch my wallet around you." As part of the consent decree, Gonnella must also provide training to its employees on civility in the workplace and must institute a policy holding managers and supervisors responsible for preventing and stopping harassment in the workplace. ***EEOC v. Gonnella Baking Co.*, Civil Action No. 15-cv-4892 (N.D. Ill. consent decree filed Jan. 10, 2017).**

- In July 2010, Area Temps, Inc., a northeast Ohio temporary labor agency, agreed to pay $650,000 to resolve an EEOC lawsuit alleging that the company engaged in a systematic practice of considering and assigning (or rejecting) job applicants by race, sex, Hispanic national origin and age. The EEOC said that Area Temps used code words to describe its clients and applicants for discriminatory purposes, such as "chocolate cupcake" for young African American women, "hockey player" for young White males, "figure skater" for White females, "basketball player" for Black males, and "small hands" for women in general. ***EEOC v. Area Temps*, No. 1:07-cv-02964 (N.D. Ohio consent decree filed July 21, 2010).**

- In April 2011, the EEOC affirmed an agency's final decision because the preponderance of the evidence of record did not establish that discrimination occurred. Complainant had filed a formal EEO complaint alleging he was subjected to discriminatory harassment while in Iraq on the basis of his race (African American) when, among other things, the word "DAN" was used by a coworker, which he learned meant "Dumb Ass Nigger," and management took no action. The evidence of record established, however, that the "DAN" comment was unlikely used in complainant's presence as he could not recall who said it and he conceded it was not directed at him. He also said he did not know what it meant until another employee told him and did not report the comment to management. Instead, another employee informed complainant's supervisor about the comment, and the supervisor promptly looked into the matter. When the supervisor was unable to establish who made the comment, he convened all the welders and threatened disciplinary action if the term was used again. There was no evidence that the term or any other racial epithet was used after this meeting. ***Battle v. McHugh*, 2011 EEOPUB LEXIS 1063, EEOC Appeal No. 0120092518 (Apr. 27, 2011).**

- In July 2010, one of the largest temporary placement agencies in the Greater Cleveland area agreed to pay $650,000 to settle an employment discrimination lawsuit brought by the EEOC. The EEOC alleged that the temp agency violated federal law by matching workers with companies' requests for people of a certain race, age, gender, and national origin and illegally profiling applicants according to their race and other demographic information using code words to describe its clients and applicants. The code words at issue included "chocolate cupcake" for young African American women, "hockey player" for a young White male, "figure skater" for White females, "basketball player" for Black males, and "small hands" for females in general. ***EEOC v. Area Temps, Inc.*, No. 1:07-cv-2964 (N.D. Ohio July 21, 2010).**

- In December 2009, a national restaurant chain settled a racial harassment lawsuit brought by the EEOC for $1.26 million and significant remedial relief in a case alleging repeated racial harassment of 37 Black workers at the company's Beachwood, OH, location. In its lawsuit, the EEOC charged that Bahama Breeze managers committed numerous and persistent acts of racial harassment against Black employees, including frequently addressing Black staff with slurs such as "n….r," "Aunt Jemima," "homeboy," "stupid n….r," and "you people." Additionally, managers allegedly imitated what they perceived to be the speech and mannerisms of Black employees and denied them breaks while allowing breaks to White employees. Despite the employees' complaints to management, the alleged race-based harassment continued. The 3-year consent decree resolving the litigation contains significant injunctive relief requiring Bahama Breeze to update its EEO policies nationwide, provide anti-discrimination and diversity training to its managers and employees, and provide written reports regarding discrimination complaints. ***EEOC v. GMRI, Inc. d/b/a Bahama Breeze*, 1:08-cv-2214 (N.D. Ohio Dec. 11, 2009).**

- In September 2007, the EEOC filed a Title VII racial harassment case against a food and beverage distributor, alleging that the company subjected a Black employee to a racially hostile work environment when a coworker repeatedly called him "Cornelius" in reference to an ape character from the movie, *Planet of the Apes*. Management officials were aware of the term's racially derogatory reference to the employee and an ape character from the movie, but terminated his employment once he objected to the racial harassment. In May 2009, the district court ruled that the distributor was not liable for racial harassment or retaliation under Title VII because the employer took prompt and remedial action once it was notified of the racial slur and because it terminated the employee misconduct, not because he opposed race discrimination. ***EEOC v. Dairy Fresh Foods, Inc.*, No. 2:07CV14085 (E.D. Mich. May 29, 2009).**

- In August 2007, a San Jose body shop agreed to pay $45,000 to settle a sexual and racial harassment lawsuit filed by the EEOC, in which a male auto body technician of Chinese and Italian ancestry was taunted daily by his foreman with sexual comments, racial stereotypes, and code words, including calling him "Bruce Lee." The company also agreed to establish an internal complaint procedure, disseminate an anti-harassment policy, and train its workforce to prevent future harassment. ***EEOC v. Monterey Collision Frame and Auto Body, Inc.*, No. 5:06-cv-06032-JF (N.D. Cal. consent decree filed August 30, 2007).**

- In August 2007, the Commission settled for $44,000 a lawsuit against a California medical clinic, alleging that a White supervisor used racial code words, such as "reggin" ("nigger" spelled backward), to debase and intimidate an African American file clerk and then fired her after she complained. The clinic also agreed to incorporate a zero-tolerance policy concerning discriminatory harassment and retaliation into its internal EEO and anti-harassment policies. ***EEOC v. Robert G. Aptekar, M.D., d/b/a Arthritis & Orthopedic Medical Clinic*, Civ. No. C06-4808 MHP (N.D. Cal. consent decree filed Aug. 20, 2007).**

- In March 2006, the Commission obtained $562,470 in a Title VII lawsuit against the eighth largest automobile retailer in the U.S. The EEOC alleged that shortly after a new White employee was transferred to serve as the new General Manager (GM), he engaged in disparate treatment of the Black employee and made racial remarks to him, such as using "BP time" (Black people time) and remarking that he'd fired "a bunch of you people already." The new GM also berated the personnel coordinator for assisting the Black employee with his complaint and intensified his harassment of him until the employee resigned. The 4-year consent decree prohibits defendants from engaging in future discrimination based on race, color, or national origin. ***EEOC v. Lithia Motors, Inc., d/b/a Lithia Dodge of Cherry Creek*, No. 1:05-cv-01901 (D. Colo. March 8, 2006).**

CHAPTER TAKEAWAYS

- There are significant financial and emotional costs to lack of diversity mindfulness and inclusion.
- Private and federal organizations were liable for workplace discrimination in the amount of $297.6 million between the years 2002–2020 as reported by the U.S. Equal Employment Opportunity Commission (EEOC)'s Educating Racism and Colorism from Employment (E-RACE).

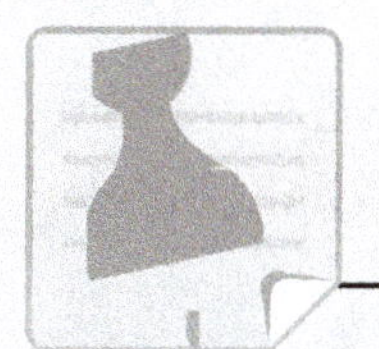

APPLICATION EXERCISES

The purpose of this exercise is to reflect upon alternatives to the financial costs of diversity mindfulness and inclusion. Part one is an individual exercise. Individuals form a group in part two to experience Diversity of Perspectives about the alternative to the financial costs.

PART I

1. Select one or more tables in the chapter to use the dollar amounts.
2. Multiply the total dollar amount times 20% to create a single virtual budget amount.
3. Identify five existing charitable nonprofit organizations to receive the virtual money.
4. Determine the amount of funds to distribute to each organization.

PART II

1. Form groups using randomly selected individuals.
2. Individuals in the group each share their charitable nonprofit organization and why they should receive the money.
3. Work together to make a final decision on distributing the money from the chapter.

PART II

- Write a brief reflection paper about how individual Diversity of Perspectives were communicated during the decision-making process for the final distribution of the funds.

CHAPTER 4

Defining Diversity of Perspectives

OVERVIEW

Organizational Diversity of Perspectives
Chapter Takeaways
Application Exercise

Diversity of Perspectives is the ability to have empathy for others through self-awareness, knowledge, choice, accountability, and new experiences. This ability contributes to positive environments while working with others who may or may not look, think, or act like you. Diversity of Perspectives can also contribute to accomplishing personal and professional goals. "Whatever it is that you want to accomplish in life, other people are probably needed to provide some thrust in support of your efforts" (Burtis & Turman, 2010, p. 7). Diversity of Perspectives contributes to effectively working with groups of people accomplishing organizational goals. "*Grouping* is people bending and blending their ideas and energies so that they can accomplish something together" (Burtis & Turman, 2010, p. 7). You bring your individual values, assumptions, beliefs, and expectations to the group. Working with a *growth mindset* (Burtis & Turman, 2010) is an opportunity to learn different ways of accomplishing organizational goals from others who may or may not look, think, or act like you.

Chapter One stated you may currently be a member of an organization as a student, adult learner, intern, entry-level, employee, manager, or leader. Now imagine working together using Diversity of Perspectives within a citizenship concept (Burtis & Turman, 2010). Organizations are comprised of people who exhibit diverse behaviors of "doer, follower, guide, manager, and leader" (Burtis & Turman, 2010, p. 14). "All grouping members play a part in giving direction to and in receiving direction from others in the group regardless of whether they are the supervisor, chairperson, president, head honcho, or prince of particularly pertinent personnel" (Burtis & Turman, 2010, p. 13). Table 4.1 identifies the roles of each behavior. The organizational citizenship concept is related to Diversity of Perspectives, because it suggests that direction giving is at every level of any organization. This implies it includes every profit and nonprofit organization providing products and services to its customers. Doers, followers, guides, managers, and leaders are direction-givers at every level of any organization.

TABLE 4.1 Defining Organizational Citizenship Roles

Role	Description
Doer	A **doer** offers direction to a group by taking the initiative to act on behalf of the group.
Follower	A **follower** offers direction to a group by providing support for the direction-giving attempt of another person.
Guide	A **guide** offers direction to a group by providing something on which the group can focus its attention for the moment.
Manager	A **manager** has the formal responsibility and authority to offer direction by attempting to marshal the resources of the group. A **manager** offers direction to a group from a position of formal authority over others in the group. The manager uses that authority to marshal some of the resources of the group (e.g., group process, personnel, budget, or supplies; the record of the group's decision-making; the group's agenda and/or long-term plans; and/or other resource(s).
Leader	A **leader** offers a transformative vision for the future of a group facing its own end. A leader (if a group has one) articulates the hopes and dreams of a group in crisis.

NOTE: Burtis, J. O., & Turman, P. D. (2010), pp. 14, 18.

Providing and receiving direction through mindfulness and inclusion while learning about others who do not look, think, or act like you is an overall benefit to any organization in times of normalcy, innovation, or crises. Behaviors of mindfulness and inclusion are critical in inspiring group members to feel welcome to participate in an organization. This should lead to individual confidence in providing input to help achieve organizational goals. Discussions will certainly have diverse perspectives but that should enrich group achievement.

Relationship building using Diversity of Perspectives is needed for innovation or unexpected crises. When innovation opportunities or crises occur, effective working relationships should have already been formed. When crises happen, it is not the time to start building working relationships. Preparation for Workforce 2030 is an opportunity to learn about others before future innovation opportunities or unexpected crises occur during that time period. For example, if you are president of your fraternity or sorority or the chief executive officer of a major corporation, you are typically considered a **leader**. If you are the treasurer of a student organization or vice president of finance in the workforce, you are typically considered to marshal resources (**manager**). When presented with organizational goals, **guides** are a beacon for others toward achieving accomplishments. **Followers** are unique in the citizenship model, because they influence others through demonstrating they either accept or reject paths toward achieving organizational results. When it comes to organizational effectiveness, **followers** exhibit the leadership trait of influence. Their behavior is observed by others in the organization who may or may not choose to follow the leader. This is another reason why building relationships using Diversity of Perspectives may benefit the work environment in individual decision-making during innovation opportunities and crises.

Earlier it was discussed that Workforce 2030 will be comprised of people of color who will become the majority, and this is a shift in the status quo working environment. It was also discussed that the ultimate human equalizer is 168 hours a week. Change is emotional; change requires heavy lifting; and change that does not sustain is a waste of time. Sustainable change goals should be intentional and with respect for people's time. Do you personally have a plan to adapt to this workforce change regardless of your organizational level? If you are a positional leader, do you have an organizational plan to adapt to change of a working environment that may or not be the same as the current? Kotter (1996) argues, "New initiatives fail far too often when employees, even though they embrace a new vision, feel disempowered by huge obstacles in their path" (p. 10). During this unique time in our world history, everyone really has an opportunity to overcome obstacles with positive intent toward achievable, sustainable change. This book will continue with how Diversity of Perspectives may help overcome obstacles to change for Workforce 2030 that is imminent.

Workforce 2030 is a major change. Kotter (1996) states "Major change is usually impossible unless most employees are willing to help, often to the point of making short-term sacrifices" (p. 9). We have discussed that it does not matter whether you are currently in the workforce. If you are reading this book, it is possible that inevitably you will be working. You currently have an opportunity to prepare for Workforce 2030 as a current student, adult learner, intern, entry-level, employee, manager, or leader that may be a doer, follower, guide, manager, and leader at any level of your organization. How will you adjust to the changing workforce? How will you contribute to help achieve organizational change of a more diverse and inclusive community? Workforce 2030 change may be a challenge for some existing companies. However, internal and external circumstances often cause the need for organizational change. Regardless of the circumstances, change shifts the comfort of the status quo, often causing individuals to resist and make it difficult for any organization to achieve a successful outcome. Gilley et al. (2008) found that "one-third to two-thirds of major change initiatives are deemed failures . . . the rate of failure to deliver sustainable change at times reaches 80–90%" (p. 153). However, this does not have to be the outcome when using a Diversity of Perspectives change readiness approach focused on willingness. When you "begin with the end in mind" (Covey, 2007) to achieve sustainable change, individuals and organizations position themselves to be ready to receive future opportunities and navigate crises that may result from a diverse workforce. Table 4.2 displays willingness categories within the Diversity of Perspectives model. It includes willingness to develop, listen, understand, communicate, learn, change, commit, develop an Individual Development Plan, be personally vulnerable when working with others, and keep trying to work with others. Chapters Five through Eight will discuss the willingness categories of self-awareness, knowledge, choice, accountability, and new experiences.

TABLE 4.2 Diversity of Perspectives: Nomenclature for Mindfulness and Inclusion

	SELF-AWARENESS—*Foundation: What we bring* ► Willingness to develop **KNOWLEDGE**—*Diversity: What we learn* ► Willingness to listen ► Willingness to understand ► Willingness to communicate **CHOICE—Actualization:** *What we decide* ► Willingness to learn ► Willingness to change ► Willingness to commit ► Willingness to develop a Personal Development Plan **ACCOUNTABILITY** ► Willingness to be personally vulnerable when working with others **NEW EXPERIENCES** ► Willingness to keep trying to work with others

In this current time in our history of sensitivity, it is especially important to implement change with mindfulness. People may experience a range of emotions like joy, sorrow, like, fear, and hate during organizational change from the status quo. A mindful approach is one that is respectful of others and intended to navigate planned organizational change that is peaceful, thoughtful, meaningful, measurable, and sustainable. Workforce 2030 should be considered planned organizational change supported by organizations and the following illuminates a way forward.

Organizational Diversity of Perspectives

Earlier you were asked how you would adjust to a changing workforce regardless of what level you were in any organization. The following may provide insight about changing diversity in the workforce although more information will be the focus of Chapters Five through Eight. When we think of an organization, we often imagine it has to have a leader. However, you have learned that leadership is at every level of any organization. Regardless of your leadership level, "leaders also need to break out of the comfort zone and develop relationships with different people, including physical, biological, political, socioeconomic, functional, and cultural differences" (Cote, 2017, p. 61). To further explain the benefit of Diversity of Perspectives in organizations, it is a formal structure that includes a positional leader who is responsible for vision. Their vision should incorporate diversity as the workforce continues to shift toward majority people of color.

Traditional vision statements developed without shared input from people who are responsible for outcomes are merely followed because of compliance (Kopaneva, 2019). This mindset presents an organizational challenge for Workforce 2030. Inclusion is the alternative. "Leaders must ensure visions are connected to the values and beliefs of others and that influences and opinions from others are incorporated into the visioning process to attract commitment and action" (Sethi & Adhikari, 2012, p. 44). A diverse workforce will have differing values, beliefs, expectations, and assumptions. Learning differing individual perspectives is one way leaders can demonstrate they value and respect workers. Transcending learned knowledge about diverse perspectives and relating its benefit to shared outcomes may result in worker synergy and commitment toward intended organizational goals. "Vision is perceived as an inspiring, motivating, and guiding force that defines the direction for change and inspires organizational members' efforts toward overcoming reluctance to embrace it" (Hague et al., 2016, p. 984). Leaders inspire workers to be motivated within to accomplish intentional organizational goals. "People are intrinsically motivated when the principal reason for their effort at work is that they find the work itself exciting, challenging, fulfilling, interesting and energizing. It is not controlled or mediated by someone else. Effective leaders strive to create an environment that is intrinsically motivating" (Kulkarni, 2015, p. 77). Chapter Two discussed definitions of culture, and leaders need to pay particular attention to cultural diversity as we journey toward Workforce 2030. "Culture is a phenomenon that surrounds us all, culture defines leadership, and to understand the *culture* is to understand the organization" (Calvin, 2015, p. 9). Culture is at the center of a changing workforce.

Leaders who are mindful about inclusiveness establish cultures that increase willingness to contribute diverse perspectives resulting in healthy work environments (Seah & Hsieh, 2015). This is especially needed during times of change like Workforce 2030. "Inclusiveness gets everyone's voices heard and is essential to getting the best of an organization's people. It encourages a culture of ownership of the mission and strategy and emboldens people to take initiative" (Bates & Atkins, 2017, p. 225). The imminent reality of Workforce 2030 will impact every worker or customer of any profit or nonprofit organization. This will result in individual mindsets about diversity that create new experiences where "taking on something new largely means giving up something else that is familiar, comfortable, and predictable" (Bruckman, 2008, p. 214). People with limited or no experience with human diversity will be impacted more significantly. Leaders should expect that some people may be resistant to the reality of a changing workforce.

> Employees play the role of change recipient and are affected the most by change initiatives. Their response to change—acceptance or resistance—is critical in affecting its success. Incorporating employees' participation in change efforts leads to lower resistance and greater potential for success. (Yanchus et al., 2015, p. 74)

Any opportunity to incorporate Diversity of Perspectives in a changing workforce should enable individuals to be respected for their contributions and result in organizational success. Leaders should begin now preparing workers for change readiness so they will "be more likely to positively contribute to the growth of an organization" (Hague et al., 2016, p. 992). The next chapter begins the discussion about each section of Diversity of Perspectives as a change readiness model of mindfulness and inclusion.

CHAPTER TAKEAWAYS

- Diversity of Perspectives is the ability to have empathy for others through self-awareness, knowledge, choice, accountability, and new experiences. This ability contributes to positive environments while working with others who may or may not look, think, or act like you.
- Diversity of Perspectives can also contribute to accomplishing personal and professional goals.
- Working with a *growth mindset* (Burtis & Turman, 2010) is an opportunity to learn about different ways of accomplishing organizational goals from others who may or may not look, think, or act like you.
- Organizations are comprised of people who exhibit diverse behaviors of "doer, follower, guide, manager, and leader" (Burtis & Turman, 2010, p. 14). "All grouping members play a part in giving direction to and in receiving direction from others in the group regardless of whether they are the supervisor, chairperson, president, head honcho, or prince of particularly pertinent personnel" (Burtis & Turman, 2010, p. 13).
- Providing and receiving direction through mindfulness and inclusion while learning about others who do not look, think, or act like you is an overall benefit to any organization in times of normalcy, innovation, or crises.
- Relationship building using Diversity of Perspectives is needed for innovation or unexpected crises. When innovation opportunities or crises arrive, effective working relationships should have already been formed. When crises happen, it is not the time to start building working relationships. Preparation for Workforce 2030 is an opportunity to learn about others before future innovation opportunities or unexpected crises occur during that time period.
- Change is emotional; change requires heavy lifting; and change that does not sustain is a waste of time. Sustainable change goals should be intentional and with respect for people's time.

- During this unique time in our world history, everyone really has an opportunity to overcome obstacles with a positive intent toward achievable, sustainable change.
- Workforce 2030 change may be a challenge for some existing companies. However, internal and external circumstances often cause the need for organizational change. Regardless of the circumstances, change shifts the comfort of the status quo, often causing individuals to resist and make it difficult for any organization to achieve a successful outcome.
- When you "begin with the end in mind" (Covey, 2007)to achieve sustainable change, individuals and organizations position themselves to be ready to receive future opportunities and navigate crises that may result from a diverse workforce.
- Table 4.2 displays willingness categories within the Diversity of Perspectives model. It includes (1) willingness to develop, listen, understand, communicate, learn, change, commit, develop an Individual Development Plan, be personally vulnerable when working with others, and keep trying to work with others to be mindful; (2) willingness to listen; (3) willingness to communicate; (4) willingness to change; (5) willingness to commit; and (6) willingness to develop a Personal Development Plan.
- In this current time in our history of sensitivity, it is especially important to implement change with mindfulness. People may experience a range of emotions like joy, sorrow, like, fear, and hate during organizational change from the status quo. A mindful approach is one that is respectful of others and intended to navigate planned organizational change that is peaceful, thoughtful, meaningful, measurable, and sustainable.
- Inclusion is the alternative to traditional vision statements that are developed without shared input from people who are responsible for the outcome. This mindset presents an organizational challenge for Workforce 2030.
- Transcending learned knowledge about diverse perspectives and relating its benefit to shared outcomes may result in worker synergy and commitment toward intended organizational goals.
- Leaders inspire workers to be motivated within to accomplish intentional organizational goals.
- Culture is at the center of a changing workforce.
- People with limited or no experience with human diversity will be impacted more significantly. Leaders should expect that some people may be resistant to the reality of a changing workforce.
- Any opportunity to incorporate Diversity of Perspectives in a changing workforce should enable individuals to be respected for their contributions and result in organizational success.

APPLICATION EXERCISE

- Write another one-page paper about a personal experience working alongside someone who did not look, think, or act like you. Reflect upon the concepts in Table 4.2 to (a) describe one *willingness* situation, (b) the situation that required you to work together, (c) whether you were willing to work together, (d) why or why not, and (e) the outcome that required you to work together.

CHAPTER 5

Self-Awareness

OVERVIEW

A Personal Lifelong Journey
Foundation: What We Bring
Mindfulness and Our Brains
Change, Diversity, and Our Brains
Willingness to Listen
Building and Sustaining Confidence
Chapter Takeaways
Application Exercises

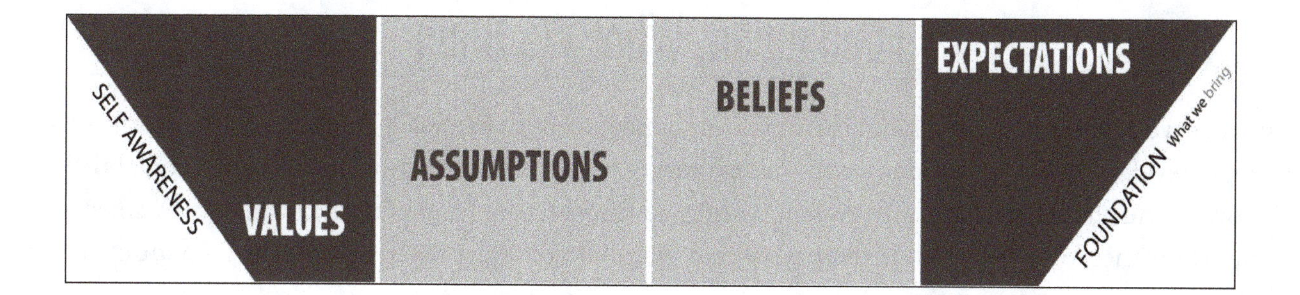

A Personal Lifelong Journey

The focus up to this point has been on the reality of Workforce 2030, defining Diversity of Perspectives, and credible outcomes of workplace behavior that is emotionally and financially costly. The idea that a single person can change the behavioral choices of an organization toward mindfulness and inclusion is nearly impossible. However, perhaps it can actually begin with the behavioral choices of one person that leads to other people changing (Black & Gregersen, 2014).

This chapter begins the discussion of the Diversity of Perspectives model and how it relates to a personal lifelong journey. The essence of communication is mindfulness and inclusion. Mindfulness begins with you! It is a challenge to be mindful of others when you do not possess self-awareness. How can you be empathetic with others if you do not have a clear focus of who you are? Ask yourself the following question using the Diversity of Perspectives model: Who am I? Your reflection for a response to this question is the first step toward your ability to be mindful and inclusive on your journey toward Workforce 2030. It begins with you, because you have a personal lifelong journey that is uniquely you. It began prior to reading this book and will continue until the end of your life. Are you ready to put in the work necessary for self-awareness?

Self-awareness begins with embracing the personal journey that has shaped your values, assumptions, beliefs, and expectations in life. This foundation is what you bring to any organization and workplace on day one. A growth mindset (Aidman & Long, 2017; Black & Gregersen, 2014) will strengthen the foundation of personal values, assumptions, beliefs, and expectations that you continue to *bring* to future organizations and workplaces. Your foundation of self-awareness is considered a significant contribution the first day of joining any organization or workplace. Life is so busy sometimes that we do not make the time to reflect upon our brand identity (Brown, 2021) that we learned about in Chapter One. You will get the opportunity to continue developing your Individual Development Plan as it relates to your brand identity in the Application Exercises section at the end of this chapter. The following provides ways to reflect upon your foundation of self-awareness.

Foundation: What We Bring

Earlier we discussed that lifelong learning is an opportunity to achieve personal growth and professional development. We also discussed that exploring your mindset may reveal strengths and abilities to overcome challenges encountered in a journey toward personal and professional goals. A constant important theme in this book is the reality that whether you are a first-year college student or have been in your career for several years, you can experience personal growth and professional development while reading this book and participating in application exercises about human diversity at the end of each chapter. This is a great time for you to "begin with the end in mind" (Covey, 2007, p. 48) as you continue developing your Individual Development Plan at the end of this chapter. Let's begin with you envisioning your personal foundation by reflecting upon things in life that you know and seek to discover what shaped your thoughts. Furthermore, does your thinking about values, assumptions, beliefs, and expectations in life match your actions?

The imminent Workforce 2030 will certainly bring about new changes in working with others who may not look, think, or act like you. Instead of waiting until that experience occurs, begin to personally examine your personal foundation and how it may contribute to a positive work environment. Do not delay your reflection until a leader of an organization decides to implement change through training initiatives like diversity, inclusion, and so forth. Begin now focusing on yourself as you prepare for the imminent changes. Perhaps you are currently in a leadership position or have it listed as a goal in your Individual Development Plan. You may recall that employers state they seek candidates with the equity and inclusion competency when hiring (NACE, 2021). A strong self-awareness with a growth mindset of lifelong learning will enable you to meet the needs of Workforce 2030 interpersonal relationships. Beginning with a focus on individual development may help you understand others through empathy as they are also adjusting to a changing workforce. Each person contributes to organizational success and deserves to be respected for their individual contributions and overcoming challenges throughout change. Your individual reflection and lifelong learning about your personal foundation may provide you the ability to help others navigate change. Perhaps you will be the one to understand why some people are hesitant about Workforce 2030 and help them navigate the changing workforce (Black & Gregersen, 2014). Don't wait for the organization to announce the workforce is changing. You may sense change and be the one that is ready and can help others navigate change.

Mindfulness and Our Brains

At the beginning of this book, a maximum 168 hours a week was discussed as a human equalizer. Another reality is that we are all born with a brain to help us navigate the functions of being a human being. This section of the book is respectfully credited to the neuroanatomist Dr. Jill Bolte Taylor who had a stroke at the age of 37. Her TED Talk in 2013 was about the human brain and is related to the Self-Awareness section of the Diversity of Perspectives model because it helps to explain why people think and act differently (Taylor, 2013).

Taylor (2013) states that "The brain cells you were born with are the brain cells you'll die with." Human beings are born with a brain which is a physiological mind filled with cells on a journey that results in only some of them surviving the developmental years. The remaining brain cells can look forward to adulthood. This is considered a very normal process of human development. However, it is important to respectfully acknowledge that all brains are not created equal. This means that some brains do not go through a normal development process and these are not the focus of this book. You should seek answers to questions about less than normal brain development from subject matter experts. This is not a book about normalcy of brain development; rather it is a book about the brain and its relationship to human beings and life experiences.

What makes us unique human beings as it relates to mindfulness is that our brain is still being developed during the early period in our life while our perspectives are beginning to take shape in the form of values, assumptions, beliefs, and expectations about our worldview. Each individual's uniqueness is the brain you are born with, the brain cells that survive, and the personal experiences you gain in early development and adulthood.

You may recall earlier in this book that there were two definitions of mindfulness. The first definition is "Mindfulness is a flexible state of mind in which we are actively engaged in the present, noticing new things and sensitive to context, with an open, nonjudgmental orientation to experience" (Langer, 1989, p. 220). The second definition is

> Mindfulness refers to an open state of mind where the leader's attention, informed by a sensitive awareness, merely observes what is taking place: worry about the future and negative ruminations or projections are brought back to the present moment where the situation is seen for what it is. (Roche et al., 2014, p. 477)

Mindfulness is essential while experiencing change toward Workforce 2030 when the majority will become people of color. The change is occurring right now, so it is not too soon to begin thinking about how to be mindful in the journey toward Workforce 2030. Taylor (2013) offers the following definition of mindfulness as it relates to our brain, and it may be a helpful tool while navigating in any aspect of change for Workforce 2030.

> We are capable of mindfulness . . . our ability to observe the neurocircuitry we are running inside of our heads. In addition to observing neurocircuitry, we are capable of changing our thought and changing our brains. We have the ability to pick and choose what's going on inside of our heads. We typically run three types of neurocircuitry: We think thoughts, we stimulate emotions and feel emotions, and we run physiological responses to what we are thinking and what we are feeling. I have the ability to think a thought, stimulate an emotional circuit, and then run a physiological response to what I am thinking. From the moment I think a thought that stimulates my anger circuit, to the time that I run my physiological response, where I dump noradrenalin into my blood stream, it flushes through me and flushes out of me. From the beginning of the thought to the time when my blood is clean of that chemistry takes less than 90 seconds. And I call this the 90-second rule. Staying angry is rethinking the thought, re-stimulating the anger circuit, which is re-stimulating the physiological response and we can stay mad for days. **I own my neurocircuitry.** You do not have the ability to stimulate and trigger my neurocircuitry without my permission. You cannot make me angry unless I stick my trigger out there for you to pounce on and stimulate my neurocircuitry. If I give you the power to stimulate my neurocircuitry, then I have given you my power. If give you my power, then I become vulnerable to you through manipulation, through advertising, through marketing, through peer pressure and through abuse. Bottom line is, we are neurocircuitry. We are this incredible celled brain filled with these beautiful cells.

We are biology. We are born with twice as many neurons as we are ever going to use. We are born with an abundance of cells. In the next 2 to 3 years, the neurons that are stimulated will connect with other neurons in neurocircuitry, and cells that are not stimulated will die away. (Taylor, 2013)

Change, Diversity, and Our Brains

Planned or unplanned change can be an experience of familiar or unfamiliar experiences. Some people may not manage their neurocircuitry to control challenging experiences during change. Other people may feel empowered by their neurocircuitry through sustaining control of it while navigating through change. Workforce 2030 will bring about some changes that are familiar. Other changes that are unfamiliar will result in personal choices to surrender your neurocircuitry through challenges or sustain empowerment of your neurocircuitry.

The following is a discussion about the brain when the surviving cells from early development are now functioning in adulthood. The cerebral cortex of our brain fuses when we become an adult about 25 years of age consisting of the ability for cognitive thinking and emotions (Taylor, 2013). This means that surviving cells process experiences as logical or emotional. A similar explanation is Toogood's (2010) description of the conscious mind and the primal mind. Taylor suggests our norm is a familiar logical state which is related to Toogood's description of the conscious mind. Taylor also suggests that unfamiliar change stimulates emotions of self-preservation which is related to Toogood's description of the primal mind. Finally, Taylor explains that the brain's **amygdala** is the information center that processes what is familiar and unfamiliar for the body to respond.

Based on this physiological state of the brain, each human being makes choices about how to navigate planned or unplanned changed. The information in this section is offered as a tool on the journey to Workforce 2030. If you know that other people's brains develop and have experiences differently than yours and use a mindful approach while working with others who do not look, think, or act like you, this may be your earliest contribution to positive results. Each person in the workforce is at a different stage of their lifelong journey. The way their unique brains were formed in early development and their unique experiences have shaped their worldview. The things they value are based upon their logical and emotional experiences. It would then make sense that their assumptions are probably based upon the outcome of previous experiences. Their beliefs stem from their cognitive, logical, conscious mindsets and can present challenges and opportunities while working together. As a result, their expectations in life may or may not align with yours due to the unique early development of your brain and experiences. Herein provides an opportunity to have a growth mindset of diversity and inclusion with mindfulness.

Edgar Schein (2004) suggests that a change in organizational culture illuminates beliefs and underlying assumptions within individuals. Schein states that "the most intriguing aspect of culture as a concept is that it points to phenomena that are below the surface, that are unconscious. In that sense culture is to a group what personality or character is to an individual" (p. 8). As we journey toward Workforce 2030 where individuals will be majority people of color, organizational culture will make a significant shift from the status quo. Culture is "a pattern of shared basic assumptions that was learned by a group as it solved its problems of external adaptation and internal integration that has worked well enough to be considered valid and, therefore, to be taught to new members as the correct way to perceive, think, and feel in relation to those problems" (Schein, 2004, p. 17).

The Self-Awareness section of the Diversity of Perspectives model includes values, beliefs, assumptions, and expectations. Schein (2004) asserts that "values are open to discussion ... but basic assumptions are so taken for granted that someone who does not hold them is viewed as a foreigner . . . and is automatically dismissed (p. 25). This will most definitely present a challenge to Workforce 2030 unless mindfulness and inclusion are central to understanding diversity of perspectives. Negative organizational interactions occur when "basic assumption comes to be strongly held in a group, members will find behavior based on any other premise inconceivable" (Schein, 2004, p. 31). As the journey toward Workforce 2030 continues and the minority people of color increases, this will inevitably be a specific change for the majority and their individual assumptions. Schein argues that "the human mind needs cognitive stability; therefore, any challenge or questioning of a basic assumption will release anxiety and defensiveness" (2004, p. 32). There will inevitably be challenges to individual assumptions throughout change toward Workforce 2030. This relates to the earlier discussion offered by Taylor (2013) and the brain's amygdala information center responding to familiar and unfamiliar changes. It also relates to Toogood (2010) and the surface level of the primal mind. According to Schein "if one does not decipher the pattern of basic assumptions that may be operating, one will not know how to interpret the artifacts correctly or how much credence to give the articulated values" (2004, p. 36). Artifacts are closely held beliefs by individuals that may be different than your own. This is why the more you get to know others that may or may not look, think, or act like you through mindfulness and willingness to listen, the more your neurocircuitry (Taylor, 2013) or primal mind (Toogood, 2010) will be able to navigate change toward a productive work environment.

Willingness to Listen

How do we listen and learn from others in the same community while navigating organizational change experiences? The following listening skills are important for effective communication at any level of every organization: Empathetic, appreciative, comprehensive, and critical. Diversity of Perspectives is an engagement model intended to inspire effective communication within organizations. The ability to communicate with others who have individual values, assumptions, beliefs, and expectations that may or may not be different from your own is crucial in the ever-growing global market. The vision and mission of an organization is *not* different for some employees. It is the intended purpose for which *all* are employed. Diversity exists in the workplace beyond federal protected classifications of race, gender, ethnicity, color of skin, religion, sexual orientation, disability, and so forth.

Individual values, assumptions, beliefs, and expectations also exist and contribute to organizational results. Differences and similarities help achieve desired organizational results. The ability to effectively communicate that diversity is personal, global, and a behavioral choice that directly connects to delivering products and services to customers is added value to any organization.

- **Empathetic**—Listening to provide emotional support for the speaker, as when a psychiatrist listens to a patient or when we lend a sympathetic ear to a friend in distress (Lucas, 2015, p. 49).
- **Appreciative**—Listening for pleasure or enjoyment, as when we listen to music, to a comedy routine, or to an entertaining speech (Lucas, 2015, p. 49).
- **Comprehensive**—Listening to understand the message of a speaker, as when we attend a classroom lecture or listen to directions for finding a friend's house (Lucas, 2015, p. 49).
- **Critical**—Listening to evaluate a message for purposes of accepting or rejecting it, as when we listen to the sales pitch of a car salesperson or the campaign speech of a political candidate (Lucas, 2015, p. 49).

The Chapter One discussion about brand identity directly relates to the Self-Awareness section of Diversity of Perspectives. Does your brand identify include a willingness to listen? Has listening and learning from others helped shape your values, assumptions, beliefs, and expectations? Do you continue to develop brand identity with a growth mindset and not be limited by your current self-awareness? The ability to embrace your foundation and feeling of empowerment through lifelong learning will help you transition through change from the status quo.

When others think of you, what stories will they tell about your brand identity? What stories will you tell?

> Stories are part of the fabric of the world, and are a portion of the inescapable human narratives that define and sustain us. With the telling of a story, a "person performs the self" evoking a sense of personal passion and sharing that links one person to another, inspiring self-reflection and a deeper consideration for the world and the systems that surround us. (Aidman & Long, 2017, p. 105)

Pereira (2019) suggests the following about brand storytelling:

> But story is not simply a mechanism that helps us to understand difficult situations outside our experience; it also serves as a safe space where we may practice interpersonal skills and learn to better navigate the world around us. . . . Research in cognitive psychology has shown that story also serves a vital function in allowing us to develop more empathy. (p. 147)

Building and Sustaining Confidence

Some people are not confident in their foundation in self-awareness of their values, beliefs, expectations, and assumptions. Others are confident, yet feel they must put in the work to sustain this confidence while adapting to ongoing changes at work. For example, Workforce 2030 will become a majority of people of color in the workforce. This unfamiliar experience will certainly require a growth mindset. A good starting point to this impending change is a positive beginning. Begin by feeling good about who you are at this stage in your life. Then accept that we are imperfect human beings that can always do better so we can be better.

We are not born self-aware of our values, assumptions, beliefs, and expectations that we bring into the workforce. It is learned through new experiences from the day we are born. Our environment helps shape our view of the world. Our imperfections as human beings are what bind us together for otherwise impossible outcomes. Instead of spending time proving ourselves, expend the energy bringing our foundation to others to create synergy that achieves far greater outcomes that one individual could make happen.

How to gain confidence? Begin by not being concerned with what others think about you. Rather, think about how you may work well with others who do not share your foundation of values, beliefs, assumptions, and expectations. Humans innately have a desire to be accepted in the workplace. For example, hiring, promotions, socializing, networking, and meeting job expectations to avoid being fired. These are all natural conditions of the workforce. When working with others, we often use the filter of our own values, assumptions, beliefs, and expectations. Empathy may be the remedy to working together. Before you can exhibit empathy for others, we must reflect upon our own values, assumptions, beliefs, and expectations. Propel yourself beyond a *fixed mindset* with mindfulness. It will not be easy for everyone. Kindness may be the necessary remedy while experiencing change. Workforce 2030 will be a challenge for many, but approaching it with kindness to coworkers may just be what creates synergy needed to produce goods and services for customers of any profit or nonprofit organization. Are you up for the challenge?

CHAPTER TAKEAWAYS

- The essence of communication is mindfulness and inclusion.
- Self-awareness begins with embracing the personal journey that has shaped your values, assumptions, beliefs, and expectations in life.
- A strong self-awareness with a *growth mindset* of lifelong learning will enable you to meet the needs of Workforce 2030 interpersonal relationships. Beginning with a focus on individual development may help you understand others through empathy as they are adjusting to a changing workforce. Each person contributes to organizational success and deserves to be respected for their individual contributions and overcoming challenges throughout change.
- Your individual reflection and lifelong learning about your personal foundation may provide you the ability to help others navigate change.
- Mindfulness is essential while experiencing change toward Workforce 2030 when the majority will be the minority people of color.
- What makes us unique human beings as it relates to mindfulness is that our brain is still being developed during the early period in our life while our perspectives are beginning to take shape in the form of values, assumptions, beliefs, and expectations about our worldview. Each individual's uniqueness is the brain you are born with, the brain cells that survive, and the personal experiences you gain in early development and adulthood.
- Planned or unplanned change can be an experience of familiar or unfamiliar experiences. Some people may permit their neurocircuitry to result in challenging experiences during change. Other people may be empowered by their neurocircuitry through sustaining control of it while navigating through change.
- The cerebral cortex of our brain fuses when we become an adult about 25 years of age consisting of the ability for cognitive thinking and emotions (Taylor, 2013). This means that surviving cells process experiences as logical or emotional.
- A similar explanation is Toogood's (2010) description of the conscious mind and the primal mind. Taylor (2008) suggests our norm is a familiar logical state of which is related to Toogood's description of the conscious mind. Taylor also suggests that unfamiliar change stimulates emotions of self-preservation which is related to Toogood's description of the primal mind.
- Each person in the workforce is at a different stage of their lifelong journey.

APPLICATION EXERCISES

Chapter Five focused on your personal foundation of values, assumptions, beliefs, and expectations that you bring to an organization the very first day. The following exercises enable you to continue developing your Individual Development Plan. It also enables you to demonstrate the competency of technology as defined by the National Association of Colleges and Employers (2021).

1. Return to Section II—Plan of your Individual Development Plan and begin to reflect upon development objectives. Identify what competencies you need to develop to strengthen confidence in your self-awareness. Identify specific resources needed (e.g., workshops, conferences, etc.). Can you think of any other activities that may help you build a stronger personal foundation of confidence? Complete this section of your Individual Development Plan.

2. Listening is one of the skills which potential employers often indicate as being critical to effective communication. Hence, many training programs and college classes provide instruction in listening. For many people, however, it is not a lack of skill that makes them a poor listener, it is their orientation toward listening. Some are just not willing to work at listening. They frequently claim (rightfully?) that they don't listen because of the poor communication skills of the speaker. Complete the **Willingness to Listen** self-assessment which is **Diversity of Perspectives • Toolkit 13.3**. This self-assessment is designed to measure your orientation to listening.

3. Earlier we discussed brand identity which is developed through self-awareness. No one knows you better than you know yourself. One way to reflect upon what has shaped your values, assumptions, beliefs, and expectations at this point in your life is personalized storytelling through words and images. Who are you and what is your brand identity based on the Diversity of Perspectives model? What is your *once upon a time* in storytelling? Create a 5-minute video of words, images, and music that communicate your brand identity as it relates to self-awareness.

CHAPTER 6

Knowledge

OVERVIEW

Lifelong Learning

The element of change is discomforting and not necessarily what is changing. Often it is the simple fact that things are changing into unfamiliar new ways that shift our norm. How is an entire workforce going to manage change if we are individual human beings with diverse perspectives? Tapping into our *growth mindset* of lifelong learning will enable us to learn about others and contribute to Workforce 2030.

In the previous chapter we discussed that people bring their personal values, assumptions, beliefs, and expectations into the workforce with them on day one. An organization of human beings has the opportunity to be accepting of one another and learn about coworkers' individual foundations of values, assumptions, beliefs, and expectations that may be similar or different than their own. This presents both growth and influence opportunities for each worker. Learning about coworkers' foundations may either reinforce or redefine what you personally brought to the organization on day one. You may recall the discussion in Chapter One about coexisting with diversity since birth. People are working longer, so multiple generations are often working alongside each other. This presents an opportunity for a *growth mindset* while approaching diversity with mindfulness. Even if you really believe you know everything, be open to the possibility that another person may know everything else while working alongside you.

Diversity matters at every level of any organization, because diverse perspectives that work together can achieve quality product and service outcomes. Lower-level position workers gain access to leadership knowledge and career opportunity. Senior-level position workers gain a perspective of meeting company goals and objectives that may not have existed when they entered the workforce. An opportunity for a win-win exists for those who embrace diversity of perspectives.

You may be thinking, alright I get it. Workforce 2030 is rapidly approaching when the majority will be people of color. You may even believe you already work well with others who do not look, think, or act like you. This may be true, but be cautious in your potential thinking that shifting workforce changes cannot bring new experiences that may impact relationships with existing or new coworkers. Chapter Two discussed the definitions of cultural, multicultural, and intercultural. We move forward with the discussion about ways to develop intercultural workplaces to prepare for Workforce 2030 and beyond. This is the opportunity to move from co-existing to thriving in an organization.

Diversity: What We Learn

One of the ways we can learn about diversity is by continuing to reflect upon how we respond to change. Are you willing to learn from others who do not look, think, or act like you? The answer to this question will help prepare you for the imminent changes of Workforce 2030. There was a lot of discussion in Chapter Five about the brain and how it responds to change. We learned about the brain's amygdala from Dr. Jill Bolte Taylor (2013) who also discusses how messages are sent to its hippocampus where we learn whether we are safe. Some people do not feel safe with change and prefer the status quo. There may have been a specific reason they came to work for the business and emotionally are not interested in external or internal changes. It may feel like a broken agreement or contract. For example, one may believe they logically agreed to work for a reason, the business agreed, and now the business is changing the persons' emotional state of work. In this example, the company is not changing the work; the work environment is changing due to the increase in people of color in the workforce. This is an external change to both the person and the business. Taylor (2013) and her "90-second rule" you learned about in Chapter Five may be a way to manage a person's disappointment of the changing workforce. You may also recall the Toogood (2010) discussion about the conscious mind (logical) versus the primal mind (emotional) in the same chapter.

As we continue the conscious mind versus primal mind discussions, we will explore the relationship between people and change through a leadership perspective. There are positional and unofficial leaders at every level of any organization. Leaders may find it difficult to implement change in organizations due to perceptions of the status quo. People become comfortable with their present status and should be introduced to change that sustains. A change that does not sustain may be viewed as a waste of time (168 hours a week). Therefore, organizational change must be viewed through the lens of workers who need to be inspired to be motivated within to change. The following information about Systems Thinking and mental models directly relate to the Diversity of Perspectives model. According to Senge et al. (1994):

> Mental models are the images, assumptions, and stories which we carry in our minds of ourselves, other people, institutions, and every aspect of the world. Like a pane of glass framing and subtly distorting our vision, mental models determine what we see. Human beings cannot navigate through the complex environments of our world without cognitive "mental maps"; and all of these mental maps, by definition, are flawed in some way. (p. 235)

This cognitive state or mental map is related to the surviving brain cells managed by the hippocampus that has learned how to work in your familiar environment (Taylor, 2013). The mental map is not the same for everyone in the same work environment and how they behave during change. Senge et al. (1994) continues by stating:

> Differences between mental models explain why two people can observe the same event and describe it differently; they are paying attention to different details. Mental models also shape how we act. For example, if we believe people are basically trustworthy, we may talk to new acquaintances far more freely than if we believe most people can't be trusted. (p. 236)

Individual experiences that may or may not be similar to others will determine how you behave during change. The primal mind of emotions becomes stirred when the brain's amygdala informs its hippocampus whether you are safe (Taylor, 2013; Toogood, 2020). Senge et al. (1994) provides the following advice for this change situation:

> But because mental models are usually *tacit,* existing below the level of awareness, they are often untested and unexamined. They are generally invisible to us—until we look for them. The core task of this discipline is bringing mental models to the surface, to explore and talk about them with

minimal defensiveness—to help us see the pane of glass, see its impact on our lives, and find ways to re-form the glass by creating new mental models that serve us better in the world. (p. 236)

Change is difficult, because it shifts the status quo. One way to participate in or inspire others while navigating change is by learning about behaviors during the experience. How do we think during change? How do we act during change? Leon deCaluwé and Hans Vermaak (2003) developed a Colors of Change self-assessment for how we think and act during change. Following are their definitions of each Color of Change:

- "Yellow print thinking assumes that people change their standpoints only if their own interests are taken into account or if you can compel them to accept certain ideas" (p. 42).
- "In blue-print thinking it is assumed that people or things will change if a clearly specified result is laid down beforehand" (p. 42).
- "Red-print thinking assumes that people and organizations will change if the right HRM (Human Resource Management) tools are employed and used correctly" (p. 43).
- "Green-print thinking . . . people change if they learn . . . are motivated to discover the limits of their competencies and to involve themselves in learning situations" (p. 43).
- "In white-print thinking, the dominant image is that everything is changing autonomously of its own accord" (p. 44).

When you take this self-assessment in the Application Exercises at the end of this chapter, you will be able to reflect upon times you have experienced change and whether you thought or acted similar to the above color description. You may find the Colors of Change helpful on the journey toward Workforce 2030 when the majority will be people of color.

Mindful Leadership During Change

Ultimately, the leader of an organization is responsible for the outcome of change. It is his or her relationship with workers in the organization that will determine change effectiveness. The ability to embrace diversity of perspectives on the journey to Workforce 2030 will define successful or unsuccessful change outcome. The following authors identify some things to consider.

Peterson (2016) states the following:

- "Having diversity of thought, approach and thinking, and being inclusive in making sure everyone feels they can make a meaningful contribution to the ultimate outcome, are some of the most important things that you as a leader can do" (p. 42).
- "World-class teams are both diverse in their perspectives and unified in sharing a common goal and purpose. The best leaders understand this and how to get the best out of each team member. But achieving this is tricky when dealing with people who have different views, perspectives, interests, motivations, personality types, experience and knowledge" (p. 43).

- "Engaging employees is challenging enough when everyone shares similar professional and personal experiences. But managers who lead teams of people with different personalities, cultures and backgrounds will struggle to fully understand each member" (p. 42).

Vangen (2017) states the following:

- " . . . culturally diverse insights, skills and experiences are in effect resources that can be brought to bear on a collaboration's tasks, enabling it to find new and alternative ways of addressing issues and producing collaborative advantage" (p. 308).
- "The current study, as well as extant research, suggests that learning how to work with cultural differences is important if collaboration is to yield advantage rather than inertia. The managers with whom I worked reflected on situations where the importance of understanding better their partners' cultural context and ways of working had been particularly apparent" (p. 315).
- " . . . each collaborative situation is, to varying degrees, distinctive in nature in its configuration of cultural 'communities of belonging.' Therefore, learning how to communicate and share understanding with others who have different 'ways of being' or 'worlds taken for granted' involves knowing how to manage the distinctive characteristics of each individual situation" (p. 316).

Parshakov et al. (2018) state the following:

- "First, speaking the same language in a team is beneficial to performance; however, a representative of another country might introduce a certain country-specific ability, which could also be beneficial, even though it increases language diversity. In other words, the benefits of diversity outweigh the drawbacks" (p. 5073).

Wang et al. (2016) state the following:

- "Cognitive diversity brings in a wide range of knowledge, skills, abilities, and ideas to the team that are distinct and non-redundant. Such a broad range of knowledge and abilities can then produce more new choices, plans, and products" (p. 3232).
- "When team members are exposed to the different preferences and opinions held by others, they must engage in systematic information processing, characterized by deeper and elaborate dissemination as well as integration of knowledge and information among team members. During this process, members may be inspired by one another and feel more competent in their team's ability to generate solutions to problems" (p. 3233).

Yusof et al. (2018) state the following:

- "Page (2008) stated that diversity in an organization trumped individual talent, allowing a group to solve complex problems in an innovative fashion. Progress and innovation might depend less on lone thinkers with enormous IQs than on diverse people working together and capitalizing on their individuality" (p. 43).

- "The influx of foreign students will dramatically change the landscape of higher institutions into a global village where each potential learner brings along her/his values, beliefs and culture against the backdrop of the existing multicultural background. This new reality demands renewed understanding of diversity engagement on campus among academe. To cater to such a diverse population, it becomes paramount that lecturers should not only be prepared with the appropriate knowledge of diverse issues, but also be well-equipped with skills to handle students with diverse personal, cultural and professional backgrounds" (p. 42).
- "Diversity in higher education would benefit students as they entered the workforce and the real world as they would be able to relate to perspectives other than their own. On the other hand, diversity also helped people to see things from different perspectives and to realize that there are many standards and perceptions. It helped to get rid of stereotypes and false beliefs; as the opportunity to work together with people with diverse cultures would enable oneself to learn about each other's backgrounds" (pp. 43–44).

Willingness to Communicate

Regardless of your current level in any organization (traditional student, adult learner, intern, entry-level, employee, manager, or leader), you are a valued member. The willingness to communicate perceptions will strengthen organizational change toward outcomes for the community engagement. During the change process, it is important to respect all forms of communication whether high- or low-verbal level. Be mindful that people communicate in varying levels and methods depending on settings. For example: group discussions, meetings, interpersonal conversations, public speaking, stranger, acquaintance, and friend. People are unique in their willingness to communicate.

Effectiveness depends on our willingness to interact with others and on developing effective communication skills. Those who engage in skillful communication are more likely to influence others. Communication professors James McCroskey and Virginia Richmond developed the Willingness to Communicate (WTC) scale to measure the predisposition to talk to a variety of situations. Taking this self-assessment in the Application Exercise will help you discover your own level of willingness to communicate in certain situations and recognize the level of others.

CHAPTER TAKEAWAYS

- The element of change is discomforting and not necessarily what is changing. Often it is the simple fact that things are changing into unfamiliar new ways that shift our norm.
- An organization of human beings have the opportunity to be accepting of one another and learn about coworkers' individual foundations of values, assumptions, beliefs, and expectations that may be similar or different than their own.
- Diversity matters at every level of any organization, because diverse perspectives that work together can achieve quality product and service outcomes.
- One of the ways we can learn about diversity is by continuing to reflect upon how we respond to change.
- Some people do not feel safe with change and prefer the status quo. There may have been a specific reason they came to work for the business and emotionally are not interested in external or internal changes.
- There are positional and unofficial leaders at every level of any organization. Leaders may find it difficult to implement change in organizations due to perceptions of the status quo. People become comfortable with their present status and must be introduced to change that sustains. A change that does not sustain may be viewed as a waste of time (168 hours a week).
- The mental map is not the same for everyone in the same work environment and how they behave during change.
- Individual experiences that may or may not be similar to others will determine how you behave during change.
- Ultimately, the leader of an organization is responsible for the outcome of change. It is his or her relationship with workers in the organization that will determine change effectiveness. The ability to embrace diversity of perspectives on the journey to Workforce 2030 will define successful or unsuccessful change outcome.

APPLICATION EXERCISES

Chapter Five focused on your personal foundation of values, assumptions, beliefs, and expectations that you bring to an organization the very first day. Begin completing the following list of Tools to help reflect upon strengths and challenges needed for your Individual Development Plan. Deadlines for completing each Tool will be determined by your instructor or trainer.

- Diversity of Perspectives • Tool 9.1 • *Willingness to Listen* (Parshakov et al., 2018; Peterson, 2016).
- Diversity of Perspectives • Tool 9.2 • *Willingness to Communicate* (Parshakov et al., 2018; Peterson, 2016).
- Diversity of Perspectives • Tool 9.3 • *Cultural Intelligence Scale—Short Version* (Taylor, 2013).
- Diversity of Perspectives • Tool 9.4 • *Diversity of Perceptions Scale* (Toogood, 2010).
- Diversity of Perspectives • Tool 9.5 • *A Color Test for Change Agents* (Vangen, 2017).
- Diversity of Perspectives • Tool 9.6 • *Leadership Communication Preference Styles Inventory* (Wang et al., 2016).
- Diversity of Perspectives • Tool 9.7 • *Individual Development Plan.*

CHAPTER 7

Choice • Behavior

OVERVIEW

Actualization: What We Decide
Change in Workplace Demographics
Teamwork

Actualization: What We Decide

What choices do you make when working with others who do not look, think, or act like you in Workforce 2030? Each individual must *decide* how to behave in the workforce. The choice to work as an individual with self-interests or in the best interest of others will certainly be influenced by your experiences. Breaking barriers to build relationships with mindfulness and inclusion on the journey to Workforce 2030 is the focus of this chapter. There can be a sort of freeing sensation when you individually choose to have a *growth mindset* where your brain's amygdala messages to its hippocampus is lifelong learning about others is familiar and a norm. The hippocampus can then tap into the tools you have learned in this book inspiring the action of valuing Diversity of Perspectives while working with others who do not look, think, or act like you. This should help to build stronger workplace and other relationships. To illustrate what has been learned up to this point, there will be a discussion about diverse personality styles you may encounter in the workplace to keep in mind and help you choose inclusiveness when working together. Personality styles will be described beyond the protected federal protection laws for "race, color, religion, sex (including pregnancy, transgender status, and sexual orientation), national origin, age (40 or older), disability or genetic information" (U.S. EEOC, 2020). This should enable you to focus on the intrinsic aspect of a person instead of what your eyes see or ears hear which is the core meaning of Diversity of Perspectives.

Change in Workplace Demographics

You will not be able to stop the impending change in workplace demographics for Workforce 2030 and beyond. However, you can choose to manage your personal experiences while change is happening. You can choose a positive mindset that learning about others who do not look, think, or act like you will help strengthen your competencies of equity, inclusion, and teamwork (National Association of Colleges and Employers [NACE], 2021). Or you can have a negative expectation of the change in workplace demographics. Experiences in your foundation of values, assumptions, beliefs, and expectations will inform your choice of a positive mindset or negative expectation. In addition, your experiences and knowledge about diversity will also inform your choices.

Goal setting of intentional mindfulness and inclusion as a choice to manage the change in the workplace demographics may help shape your experiences. Set positive goals you can achieve to enhance your brand identity while experiencing change.

Strive to have personally rewarding Diversity of Perspectives workplace experiences during the journey toward Workforce 2030. "If a person perceives that the event is contingent upon his own behavior or his own relatively permanent characteristic, we have termed this a belief in *internal control*" (Rotter, 1966, p. 1). Intentionally seek positive experiences as a way to limit a life of negative ones.

Teamwork

One of the ways to develop the competency of teamwork as defined by the National Association of Colleges and Employers (NACE) is to consider experiencing a *learning organization* on the journey toward Workforce 2030 and beyond. Regardless of your current level in any organization (traditional student, adult learner, intern, entry-level, employee, manager, or leader), you will soon experience a changing workforce that will become majority people of color as early as the year 2030.

A learning organization is a system of people working together toward a common goal. It should not matter what people look like. Rather, how people think and act does matter when working toward an intended organizational outcome. The following discussion about systems thinking and learning organizations is attributed to Peter Senge et al. (1994). "Learning in organizations means the continuous testing of experience, and the transformation of that experience into knowledge—accessible to the whole organization, and relevant to its core purpose" (p. 49). He relates organization of people as systems working toward a common goal. Senge's (1994) system thinking and learning organization statements illuminate the importance of Diversity of Perspectives. "A system is a perceived whole whose elements 'hang together' because they continually affect each other over time and operate toward a common purpose" (p. 90). The vision and mission is not intended for only some people in the organization. It is the intended purpose for everyone!

The journey toward Workforce 2030 will inevitably stir up familiar and unfamiliar feelings within each of us. These feelings may not necessarily be due to working with others who do not look, think, or act like you. The very existence of rapid change through people with unique ideas about how to develop and deliver products and services will inevitably shift the status quo for any organization. Senge (1994) has some things to keep in mind that may be helpful.

> At its essence, every organization is a product of how its members think and interact. This emphasis on thinking and interacting makes many people in mainstream organizations feel disoriented. It means shifting their point of orientation from outward to inward. To look inward, the first step is becoming aware of, and studying the tacit "truths" that we take for granted, and the aspirations and expectations that govern what we choose from life. Once we start to become conscious of how we think and interact, and begin developing capacities to think and interact differently, we will already have begun to change our organizations for the better. Those changes will ripple out around us, and reinforce a growing sense of capability and confidence. (p. 48)

Your experiences in the workforce will undoubtedly influence your behavioral decision-making. A focus on internal control about how you work with others may help balance any external variable during your experiences. You are accountable for your behavior in the workplace, so be responsible for contributing to a positive work environment. The next chapter will make the connection of your accountability to your brand identity you are developing that we discussed earlier in the book.

CHAPTER 8

Storytelling Your Brand Identity

OVERVIEW

Your Brand Identity and Workforce 2030
Storytelling Experiences

ACCOUNTABILITY

Your Brand Identity and Workforce 2030

How will your brand identity contribute to this unique time in our world history? How will you be remembered? How do individual experiences influence broader accountability? Your toolkit in Chapter Nine should help when interacting with people. Do you consider yourself a leader regardless if it is a positional title? Leaders are at every level of any organization and matter in its effectiveness when working with other people. "Leadership is social influence. It means leaving a mark, it is initiating and guiding, and the result is change. The product is new character or direction that otherwise would never be" (Manning & Curtis, 2015, p. 2). What will be your mark? What stories will you tell about your experiences throughout the journey toward Workforce 2030? Your brand identity may mean more now than ever!

Storytelling Experiences

The following by Burtis (2010) illuminates why a positive work environment where everyone has the opportunity to thrive leads to effective organizations.

> We want to feel positive and optimistic about our team, organization, or community. We want to be personally effective when we act as doer, follower, guide, manager, or leader. We want our various groups to succeed and to thrive because then we feel as though we are succeeding and thriving. To get what we want, we communicate with others, creating and sharing accounts of what we are doing as a group and of what we should be doing. We frame and shape group experiences as we communicate about them. Our talk changes the group's experience story. (p. 163)

FIGURE 8.1 Diversity of Perspectives: Brand Identity

Storytelling Your Brand Identity

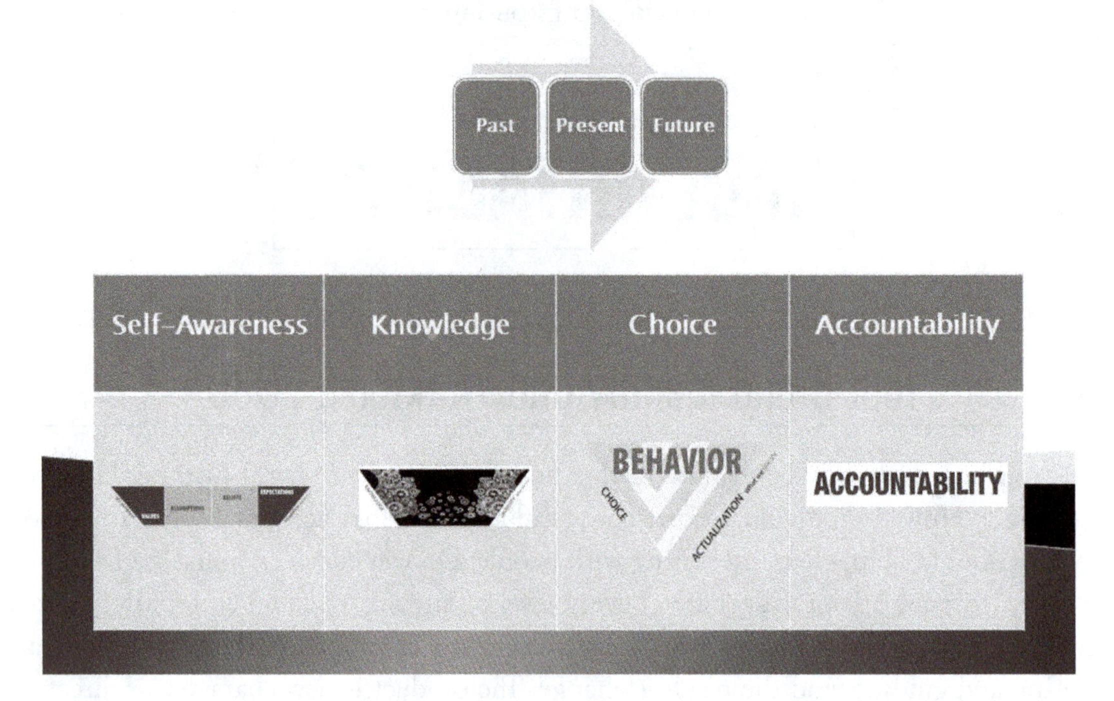

Prior to reading this book, you already had a personal foundation within the Diversity of Perspectives model. All of your life you have been interacting with people. Some people may or may not have looked, thought, or acted like you. You've made behavioral choice decisions while working with others and will continue to do so. Only you know whether you have thought about accountability of your actions before behaving in certain ways. If someone else would be telling your story as you journey toward Workforce 2030, how would they describe your brand identity?

SELF-AWARENESS

Foundation: What we bring

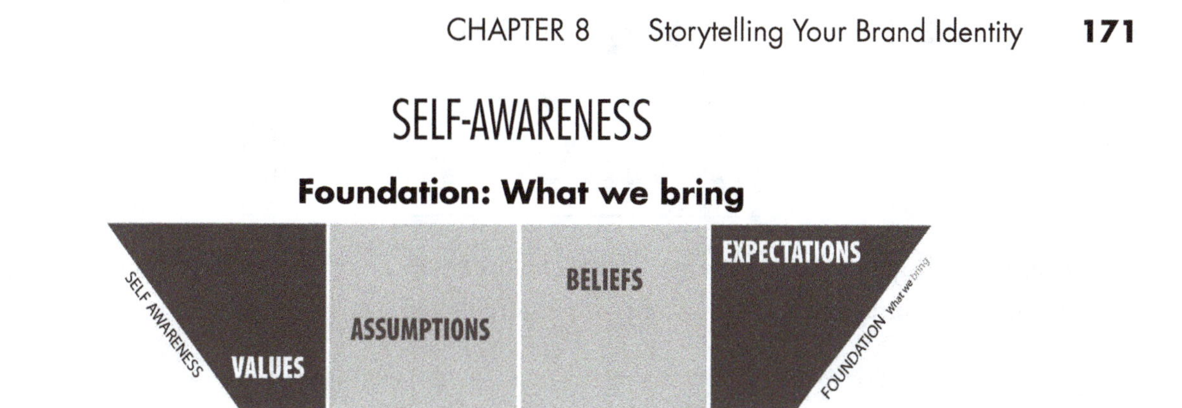

Perhaps you only need to awaken your self-awareness through reflection. Reflecting upon your values, assumptions, beliefs, and expectations in life is important. This is the value you bring to any workforce organization to contribute to its effectiveness while working with others.

KNOWLEDGE

Diversity: What we learn

Take advantage of opportunities to participate in a learning and social citizenship community of others who want to learn from each other. Knowledge gained through participating in experiences at work may build stronger organizations toward its mission and vision. Navigating a changing workforce will not be easy for everyone. Increased people of color will be the norm, but imagine using Diversity of Perspectives as a tool while navigating the change toward Workforce 2030 and beyond.

CHOICE

Actualization: What we decide

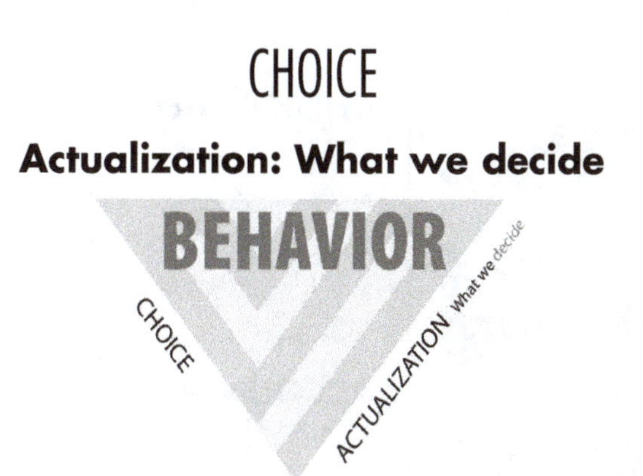

Reflect upon missed mindfulness and inclusion opportunities of the past while anticipating new ones on the journey toward Workforce 2030. Intentionally act upon new opportunities as a valued contributor to any organization and commit to sustain your efforts.

ACCOUNTABILITY

Demonstrate courageous accountability through willingness to be personally vulnerable while working with others. Courageous accountability is vulnerable but also admirable.

EXPERIENCES

Demonstrate willingness to keep trying to work with others. Envision the near-future of Workforce 2030. Ultimately, demonstrate brand identity sustainability through self-awareness, knowledge, choice, accountability, and new experiences.

TABLE 8.1 Diversity of Perspectives: Nomenclature for Mindfulness and Inclusion

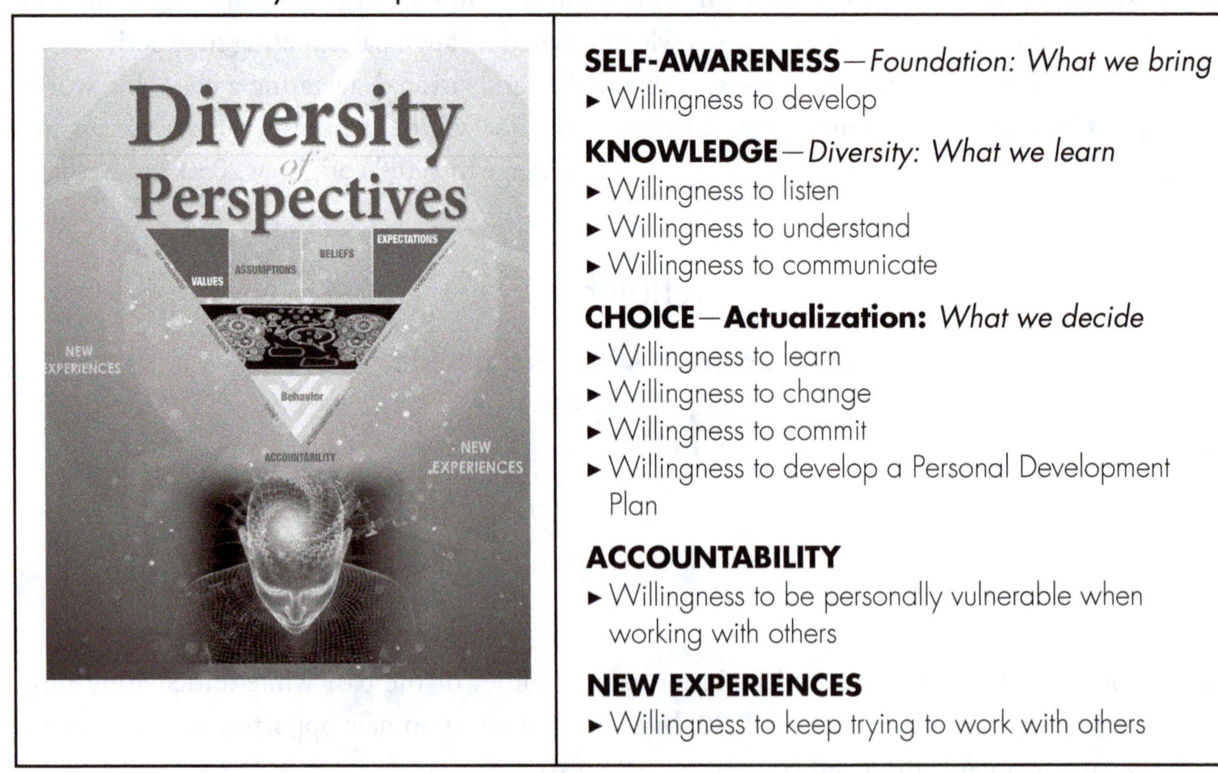

SELF-AWARENESS—*Foundation: What we bring* ▸ Willingness to develop
KNOWLEDGE—*Diversity: What we learn* ▸ Willingness to listen ▸ Willingness to understand ▸ Willingness to communicate
CHOICE—Actualization: *What we decide* ▸ Willingness to learn ▸ Willingness to change ▸ Willingness to commit ▸ Willingness to develop a Personal Development Plan
ACCOUNTABILITY ▸ Willingness to be personally vulnerable when working with others
NEW EXPERIENCES ▸ Willingness to keep trying to work with others

CHAPTER 9

Diversity of Perspectives Toolkit

OVERVIEW

Self-Assessments

This section of the textbook provides *tools* for individual development as you journey toward Workforce 2030. There are a variety of assessments that explore and help you reflect upon your self-awareness, knowledge, choices, accountability, and new experiences as it relates to Diversity of Perspectives. After taking the assessments, analyze your effectiveness in communicating with others by responding to the following questions. Were there any communication discoveries? About yourself? Others? Were the content of assessments a gentle reminder of diversity in communication within your organization? The most important part of this section is your intentional choice of a *growth mindset* versus a *fixed mindset*. The final part of this section is the Individual Development Plan.

DIVERSITY OF PERSPECTIVES • TOOL 9.1
WILLINGNESS TO LISTEN

Listening is one of the skills which potential employers often indicate as being critical to effective communication. Hence, many training programs and college classes provide instruction in listening. For many people, however, it is not a lack of skill that makes them a poor listener, it is their orientation toward listening. Some are just not willing to work at listening. They frequently claim (rightfully?) that they don't listen because of the poor communication skills of the speaker. This instrument is designed to measure this kind of an orientation. Alpha reliabilities for this instrument should be expected to be well above .85.

DIRECTIONS: The following 24 statements refer to listening. Please indicate the degree to which each statement applies to you by marking whether you:

Strongly Disagree = 1; Disagree = 2; Are Neutral =3;
Agree = 4; Strongly Agree = 5

____ 1. I dislike listening to boring speakers.

____ 2. Generally, I can listen to a boring speaker.

____ 3. I am bored and tired while listening to a boring speaker.

____ 4. I will listen when the content of a speech is boring.

____ 5. Listening to boring speakers about boring content makes me tired, sleepy, and bored.

____ 6. I am willing to listen to boring speakers about boring content.

____ 7. Generally, I am unwilling to listen when there is noise during a speaker's presentation.

____ 8. Usually, I am willing to listen when there is noise during a speaker's presentation.

____ 9. I am accepting and willing to listen to speakers who do not adapt to me.

____ 10. I am unwilling to listen to speakers who do not do some adaptation to me.

____ 11. Being preoccupied with other things makes me less willing to listen to a speaker.

Willingness to Listen (McCroskey, 1992). Permission granted by the James McCroskey estate.

____ 12. I am willing to listen to a speaker even if I have other things on my mind.

____ 13. While being occupied with other things on my mind, I am unwilling to listen to a speaker.

____ 14. I have a willingness to listen to a speaker, even if other important things are on my mind.

____ 15. Generally, I will not listen to a speaker who is disorganized.

____ 16. Generally, I will try to listen to a speaker who is disorganized.

____ 17. While listening to a non-immediate, non-responsive speaker, I feel relaxed with the speaker.

____ 18. While listening to a non-immediate, non-responsive speaker, I feel distant and cold toward that speaker.

____ 19. I can listen to a non-immediate, non-responsive speaker.

____ 20. I am unwilling to listen to a non-immediate, non-responsive speaker.

____ 21. I am willing to listen to a speaker with views different from mine.

____ 22. I am unwilling to listen to a speaker with views different from mine.

____ 23. I am willing to listen to a speaker who is not clear about what he or she wants to say.

____ 24. I am unwilling to listen to a speaker who is not clear, not credible, and abstract.

SCORING: Scores can range from 24 to 120. To compute the score on this instrument, complete the following steps:

Step 1: Add scores for items 2, 4, 6, 8, 9, 12, 14, 16, 17, 19, 21, and 23.
Step 2: Add scores for items 1, 3, 5, 7, 10, 11, 13, 15, 18, 20, 22, and 24.
Step 3: Total score = 72 – Total from Step 1 + Total from Step 2.

Scores above 89 indicate a high willingness to listen.
Scores below 59 indicate a low willingness to listen.
Scores between 59 and 89 indicate a moderate willingness to listen.

DIVERSITY OF PERSPECTIVES • TOOL 9.2
WILLINGNESS TO COMMUNICATE

Willingness to communicate is the most basic orientation toward communication. Almost anyone is likely to respond to a direct question, but many will not continue or initiate interaction. This instrument measures a person's willingness to *initiate* communication. The face validity of the instrument is strong, and results of extensive research indicate the predictive validity of the instrument. Alpha reliability estimates for this instrument have ranged from .85 to well above .90. Of the 20 items on the instrument, 8 are used to distract attention from the scored items. The 12 remaining items generate a total score, 4 context-type scores, and 3 receiver-type scores. The sub-scores generate lower reliability estimates, but generally high enough to be used in research studies.

DIRECTIONS: Below are 20 situations in which a person might choose to communicate or not to communicate. Presume you have completely free choice. Indicate the percentage of times you would choose to communicate in each type of situation. Indicate in the space at the left of the item what percent of the time you would choose to communicate.

(0 = Never to 100 = Always)

____ 1. Talk with a service station attendant.
____ 2. Talk with a physician.
____ 3. Present a talk to a group of strangers.
____ 4. Talk with an acquaintance while standing in line.
____ 5. Talk with a salesperson in a store.
____ 6. Talk in a large meeting of friends.
____ 7. Talk with a police officer.
____ 8. Talk in a small group of strangers.
____ 9. Talk with a friend while standing in line.
____ 10. Talk with a waiter/waitress in a restaurant.
____ 11. Talk in a large meeting of acquaintances.
____ 12. Talk with a stranger while standing in line.

Willingness to Communicate (Ang & Van Dyne, 2008; McCroskey & Richmond, 1987). Permission granted by the James McCroskey estate.

____ 13. Talk with a secretary.
____ 14. Present a talk to a group of friends.
____ 15. Talk in a small group of acquaintances.
____ 16. Talk with a garbage collector.
____ 17. Talk in a large meeting of strangers.
____ 18. Talk with a spouse (or girl/boyfriend).
____ 19. Talk in a small group of friends.
____ 20. Present a talk to a group of acquaintances.

SCORING:

Context-type sub-scores—

Group Discussion: Add scores for items 8, 15, & 19; then divide by 3.
Meetings: Add scores for items 6, 11, 17; then divide by 3.
Interpersonal: Add scores for items 4, 9, 12; then divide by 3.
Public Speaking: Add scores for items 3, 14, 20; then divide by 3.

Receiver-type sub-scores—

Stranger: Add scores for items 3, 8, 12, 17; then divide by 4.
Acquaintance: Add scores for items 4, 11, 15, 20; then divide by 4.
Friend: Add scores for items 6, 9, 14, 19; then divide by 4.
To compute the total WTC score, add the sub-scores for stranger, acquaintance, and friend. Then divide by 3.
All scores, total and sub-scores, will fall in the range of 0 to 100.

Norms for WTC Scores—

Group discussion >89 High WTC, <57 Low WTC
Meetings >80 High WTC, <39 Low WTC
Interpersonal conversations >94 High WTC, <64 Low WTC
Public Speaking >78 High WTC, <33 Low WTC
Stranger >63 High WTC, <18 Low WTC
Acquaintance >92 High WTC, <57 Low WTC
Friend >99 High WTC, <71 Low WTC
Total WTC >82 High Overall WTC, <52 Low Overall WTC

DIVERSITY OF PERSPECTIVES • TOOL 9.3
CULTURAL INTELLIGENCE SCALE—SHORT VERSION

DIRECTIONS: Read each statement and select the response that best describes your capabilities. Select the answer that BEST describes you AS YOU REALLY ARE

(1 = strongly disagree; 7 = strongly agree).

____ 1. I enjoy interacting with people from different cultures.

____ 2. I am sure I can deal with the stresses of adjusting to a culture that is new to me.

____ 3. I know the cultural values and religious beliefs of other cultures.

____ 4. I know the legal and economics systems of other cultures.

____ 5. I know the rules (e.g., vocabulary, grammar) of other languages.

____ 6. I am conscious of the cultural knowledge I use when interacting with people with different cultural backgrounds.

____ 7. I check the accuracy of my cultural knowledge as I interact with people from different cultures.

____ 8. I change my verbal behavior (e.g., accent, tone) when a cross-cultural interaction requires it.

____ 9. I change my nonverbal behavior when a cross-cultural situation requires it.

SCORING: Scores range from 9 to 63. The higher the score, the higher your perceived level of cultural intelligence.

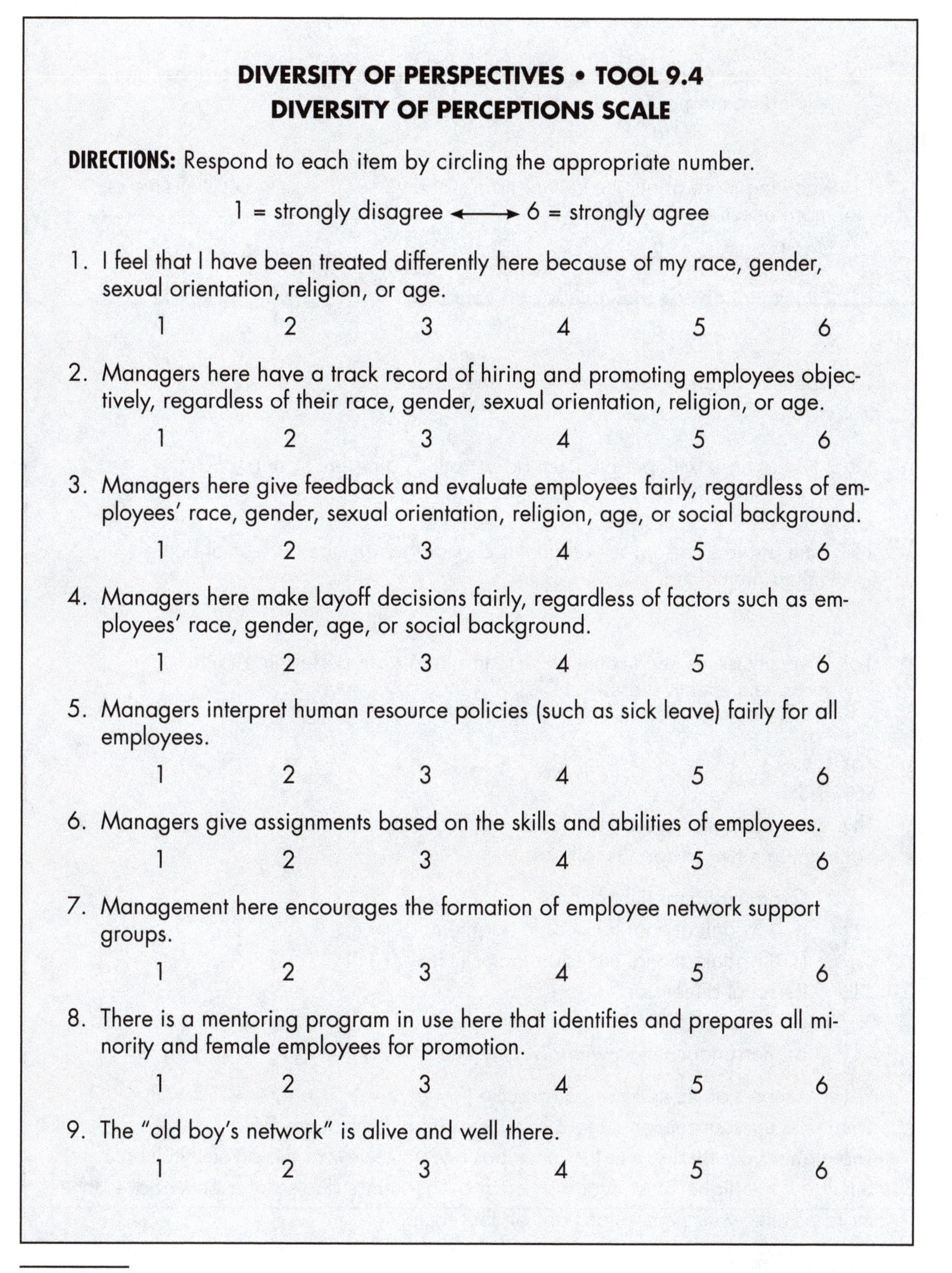

DIVERSITY OF PERSPECTIVES • TOOL 9.4
DIVERSITY OF PERCEPTIONS SCALE

DIRECTIONS: Respond to each item by circling the appropriate number.

1 = strongly disagree ⟷ 6 = strongly agree

1. I feel that I have been treated differently here because of my race, gender, sexual orientation, religion, or age.

   1 2 3 4 5 6

2. Managers here have a track record of hiring and promoting employees objectively, regardless of their race, gender, sexual orientation, religion, or age.

   1 2 3 4 5 6

3. Managers here give feedback and evaluate employees fairly, regardless of employees' race, gender, sexual orientation, religion, age, or social background.

   1 2 3 4 5 6

4. Managers here make layoff decisions fairly, regardless of factors such as employees' race, gender, age, or social background.

   1 2 3 4 5 6

5. Managers interpret human resource policies (such as sick leave) fairly for all employees.

   1 2 3 4 5 6

6. Managers give assignments based on the skills and abilities of employees.

   1 2 3 4 5 6

7. Management here encourages the formation of employee network support groups.

   1 2 3 4 5 6

8. There is a mentoring program in use here that identifies and prepares all minority and female employees for promotion.

   1 2 3 4 5 6

9. The "old boy's network" is alive and well there.

   1 2 3 4 5 6

10. The company spends enough money and time on diversity awareness and related training.

    1 2 3 4 5 6

11. Knowing more about the culture norms of diverse groups would help me be more effective in my job.

    1 2 3 4 5 6

12. I think that diverse viewpoints add value.

    1 2 3 4 5 6

13. I believe diversity is a strategic business issue.

    1 2 3 4 5 6

14. I feel at ease with people from backgrounds different from my own.

    1 2 3 4 5 6

15. I am afraid to disagree with members or other groups for fear of being called prejudiced.

    1 2 3 4 5 6

16. Diversity issues keep some work teams here from performing to their maximum effectiveness.

    1 2 3 4 5 6

SCORING:

This scale measures two dimensions—the organizational and the personal—which each contain two factors as follows:

I. Organizational dimension
   a. Organizational fairness factor (items 1–6)
   b. Organizational inclusion factor (items 7–10)

II. Personal dimension
   a. Personal diversity value factor (items 11–13)
   b. Personal comfort with diversity items (items 14–16)

Reverse scores on items 1, 9, 15, and 16 (1 = 6, 2 = 5, 3 = 4, 4 = 3, 5 = 2, 6 = 1).
Then add up your responses to all 16 items (maximum score 96).
The higher your total score, the more positive your view of the diversity climate.
Similarly, the higher your score on each of the item subsets described above, the more positive your perceptions are on that factor.

DIVERSITY OF PERSPECTIVES • TOOL 9.5
A COLOR TEST FOR CHANGE AGENTS

Léon de Calwué and Hans Vermaak (2003) describe their following "A Color Test for Change Agents" in their book, *Learning to Change: A Guide for Organization Change Agents*.

This test is designed to give you some insight into the ways you are inclined to think about and act during change processes. It will highlight your relative preferences among the five change paradigms, each of which is represented by a different color. The test will also show the degree to which your thoughts and actions are consistent with one another.

The test can be useful for anybody; after all, at times we all try to bring change about in our lives. Whether you are a manager, a consultant, a secretary, a teacher, or a lawyer, we assume that you have more than once attempted to initiate or influence change and thus are a change agent of sorts.

On the following pages pairs of statements are listed that apply to changes within organizations. Please circle the statement in each pair that most reflects your view.

In a number of cases you will find that neither A nor B captures your view accurately. In these cases, choose the statement that most closely resembles your opinion.

Do not take too long to decide on your answers; trust your initial reaction and opt for the statement that makes sense to you at first glance.

Testing Your "Thoughts"

The first part of the color test is meant to characterize your vision and ideas on change. Read the following statements and choose the statement closest to your viewpoint. The focus here is on your convictions, what you think will work well, what you regard as being a desirable and realistic approach.

Circle your answers:

1. A. Change can be successful only when it is supported by the major players.
   B. Change can be successful only when you tap the energy and the strength of the people involved.

2. A. Things will change if you stimulate people the right way and entice them to come on board.
   B. Things will change if you take power, status, or influence into account and make use of them.

---

3. A. Organizations change as a result of people holding up mirrors for one another.
   B. Organizations change when you organize around people's energy and strength.

4. A. Things change when you offer those involved a brighter future and an (personally) attractive proposition.
   B. Things change when real dialogue takes place between people.

5. A. A change agent must ensure that the most important players adjust their positions in such a way that they do not counteract each other.
   B. A change agent must ensure that people listen to and learn from one another.

6. A. Organizations change when people develop themselves.
   B. Organizations change when people know what the organization wants to achieve.

7. A. It is important to allow people to link their thoughts and their actions.
   B. It is important to stimulate people and give them incentives.

8. A. You can change organizations only when you first analyze what the best solution is.
   B. You can change organizations only when you can get the most influential people in the organization to agree with a solution.

9. A. Organizations change when you invest in people.
   B. Change should not be dependent on the people who make it happen.

10. A. You should reduce complexity to a minimum during change processes.
    B. You should make full use of the dynamics and complexity of the situation during the change process.

11. A. Time constraints and deadlines are instrumental in pushing important decisions through.
    B. Creating space (by loosening up constricting norms and values or by breaking through entrenched positions) is instrumental in getting things moving.

12. A. For change to succeed, a good atmosphere and team spirit are important.
    B. To bring about change, it is important to form coalitions.

13. A. Change occurs only when a clear result or goal has been determined beforehand.
    B. Change occurs only when individuals put their heart and soul into it.

14. A. In an effective change process there must be scope for consultation and room for negotiations.
    B. For a change process to be effective, the end result must be clear-cut from the start.

15. A. A change needs first to create a safe learning environment by clarifying rules and acting as a role model.
    B. A change agent first needs to discern underlying patterns that drive the organization and explicitly make sense of them.

16. A. A change agent should be knowledgeable about the subject matter and ensure that all activities contribute to the intended result.
    B. A change agent should be empathic in order to help create an environment for people to communicate openly and effectively.

17. A. Something changes when you reward the people involved for their contributions to that change.
    B. Something changes when you help the people involved to explore and gain new insights.

18. A. Change requires space; people need to have room to breathe and to explore.
    B. Change needs to be embedded in the organization and its policies; people shouldn't be left hanging.

19. A. A change agent should offer the employees opportunities and perspectives.
    B. A change agent should monitor progress and adjust the planning based on previously determined criteria and standards.

20. A. For organizations to change, policies need to change first.
    B. For organizations to change, people need to change first.

21. A. In order to design interventions, the change agent has to discern the underlying causes behind current problems.
    B. The change agent should have expertise on the problems at hand and be able to handle them systematically.

22. A. The change agent should ensure that the change progresses steadily and controllably.
    B. The change agent should monitor and maintain the balance of power behind a change program.

23. A. Things change when you make it pleasant for people to go along with the change.
    B. Things change when they are framed differently and take on new meaning.

24. A. First and foremost, change agents need to be empathic.
    B. First and foremost, change agents need to exercise care.

25. A. Communication among all those concerned is an indispensable ingredient of a change process.
    B. A thorough analysis carried out beforehand is indispensable if a change is to succeed.

26. A. The change agent must be authentic no matter how confrontational this might seem to others.
    B. The change agent must show empathy to others.

27. A. If the change agent is forced to choose, he or she should give preference to changing a "hard" aspect within the organization; for example, its structure, systems, or strategy.
    B. If the change agent is forced to choose, he or she should give preference to changing a "soft" aspect within the organization; for example, management style, culture, or personnel.

28. A. It is important to offer people support and safety while they are creating and implementing solutions.
    B. It is important to limit the number of options before decision-making takes place because agreements are otherwise hard to reach.

29. A. A change agent must ensure that people reach agreements.
    B. A change agent must motivate people.

30. A. A change agent must gain substantial insight into the context of the problem and the networks of people associated with it.
    B. A change agent must gain substantial insight into the underlying patterns that sustain the problem.

Scoring Your "Thinking"

Circle the letter you have chosen for each of the thirty statements.

Number	Yellow	Blue	Red	Green	White
1	A				B
2	B		A		
3				A	B
4			A		B
5	A			B	
6		B	B	A	
7				A	
8	B	A			
9		B	A		
10		A			B
11	A				B
12	B				
13		A			B
14	A	B			
15				A	B
16		A		B	
17			A	B	
18			B		A
19		B	A		
20	A			B	
21		B			A
22	B	A			
23			A		B
24			B	A	
25		B		A	
26				B	A
27		A	B		
28	B			A	
29	A		B		
30	A				B
Total number of circled letters for each column	**Yellow**	**Blue**	**Red**	**Green**	**White**

TESTING YOUR "ACTIONS"

The second part of the Color Test is designed to characterize the way you act as a change agent.

Before completing this part of the test, think of three change processes in which you have played an important role. The test works best if your role and style in these processes are representative of your behavior during most change processes. Preferably, they should concern change processes that took place within the past 2 years. First, try to recall the circumstances of the three change processes, the aims of these processes, and your contribution to them.

Now turn your attention to the statements listed below. Base your choice of statement as much as possible on your actual behavior in the three change processes.

Circle your answers:

1. A. I was a role model for others.
   B. I ensured that new role models were given enough space.

2. A. I supported solutions that generated lively interactions.
   B. I supported the best solution.

3. A. I helped management agree with each other on solutions and assisted further implementation from the top down.
   B. I attempted to find and catalyze intrinsic drivers for change whenever I could find them in the organization.

4. A. I encouraged and supported people to make change happen in their work arenas.
   B. I ensured that the previously formulated outcome was not amended by those carrying out the implementation.

5. A. I held a mirror up to people, I gave them feedback.
   B. I persuaded the staff to act in the right direction.

6. A. In the change process, I supported people in developing their talents.
   B. In the change process, I tried to spot and create new "heroes."

7. A. People remarked on my carefulness and meticulousness when dealing with others.
   B. People remarked on my systematic, planned way of working.

8. A. I ensured that none of the major parties involved suffered loss of face.
   B. I ensured that everyone's performance was rewarded or criticized based on the same procedure and criteria.

9. A. I opted for the best solution.
   B. I opted for the most feasible solution.

10. A. When facilitating groups, I used my position (of authority) when needed.
    B. When facilitating groups, I left the responsibility for the results with them.

11. A. I made clear agreements with all those concerned and made sure that I and everyone else stuck to them.
    B. I allowed people to reach agreement concerning the direction we were going without involving myself too much with the details.

12. A. I always ensured I had room to maneuver.
    B. I always ensured complete openness: Everyone involved knew the score.

13. A. I measured progress using predetermined criteria and norms.
    B. I helped people discuss progress with one another. I concentrated on the way they communicated while doing so.

14. A. During the change process, I helped people develop the competencies that we had identified as crucial.
    B. During the change process, I helped people become aware of the many aspects involved and their interrelationships.

15. A. I created situations that enabled people to work on their own learning goals.
    B. I ensured that there were training programs where specific groups could master predetermined competencies.

16. A. I managed conflicts in order to reach a consensus between the major players.
    B. I optimized conflicts to create dynamics and energy within the organization.

17. A. I strived for the best solution within the stated margins.
    B. I encouraged people to find their own solutions and to implement them.

18. A. I concentrated on neutralizing the forces that block new initiatives and emerging solutions.
    B. I concentrated on clearly defining the desired end result and planning its implementation.

19. A. I stimulated the exchange of ideas and experiences.
    B. I uncovered and shared more fundamental ways of looking at things.

20. A. I strived for open communication and showed empathy.
    B. I guarded my independent position and was self-controlled.

21. A. I attempted to create and retain support for a solution.
    B. I ensured that all activities were goal-oriented.

22. A. I carefully recorded my goals and stuck to them.
    B. I constantly reflected on what was going on and based my actions on that from moment to moment.

23. A. I always acted diplomatically in keeping with the situation.
    B. I stuck my neck out and stood up for what I believe in.

24. A. I motivated people by rewarding good performance.
    B. I assisted learning by giving people feedback on their performance.

25. A. I held up a mirror to people.
    B. I stuck to agreements and ensured that others did so as well.

26. A. I acted as an arbiter in conflict situations.
    B. I coached people to improve their communication skills.

27. A. I made the change process manageable.
    B. I created room for change.

28. A. I encouraged people to change their standpoints when doing so would break deadlock situations.
    B. I attempted to create a good atmosphere and to motivate people.

29. A. I aimed at achieving a result that would hurt or compromise no one.
    B. I aimed at achieving the best possible result.

30. A. I aimed at creating a secure learning environment.
    B. I aimed at creating constructive conflicts and dialogues.

Scoring Your "Actions"

Circle the letter you have chosen for each of the thirty statements.

Number	Yellow	Blue	Red	Green	White
1				A	B
2		B			A
3	A				B
4		B	A		
5			B	A	
6			A		B
7		B	A		
8	A		B		
9	B	A			
10	A			B	
11	B	A			
12	A		B		
13		A		B	
14			A		B
15			B	A	
16	A				B
17		A		B	
18		B			A
19				A	B
20	B			A	
21	A	B			
22			A		B
23	A				B
24			A	B	
25		B		A	
26	A			B	
27		A			B
28	A		B		
29		B	A		
30				A	B
Total number of circled letters for each column	**Yellow**	**Blue**	**Red**	**Green**	**White**

DIVERSITY OF PERSPECTIVES • TOOL 9.6
LEADERSHIP COMMUNICATION PREFERENCE STYLES INVENTORY

BACKGROUND: One factor that contributes to variations in leader effectiveness is communication style. Leadership communication style is a relatively enduring set of communicative behaviors in which a leader engages when interacting with followers. A leader's communication style may reflect a philosophical belief about human nature, or it may simply be a strategy designed to maximize outcomes in a given situation. The communication style a leader selects contributes to the success or failure of any attempt to exert influence.

DIRECTIONS: To explore your own leadership style preference, complete the self-assessment. Read the 12 statements below. For each statement indicate your level of agreement.

SELF-ASSESSMENT

		Strongly Disagree	Disagree	Unsure	Agree	Strongly Agree
1.	A leader should set direction without input from followers.	1	2	3	4	5
2.	A leader should set direction with input and consultation with followers.	1	2	3	4	5
3.	A leader should set direction based on the wishes of followers.	1	2	3	4	5
4.	A leader should use a task force or committee rather than making a decision alone.	1	2	3	4	5
5.	A leader should evaluate the progress of work with little input from followers.	1	2	3	4	5
6.	A leader should leave it up to followers to initiate informal day-to-day communication.	1	2	3	4	5
7.	A leader should encourage followers to initiate decision-making without first seeking approval.	1	2	3	4	5

		Strongly Disagree	Disagree	Unsure	Agree	Strongly Agree
8.	A leader should closely monitor rules and regulations—punishing those who break the rules.	1	2	3	4	5
9.	A leader should keep followers up to date on issues affecting the work group.	1	2	3	4	5
10.	A leader should explain the reasons for making a decision to his/her followers.	1	2	3	4	5
11.	A leader should remain aloof and not get too friendly with his/her followers.	1	2	3	4	5
12.	A leader should provide broad goals and leave decisions regarding the methods for achieving the goals to followers.	1	2	3	4	5

SCORING: Tally your score on each of the leadership communication styles listed below by totaling your points as indicated.

Authoritarian	Democratic	Laissez-Faire
Question 1 ____________	Question 2 ____________	Question 3 ____________
Question 5 ____________	Question 4 ____________	Question 6 ____________
Question 8 ____________	Question 9 ____________	Question 7 ____________
Question 11 ____________	Question 10 ____________	Question 12 ____________
TOTAL ____________	**TOTAL** ____________	**TOTAL** ____________

The higher your score, the greater your preference for a given leadership communication style. An unequal distribution of scores generally indicates a stronger preference for a certain style. Relatively equal scores indicate a more balanced preference of styles. This likely indicates a blended approach in which styles are based on situational factors.

DIVERSITY OF PERSPECTIVES • TOOL 9.7
INDIVIDUAL DEVELOPMENT PLAN

First Name	**Last Name**	**Current Position**
Education Level	**Department/Organization**	**University/Business**

Section I • Career Goals	
Short-Term Goals (1–2 years):	Long-Term Goals (3–5 years):

Section II • Plan		
Development Objectives Needed *(competencies to be developed)*	Developmental Opportunities Requested (workshops, conferences, etc.)	Other Activities Requested (any other activity to strengthen desired competencies development)

Section III • Accomplishment Schedule and Cost	
Development Organization and Location	Development Description of Services

Projected Cost	Target Completion Date	Actual Completion Date

Individual's Signature / Date	Note: This IDP is subject to change depending on availability of opportuities and activities for individual requests.

Source: Federal Aviation Administration (https://www.faa.gov/regulations_policies/orders_notices/index.cfm/go/document.information/documentID/3661)

References

Aidman, B., & Long, T. A. (2017, October). Leadership and storytelling: Promoting a culture of learning, positive change, and community. Retrieved April 2020 from https://files.eric.ed.gov/fulltext/EJ1160822.pdf

Anderson, L. W., & Krathwohl, D. R. (2001). *A taxonomy for learning, teaching, and assessing: A revision of bloom's taxonomy of educational objectives* (Complete). Longman.

Ang, S., & Van Dyne, L. (Eds.) (2008). *Handbook of cultural intelligence: Theory, management, and applications.* Sharpe, Appendix C, p. 391. Used by permission of Taylor & Francis.

Baker, B. B., & Boyle, C. B. (2009). The timeless power of storytelling. *Journal of Sponsorship*, *3*(1), 79–87.

Bates, S., & Atkins, A. (2017). Bridge the gap from strategy to execution: Culture change that sticks. *Strategic HR Review, 16*(5), 222–228.

Bebber, B. (2020). The architects of integration: Research, public policy and the Institute of Race Relations in Post-imperial Britain. *The Journal of Imperial and Commonwealth History, 48*(2), 319–350.

Black, J., & Gregersen, H. (2014). *It starts with one, changing individuals changes organizations* (3rd ed.). Pearson Education, Inc.

Brown, S. K. (2021, Feb. 2). Actor in *This Is Us*. NBC Celebrating Black Leaders.

Bruckman, J. (2008). Overcoming resistance to change: Causal factors, interventions, and critical values. *The Psychologist-Manager Journal, 11*(2), 211–219.

Bureau of Labor Statistics, US Department of Labor. Retrieved from https://www.bls.gov/news.release/pdf/nlsoy.pdf

Burtis, J. O., & Turman, P. D. (2010). *Leadership communication as citizenship*. Thousand Oaks, CA: SAGE Publications, Inc.

Calvin, James R. (2015). Leadership for developing empowering culture in organizations: Outreach empowerment. *Academy of Business Journal*, (1), pp. 7–15.

Capezio, P., & Morehouse, D. (1997). *Secrets of breakthrough leadership.* Career Press.

Carr, A. N., & Ann, C. (2011). The use and abuse of storytelling in organizations. *Journal of Management Development, 30*(3), 236–246.

Challita, M. (2014). The empathetic brain as the neural basis of moral behavior—Presented from interdisciplinary perspectives. Roma: Regina Apostolorum.

Challita, M. (2016). From empathetic mind to moral behavior: The "who," "why", and "how." *Medicine, Health Care and Philosophy, 19*, 517–522.

Chrobot-Mason, D., & Aramovich, N. (2013). The psychological benefits of creating an affirming climate for workplace diversity. *Group & Organization Management*, *38*(6), 659.

Cote, R. (2017). Vision of effective leadership. *Journal of Leadership, Accountability, and Ethics, 14*(4), 52–63.

Covey, S. R. (2007). Begin with the end in mind. *Training 44*(8), 48.

de Caluwé, L., & Vermaak, H. (2003). *Learning to change: A guide for organization change agents.* Sage Publications, Inc.

Dimock, M. (2018). Defining generations: Where Millennials end and post-Millennials begin. Retrieved from http://www.pewresearch.org/fact-tank/2018/03/01/defining-generations-where-millennials-end-and-post-millennials-begin/

Dimock, M. (2019). Defining generations: Where Millennials end and Generation Z begins. Retrieved from https://www.pewresearch.org/fact-tank/2019/01/17/where-millennials-end-and-generation-z-begins/

Dubrin, A. J. (1995). *Leadership.* Houghton Mifflin.

Dweck, C. S., & Reppucci, N. (1973). Learned helplessness and reinforcement responsibility in children. *Journal of Personality and Social Psychology, 25*(1), 109–116.

Dweck, C. S. (2016). *Mindset : the new psychology of success* (Updated). Random House.

Ely, R., & Thomas, D. (2001). Cultural diversity at work: The effects of diversity perspectives on work group processes and outcomes. *Administrative Science Quarterly, 46*(2), 229–273. https:/doi.org/10.2307/2667087

Evans, C., Williams, D., Onnela, J.-P., & Subramanian, S.V. (2017, Nov. 9). A multilevel approach to modeling health inequalities at the intersection of multiple social identities. *Social Science & Medicine,* S0277–9536. https://doi.org/10.1016/j.socscimed.2017.11.011

Gilley, A., Dixon, P., & Gilley, W. (2008). Characteristics of leadership effectiveness: Implementing change and driving innovation in organizations. *Human Resource Development Quarterly, 19*(2), 153–169. http://dx.doi.org/10.1002/hrdq.1232

Halal, W. E., & Taylor, K. B. (Ed.) (1999). Twenty-first century economics: Perspectives of socioeconomics for a changing world. New York.

Haque, M., TitiAmayah, A., & Liu, Lu. (2016). The role of vision in organizational readiness for change and growth. *Leadership & Organization Development Journal, 37*(7), 983–999.

Hersted, L., & Frimann, S. (2016). Constructing leadership identities through stories. *Tamara - Journal for Critical Organization Inquiry, 14*(4), 149–162.

Hideg, I., & Ferris, D. L. (2017). Dialectical thinking and fairness-based perspectives of affirmative action. *Journal of Applied Psychology, 102*(5), 781–801.

Kim, C., & Kim, T. (2020). *Dedication: Leader, scholar, athlete, and beyond.*

Kopaneva, I. M. (2019). Left in the dust: Employee constructions of mission and vision ownership. *International Journal of Business Communication, 56*(1), 122–145.

Kotter, J. P. (1996). *Leading change.* Harvard Business School Press.

Kravitz, D. A., Harrison, D. A., Turner M. E., Levine, E. L., Chaves, W., Brannick, M. T., Denning, D. L., Russell, C. J., & Conrad, M. A. (1997). Affirmative action: A review of psychological and behavioral research. Bowling Green, OH: Society for Industrial and Organizational Psychology

Kulkarni, S. M. (2015). A review on intrinsic motivation: A key to sustainable and effective leadership. *Review of Integrative Business and Economics Research, 4*(3), 74–88.

Langer, E. J. (1989). *Mindfulness.* Da Capo.

Lucas, S. E. (2015). *The art of public speaking* (12th ed.). McGraw Hill.

Manning, G., & Curtis, K. (1988). *Leadership: Nine keys to success.* South-Western.

Manning, G., & Curtis, K. (2015). *The art of leadership* (5th ed.). McGraw-Hill.

Maya, J., Audibert, J., Sipala, Z., Vandis, C., Carson, C., & Prudente, E. (Winter 2020). Responsibilities and rights of employers and employees doing the COVID-19 pandemic. *Labor Law Journal,* pp. 220–254.

McCormick, A. L. (2014). *The industrial revolution in United States history.* Enslow Publishers, Inc.

McCroskey, J. C. (1992). Reliability and validity of the willingness to communicate scale. *Communication Quarterly, 40,* 16–25.

McCroskey, J. C., & Richmond, V. P. (1987). Willingness to communicate. In J. C. McCroskey & J. A. Daly (Eds.), *Personality and interpersonal communication* (pp. 119–131). Sage.

McCroskey, J. C., & Richmond, V. P. (1996). *Fundamentals of human communication: An interpersonal perspective.* Waveland Press.

Merriam-Webster. Retrieved on January 3, 2021, from https://www.merriam-webster.com/dictionary/equity

Minkes, A. L., Small, M. W., & Chatterjee, S. R. (1999). Leadership and business ethics: Does it matter? Implications for management. *Journal of Business Ethics, 20*(4), 327–335.

Mor Barak. (2016). *Managing diversity* (pp. 328–329). Sage Publications.

Muindi, F., Ramachandran, L., & Tsai, J. W. (2020, March). Human narratives in science: The power of storytelling. *Trends in Molecular Medicine, 26*(3), 249–251.

National Association of Colleges and Employers (2019). *Career Readiness Defined.* https://www.naceweb.org/career-readiness/competencies/career-readiness-defined/

National Association of Colleges and Employers (NACE). (2021). *Career readiness: Competencies for a career-ready workforce.* http://naceweb.org/career-readiness-competencies

Parshakov, P., Zavertiaeva, C., & Zavertiaeva, M. (2018). Is diversity good or bad? Evidence from eSports teams analysis. *Applied Economics, 50*(47), 5064–5075. https:/doi.org/10.1080/00036846.2018.1470315

Pereira, G. (2019). Brand storytelling: Three-dimensional perspective. *Journal of Brand Strategy, 8*(1), 146–159.

Peterson, R. S. (2016). Four steps to leading diverse teams effectively. *London Business School Review, 27*(3), 40–43.

Pew Research Center. (2015, September 3). Retrieved from https://www.pewresearch.org/politics/2015/09/03/the-whys-and-hows-of-generations-research/

Quinn, G. P., Gwede, C. K., & Meade, C. D. (2018). Diversity beyond race and ethnicity: Enhancing inclusion with an expanded definition of diversity. *The American Journal of Bioethics, 18*(4), 47–48.

Richmond, V. P., & Hickson, M. III. (2001). *Going public: A practical guide to public talk.* Allyn & Bacon.

Roche, M., Haar, J. M., & Luthans, F. (2014). The role of mindfulness and psychological capital on the well-being of leaders. *Journal of Occupational Health Psychology, 19*, 476–489. http://dx.doi.org/10.1037/ a0037183

Ross, R., Smith, B., Roberts, C., & Kleiner, A. (1994) as cited in Senge, P. M., Kleiner, A., Roberts, C., Ross, R. B., and Smith, B. J. (1994). *The fifth discipline: Strategies and tools for building a learning organization.* Doubleday Dell Publishing Group Inc.

Rotter, J. B. (1966). Generalized expectations for internal versus external control of reinforcement. *Psychological Monographs: General and Applied, 8)*(1), 1–28.

Salicru, S. (2018). Storytelling as a leadership practice for sensemaking to drive change in times of turbulence and high velocity. *Journal of Leadership, Accountability and Ethics, 15*(2), 130–140.

Schein, E. (2004). *Organizational Culture and Leadership* (3rd ed.). Jossey-Bass.

Seah, M., & Hsieh, M. H. (2015). Impact of leader adaptability on organizational change and adaptation: The case of Savecom Communication. *Journal of Asia Business Studies, 9*(3), 213–231.

Senge, P., Kleiner, A., Roberts, C., Ross, R. B., & Smith, B. J. (1994). *The fifth discipline fieldbook: Strategies and tools for building a learning organization.* Doubleday.

Sethi, A., & Adhikari, B. (2012). Impact of communicating 'vision' on organizational communication effectiveness. *International Journal of Marketing & Business Communication, 1*(3), 43–48.

Sole, D., & Wilson, D. G. (2002), Storytelling in Organizations: The Power and Traps of Using Stories to Share Knowledge in Organizations, Harvard Graduation School of Education, LILA.

Snyder, K., Hedlund, C., Ingelsson, P., & Bäckström, I. (2017). Storytelling: A co-creative process to support value-based leadership. *International Journal of Quality and Service Sciences, 9*(3/4), 484–497. https://doi.org/10.1108/ijqss-02-2017-0009

Spring Institute. (2016, April 8). What's the difference between multicultural, intercultural, and cross-cultural communication? Retrieved January 2 , 2021, from https://springinstitute.org/whats-difference-multicultural-intercultural-cross-cultural-communication/

Strauss, W., & Howe, N. (1991). *Generations: The history of America's future, 1584 to 2069*. Quill/William/Morrow.

Strauss, W., & Howe, N. (1997). *The fourth turning: An American prophecy—What the cycles of history will tell us about America's next rendezvous with destiny.* Broadway Books.

Taylor, J. B. (2008). *My stroke of insight: A brain scientist's personal journey.* Plume.

Taylor, J. B. (2013, Feb. 23). *The neuroanatomical transformation of the teenage brain* [Video]. TEDxYouth@Indianaolis. https://www.youtube.com/watch?v=PzT_SBl31-s

Taylor, E. (2021). *Diversity of Perspectives.* Kendall Hunt Publishing Company.

Toogood, G. N. (2010). *The new articulate executive: Look, act, and sound like a leader* (2nd ed.). McGraw-Hill.

Vespa, J., Medina, L., & Armstrong, D. M. (2020*). Demographic turning points for the United States: Population projections for 2020 to 2060.* U.S. Department of Commerce, U.S. Census Bureau. https://www.census.gov/content/dam/Census/library/publications/2020/demo/p25-1144.pdf

U.S. Equal Employment Opportunity Commission. *E-RACE Educating Racism and Colorism From Employment*, https://www.eeoc.gov/initiatives/e-race/significant-eeoc-racecolor-casescovering-private-and-federal-sectors

U.S. Equal Employment Opportunity Commission (EEOC). (2020). https://www.eeoc.gov/overview

Vangen, S. (2017). Culturally diverse collaborations: A focus on communication and shared understanding. *Public Management Review, 19*(3), 305–325. https://doi.org/10.1080/14719037.2016.1209234

Vespa, J., Medina, L., & Armstrong, D. M. (2020). *Demographic turning points for the United States: Population projections for 2020 to 2060.* U.S. Department of Commerce, U.S. Census Bureau. https://www.census.gov/content/dam/Census/library/publications/2020/demo/p25-1144.pdf

Wang, X., Kim, T., & Lee, D. (2016). Cognitive diversity and team creativity: Effects of team intrinsic motivation and transformational leadership. *Journal of Business Research, 69*(9), 3231.

Wilson, V. (2016). *People of color will be a majority of the American working class in 2032*. Economic Policy Institute. https://files.epi.org/pdf/108254.pdf

Wilson, A. O. (2019). The role of storytelling in navigating through the storm of change. *Journal of Organizational Change Management*, *32*(3), 385–395. https:/doi.org/10.1108/jocm-12-2018-0343

Yanchus, N. J., Shoda, E. A., Derickson, R., & Osatuke, K. (2015). Organizational change and sensemaking in the veterans health administration. *Journal of Organizational Psychology, 15*(1), 74–89.

Yusof, N., Hashim, R. A., Valdez, N. P., & Yaacob, A. (2018). Managing diversity in higher education: A strategic communication approach. *Journal of Asian Pacific Communication, 28*(1), 41–60.

Index

D

K

L

M

N

O

P

R